HISTORICAL FOUNDATIONS
OF EDUCATION

Educational Foundations

edited by Bruce Maxwell and Lauren Bialystock

Education, as an academic field taught at universities around the world, emerged from a range of older foundational disciplines. The *Educational Foundations* series comprises six volumes, each covering one of the foundational disciplines of philosophy, history, sociology, policy studies, economics, and law. This is the first reference work to provide an authoritative and up-to-date account of all six disciplines, showing how each field's ideas, methods, theories, and approaches can contribute to research and practice in education today. The six volumes cover the same set of key topics within education, which also form the chapter titles:

– Mapping the Field
– Purposes of Education
– Curriculum
– Schools and Education Systems
– Learning and Human Development
– Teaching and Teacher Education
– Assessment and Evaluation

This structure allows readers to study the volumes in isolation, by discipline, or laterally, by topic, and facilitates a comparative, thematic reading of chapters across the volumes. Throughout the series, attention is paid to how the disciplines comprising the educational foundations speak to social justice concerns such as gender and racial equality.

Volume 1: Philosophical Foundations of Education
edited by Winston C. Thompson

Volume 2: Historical Foundations of Education
edited by Theodore Michael Christou

Volume 3: Sociological Foundations of Education
edited by Claire Maxwell, Miri Yemini, and Laura Engel

Volume 4: Policy Foundations of Education
edited by Andrew Wilkins

Volume 5: Economic Foundations of Education
edited by Álvaro Choi

Volume 6: Legal Foundations of Education
edited by J.C. Blokhuis

HISTORICAL FOUNDATIONS
OF EDUCATION

edited by Theodore Michael Christou

BLOOMSBURY ACADEMIC
LONDON • NEW YORK • OXFORD • NEW DELHI • SYDNEY

BLOOMSBURY ACADEMIC
Bloomsbury Publishing Plc
50 Bedford Square, London, WC1B 3DP, UK
1385 Broadway, New York, NY 10018, USA
29 Earlsfort Terrace, Dublin 2, Ireland

BLOOMSBURY, BLOOMSBURY ACADEMIC and the Diana logo are
trademarks of Bloomsbury Publishing Plc

First published in Great Britain 2023

Cover design: Charlotte James
Cover image © CSA Images/ Getty Images

A catalogue record for this book is available from the British Library.

A catalog record for this book is available from the Library of Congress.

ISBN: HB: 978-1-3501-7092-6
       ePDF: 978-1-3501-7093-3
       eBook: 978-1-3501-7094-0
       Set: 978-1-3501-7152-7

Typeset by Integra Software Services Pvt. Ltd.
Printed and bound in Great Britain

To find out more about our authors and books visit www.bloomsbury.com
and sign up for our newsletters.

CONTENTS

LIST OF ILLUSTRATIONS   vii

GENERAL EDITORS' PREFACE   viii
Bruce Maxwell and Lauren Bialystok

Introduction   1
Theodore Michael Christou

1   Mapping the Field: New Foundations for Making Meaning
of the Past   15
*Theodore Michael Christou, Rebecca S. Evans, and Christopher
McCuaig*

2   Purposes of Education: Unsettling Historical Accounts of
Settler Colonial Public Education   39
*Nicholas Ng-A-Fook, Patrick Phillips, Mark T.S. Currie,
and Jackson Pind*

3   Curriculum: The Educational Experience in the School Curriculum   65
Peter Hlebowits

4   Schools and Education Systems: Oscillating between a Force
for Change and an Agent of Social Stagnation   87
Ryan W. Coughlan

5   Learning and Human Development: Thinking Historically About
Studying Childhood   111
Shawn Michael Bullock and Cécile Sabatier Bullock

6   Teaching and Teacher Education: The Interplay of Bureaucratic
Rationalization and Occupational Professionalism   137
Dorothea Anagnostopoulos and Jack Schneider

7 Assessment and Evaluation: Assessment is Posited within Evaluation 157
Corrie Rebecca Klinger and Don A. Klinger

LIST OF CONTRIBUTORS 184
INDEX 187

ILLUSTRATIONS

FIGURE

0.1   Education Is Bigger Than School   3

TABLE

7.1   Summary of the *Taxonomy of Educational Objectives Handbook I: The Cognitive Domain* (1956) by Benjamin S. Bloom, Max Englehart, Edward J. Furst, Walker Hill, and David Krathwohl   169

GENERAL EDITORS' PREFACE

BRUCE MAXWELL

UNIVERSITY OF MONTREAL

LAUREN BIALYSTOK

UNIVERSITY OF TORONTO

Readers of a certain age will undoubtedly remember Choose Your Own Adventure children's books. In a normal novel, the author leads the reader through a series of fixed events and experiences lived by some other person. Choose Your Own Adventure books were different because they made the reader the protagonist. Every few pages, options were proposed about what to do next so that the story unfolded in different ways depending on the reader's choices. The net effect, enhanced by the uncustomary use of the second person throughout, is that readers themselves determine the reading experience. We offer this six-volume book series on educational foundations in much the same spirit. It does not have to be read sequentially, but rather can be delved into according to one's personal, academic, or professional interests and informational needs. These are books made for exploration.

THE AIM AND STRUCTURE OF THE SERIES

If a reference work in educational foundations like this one is to be comprehensive, it must necessarily be extremely long. If conciseness is the aim, comprehensiveness is out of the question. The foundations, after all, comprise a set of disciplinary approaches to education whose boundaries are porous and contested, and which take up a vast array of topics. The relevant literatures span centuries and their influence is global. Yet at the same time, the study of educational foundations is nearly always, and rightly so, adapted to local contexts and current educational unknown—what topics and issues are examined under this heading, and even the very academic disciplines it is thought to include, can thus vary considerably from place to place and shift as the decades recede behind us. From an editorial standpoint, faced with this surfeit of material, the choice between offering selected tidbits from the great canvass of the education foundations or taking a deep dive into one particular conception of the educational foundations may seem inevitable. The result of the first choice is superficiality. The result of the second is neglect.

In the design of this series, we have attempted to avoid these compromises. We have tried to offer a substantial but also comparative view of educational foundations that highlights the distinct contributions of six selected foundations disciplines. The six volumes are devoted, respectively, to the disciplines of philosophy (Volume 1), history (Volume 2), sociology (Volume 3), politics (Volume 4), economics (Volume 5), and law (Volume 6), but the structure of the volumes is consistent in that the same set of chapter headings appears in each of the volumes and in the same order. The goal of this parallel structure is to encourage the chapter authors, all internationally recognized experts in their fields, to explore the same key topics in education from the vantage point of their respective disciplines. Using a style accessible to a wide audience of education students, teacher educators, and others interested in educational issues, their writ was to produce informative and rigorous statements on how their home academic discipline approaches the topic they were assigned and how their field has contributed to the advancement of knowledge in these areas.

In the first chapter of each volume in this series, "Mapping the Field," the volume editors survey the characteristic sources, methods, and concerns of their field as it has engaged with education. In the ensuing chapters, the contributing authors address the six themes that we selected to encompass a range of broad topics that have been of perennial interest to educational thinkers across cultures at least since the advent of mass, compulsory schooling. The first three chapters in each volume are concerned with the wider conceptual and institutional contexts of schooling. The chapters titled "Purposes of Education" (Chapter 2) address the general aims of teaching and learning as they occur within schools and education systems. The chapters on "Curriculum" (Chapter 3) and "Schools and Education Systems" (Chapter 4) deal with what children and young people are taught in school and why, and the institutional frameworks through which the curriculum is transmitted and particular aims are pursued. The final three chapters in the volumes turn to matters closer to pedagogy and instruction. The chapters on "Learning and Human Development" (Chapter 5) consider how children and young people acquire what is taught in school and how education shapes them as persons. The chapters on "Teaching and Teacher Education" (Chapter 6) examine how adults help children and young people acquire what is taught in school and how to prepare adults to occupy the educator role. The final chapter in each volume deals with "Assessment and Evaluation" (Chapter 7), or how we judge students' progress in acquiring what is taught in school as well as the outcomes of educational systems.

The advantage of the overarching structure of the series is that it facilitates a vertical and horizontal reading, which makes the set of books conducive to exploration. Readers interested in one disciplinary perspective only could study that volume in depth. And, since each volume covers the same set of topics and the common themes appear as the titles of the chapters, readers interested in a particular topic can read across the volumes to find out what different academic disciplines have to say about it.

THE EDUCATIONAL FOUNDATIONS IN CONTEXT

The publication of this book series comes at a curious moment in the history of the field of educational foundations. The choices that led to the design of this series were very much the product of this historical context.

Educational foundations as a core subject in teacher education has never been so uncertain (Neuman 2009; Shutz and Butin 2013). The widespread belief among teacher educators that future teachers need to be versed to some extent in the educational foundations is a vestige of a once-dominant liberal arts model of teacher education. Taking hold during the first half of the twentieth century under the influence of John Dewey and likeminded progressivists (see Butin 2005b), the idea that the humanities should be central to teacher education came increasingly under attack after the Second World War, and has lost ground steadily through to the present. Under pressure from government and trustee institutions, faculties of education in North America and Europe have been gravitating for some time toward a professional training model for teachers and away from the liberal arts model that made humanistic studies so central to teacher education (Colgan and Maxwell 2019). With these changes came the slow but ineluctable erosion of educational foundations content in teacher education. While instruction in the foundations of education was once typically separated into discrete areas of study, under the influence of a professional training model and neoliberal pressures, professional preparation in the foundations has been consolidated and diluted. Two generations ago, education students could expect tens of hours of instruction dedicated exclusively to educational philosophy and theory, the history of educational systems and ideas, and the sociological analysis of educational methods and institutions. Today, the curricular diet of the average education student contains but a few hours of educational foundations material, in which the constitutive disciplines may be blurred together. Although the phrase "foundations of education" promises to transmit the collected wisdom of multiple traditions, most courses in educational foundations are taught by a single instructor with relevant expertise and qualifications in at most one discipline in the humanities or social sciences.

Furthermore, the great variety of topics addressed under the heading of "educational foundations" is testimony to a state of deep uncertainty among teacher educators and foundations scholars themselves about what the educational foundations are all about (see Butin 2005a; Ryan 2006; Neumann 2006; Kerr, Mandzuk, and Raptis 2011; Hartlep et al. 2015). Some adopt a discipline-based view, limiting educational foundations to three areas of scholarly inquiry: philosophy of education, history of education, and sociology of education, usually in that order (e.g., Semel 2010). Others add to the list of disciplinary lenses that constitute the educational foundations anthropology, policy studies, law, and economics (e.g., Pope and Stemhagen 2008). Still others expand educational foundations to include such diverse forms of scholarship as cultural studies, gender studies, religious studies, indigenous ontologies, critical theory, and comparative and international education (see Committee on Academic Standards and Accreditation 2013; Hartlep et al. 2015). In the United Kingdom, much more so than in North America, psychology is often considered a foundations discipline. Indeed, the lists of topics and fields that have been proposed to define "the foundations of education" give the impression it is a catch-all term for anything to do with education that is theoretical, critically reflective, or abstract, as opposed to content that relates to the practical matters of effective instruction, evaluation, and classroom management. The scales fall from one's eyes, however, when one peruses the tables of contents of textbooks explicitly positioned as works on the educational foundations, social foundations of education, or education studies. Such books routinely contain chapters on assessment, classroom management, and reflective teaching practice (e.g., Curtis et al. 2013; Edmunds et al. 2015). In the end, perhaps the practical and the theoretical in teaching are not that distinct.

It is common knowledge that the foundations of education—which we take to be essentially coextensive with "social foundations of education" and "education studies"—lie at the epicenter of an ideological earthquake that has been shaking teacher education and educational research since about the turn of the twenty-first century. Given the depth of the identity crisis facing the educational foundations, it is a small wonder that a consensus has emerged around educational foundations as a vehicle for advancing the cause of social justice concerns in education and denouncing data-driven educational decision-making. If those invested in educational foundations are looking for a way to demonstrate its relevance to teacher education, who can deny that the problem of educational inequality is bad and getting worse and that unbridled managerialism in education can create more problems than it solves? Teachers need to know this.

As the debates rage on about what the educational foundations are and what role they should play in teacher preparation, over the last thirty years, interest in educational issues has quietly grown, not only within academic disciplines typically associated with educational foundations—philosophy, history, sociology—but also in other disciplines that fall outside the educational foundations' customary sphere. The latter include political science, economics, and law. This newfound interest in educational research has led to a proliferation of research associations, academic journals, and scholarly conferences dedicated to the study of education from a particular disciplinary perspective. At their best, these sites operate as a meeting ground where fruitful exchange occurs between researchers based in education departments and faculties (who tend to be better versed in the realities of classroom instruction, mass schooling, and teacher formation) and researchers who are more inclined to tackle educational issues from within the boundaries of specific academic disciplines. Academic expertise in educational issues is no longer the exclusive purview of scholars affiliated with education departments in universities.

This book series seeks to leverage this exciting new scholarly interest in educational matters, both for the benefit of those engaged in educational theory, research, and practice, and for the benefit of the field of educational foundations itself. We believe that educational justice can be served by asking what we can learn from specific academic disciplines in the social sciences and humanities and how they frame, study, and understand the universal and recurrent questions in education, as well as how they can help us to think about evolving realities within and outside schools.

SELECTING THE SIX FOUNDATIONS DISCIPLINES

Setting out the general objectives for the book series was, relatively speaking, the easy part. Settling on which disciplinary perspectives would (and would not) be represented in the series involved some tough choices. As we saw above, there is no authoritative list of the fields that make up educational foundations. Our gambit in this series is that certain disciplines deserve to be read independently as part of the mosaic that makes up educational studies. Our selection of the six disciplines that were elected for inclusion in this series—philosophy, history, sociology, policy studies, economics, and law—reflects some degree of overlapping consensus among those who debate the contents of educational foundations, but does not purport to be definitive or immutable. We chose these six fields, not as a function of how frequently they are recognized as foundational, but because they met our criteria for the kinds of disciplines that would work in this series.

First, we wanted to include only fields with a long-standing and recognized history in academia, ones characterized by fairly well-defined objects of study as well as methods of inquiry proper to them. The application of this criterion led us to exclude, most notably, a volume on the cultural foundations of education. Cultural studies is a relative newcomer on the academic scene and its distinctive area of concern and methodological and analytic approaches are still very fluid. Nevertheless, many of the concerns of cultural studies are captured within more established disciplines, especially critical sociology, for which the sociological foundations volume gives a forum. Second, we wanted to ensure that each volume had a relatively distinct identity in terms of content and to avoid undue overlap with any other volume in the series. The application of this criterion led us to exclude, most notably, a volume on the anthropological foundations of education, as we felt that repetition with a sociology volume would have been inevitable. Third, we wanted to make sure that any discipline selected for the series would have something substantive to say about the wide range of recurrent issues in education articulated in the series' chapter headings. The application of this criterion led us to rule out a volume on the psychological foundations of education. While psychologists undoubtedly have much to say on such topics as learning and human development and assessment, topics such as the purposes of education and the curriculum generally fall outside psychology's individual-oriented scope.

While the six disciplines retained for this series all met our criteria, there are noteworthy differences between them as well. Some, history and philosophy in particular, have been recognized as areas of formal inquiry for millennia. Indeed, philosophy, previously known as the "queen of the sciences," may have hitherto subsumed many of the methods and areas of inquiry that branched into their own disciplines during modernity, and which are still splintering today. Moreover, educational questions were always present in philosophical thought, going back in the Western tradition at least as far as Plato's *Republic*. In the contemporary academy, educational questions are less often addressed in philosophy departments, but philosophical questions seem to permeate the study of education. Along with philosophy, the trio of classical foundational disciplines most commonly taught today includes history and sociology. Understood in opposition to the technical or practical dimensions of teaching, these disciplines are now widely regarded as constituting the core of the "educational foundations" and often operate as a beachhead for the social sciences and humanities in faculties of education.

In contrast to the classical foundations, economics, policy studies, and law have developed as branches of educational study only recently, but now provide perspectives on all aspects of formal schooling. These fields have rapidly gained substantial influence and may be, in the eyes of educational policymakers and administrators at any rate, the most important areas of educational study. Educational economics has shaped the twenty-first-century view of education as an investment good that is crucial to microeconomics as well as to global markets and national growth. This focus follows naturally from global shifts in economic policy toward neoliberalism and privatization, which have resulted in stronger connections between education and labor markets. However, contrary to popular belief, perhaps, educational economists are also concerned with the effects of inequality, both as inputs into educational systems and as outcomes of educational marketization. Policy studies uses empirical and theoretical methods to examine political forces in education, and especially the processes by which governments make educational choices. Drawing from other critical social sciences, policy studies is especially well suited to understanding relations of power and authority in education. The discipline of law traditionally studies how legal systems determine and interpret legal norms, but educational law has become a focus of legal scholarship only comparatively recently. Developing in tandem with the judicialization of American education, educational law focuses on the analysis of case law from around the world on such issues as parents' rights in education, the need for schools to respect students' basic rights, and the role the courts have played in advancing the cause of educational justice and equality.

As much as philosophy, history, sociology, policy studies, economics, and law offer distinct perspectives and resources for understanding educational phenomena, these disciplines all broadly apply the methods of the humanities and social sciences to questions of curriculum, learning, teaching, and schooling. We do not conceive of a discipline as a monolithic tradition of study; educational scholars borrow liberally from one another and move toward similar goals, all while advancing their respective traditions. The layout of this series is intended to showcase similarities across disciplines that tend to work on parallel problems in relative isolation from one another. These volumes feature recurrent methods of analysis—for instance, critiques of power and interpretations of social processes—as well as appeals to shared intellectual ancestors—such as John Dewey, Michel Foucault, or Émile Durkheim. Taken together, the six disciplines that anchor this book series provide panoramic perspectives on a battery of educational issues. By presenting them as a symmetrical set, we hope to advance understanding of the meaning and importance of educational foundations, separately and collectively.

ADVANCING EDUCATIONAL JUSTICE WITH THE SOCIAL SCIENCES AND HUMANITIES

While the academic origins of much educational research have been pushed out of teacher education, the critical spirit of the humanities and social sciences is alive and well in many faculties of education. As mentioned earlier, when teacher education tips into the non-technical, it is often oriented toward a social justice agenda that highlights how education systems reproduce and can exacerbate patterns of oppression and inequality. These concerns have gained traction in the context of global racial reckonings, the climate crisis, and the COVID-19 pandemic, which intensified all manner of disparities and challenges in education.

We take seriously the demands of educational justice in both research and practice, but social justice education is not a discipline in its own right, nor can it be said to be an academic foundation that has shaped the study of education through modernity. We believe it is through an appreciation of the educational foundations that social justice concerns can best be understood and leveraged to create change. Concerns about equity and the injustice of background conditions suffuse these volumes, highlighting the ongoing relevance of educational foundations for interpreting the world and challenging educational practices. Schools and universities, like other institutions, are presently in the throes of diversity, equity, and inclusion (DEI) discourse and corresponding mandates to rid themselves of racist legacies and biases. Severed from historical understanding or reasoned explanation, these institutional positions have at times been criticized for paying lip service to social justice while reinforcing neoliberal structures. By engaging deeply with the academic work that calls these structures into question, these volumes offer a means of contextualizing and interpreting the need for DEI in all aspects of formal education.

Given the political context and professional pressures we have described, this series is intended to be both backward-looking and forward-looking. The contributors—a diverse group hailing from five continents—are leading scholars who have their finger on the pulse of their fields and directions for future research. By articulating the contributions of academic disciplines to educational studies and the state of research in those fields, these volumes can inform rigorous scholarship, educational policy, and professional practice. However much of the series you read, and in whatever order, we hope that these books will leave you enlightened and with a renewed appreciation for the richness that the social sciences and humanities have to offer the study of education.

REFERENCES

Butin, Dan W. (2005a), "Guest Editor's Introduction: How Social Foundations of Education Matters to Teacher Preparation: A Policy Brief," *Educational Studies*, 38 (3): 214–29.

Butin, Dan W. (2005b), *Teaching Social Foundations of Education*, New York: Routledge.

Colgan, Andrew D. and Bruce Maxwell, eds. (2019), *The Importance of Philosophy in Teacher Education: Mapping the Decline and its Consequences*, Abingdon, UK: Routledge.

Committee on Academic Standards and Accreditation: Sandra Winn Tutweiler (Chair), Kathleen deMarrais, David Gabbard, Andrea Hyde, Pamela Konkol, Huey-li Li, Yolanda Medina, Joseph Rayle, and Amy Swain (2013), "Standards for Academic and Professional Instruction in Foundations of Education, Educational Studies, and Educational Policy Studies, third edition, 2012, draft presented to the educational

community by the American Educational Studies Association's Committee on
   Academic Standards and Accreditation," *Educational Studies*, 49 (2): 107–18.
Curtis, Will, Stephen Ward, John Sharp, and Les Hankin, eds. (2013), *Education
   Studies: An Issue Based Approach*, London: Learning Matters.
Edmunds, Alan, Jodi Nickel, Kenneth Rea Badley, and Gail Edmunds (2015),
   Educational Foundations in Canada, Don Mills, ONT: Oxford University Press.
Hartlep, Nicholas D., Bradley J. Porfilio, Stacy Otto, and Kathleen O'Brien (2015),
   "What We Stand *For*, Not *Against*: Presenting our Teacher Education Colleagues
   with the Case for Social Foundations in PK–12 Teacher Preparation Programs,"
   Educational Foundations, 28: 135–50.
Kerr, Donald, David Mandzuk, and Helen Raptis (2011), "The Role of the Social
   Foundations of Education in Programs of Teacher Preparation in Canada,"
   Canadian Journal of Education, 34 (4): 118–34.
Neumann, Richard (2009), "Highly Qualified Teachers and the Social Foundations of
   Education," *Phi Delta Kappan*, 91 (3): 81–5.
Plato (1974), *The Republic*, trans. G.M.A. Grube, Indianapolis, IN: Hackett.
Pope, Nakia S. and Kurt Stemhagen (2008), "Social Foundations Educators of the
   World Unite! An Action Plan for Disciplinary Advocacy," *Educational Studies*,
   44 (3): 247–55.
Ryan, Ann Marie (2006), "The Role of Social Foundations in Preparing Teachers for
   Culturally Relevant Practice," *Multicultural Education*, 13 (3): 10–13.
Schutz, Aaron, and Dan W. Butin (2013), "Beyond Dependency: Strategies for Saving
   Foundations," *Critical Questions in Education*, 4 (2): 60–71.
Semel, Susan F., ed. (2010), *Foundations of Education: The Essential Texts*,
   New York: Routledge.

Introduction

THEODORE MICHAEL CHRISTOU

On November 8, 2021, just as several years' of work on this volume came to completion, Elon Musk used the global medium Twitter to tweet: "'We are choked with news and starved of history' – Durant" (Musk 2021). More than 250,000 engagements in a day signify less than 1 percent of Musk's ~68,000,000 followers; yet the Will Durant Society members must have appreciated the attention.[1] The original text of Durant's text, *Invitation to History*, is a polemic about the teaching of history, opening as follows:

> "History" said Henry Ford, "is bunk." As one who has written history for twenty-five years, and studied it for forty-five, I should largely agree with the great engineer who put half the world on wheels. History as studied in schools – history as a dreary succession of dates and kings, of politics and wars, of the rise and fall of states – this kind of history is verily a weariness of the flesh, stale and flat and unprofitable. No wonder so few students in school are drawn to it; no wonder so few of us learn any lessons from the past.
>
> (Durant 1945)

Unsurprisingly, Durant's text sprawls with ambition, entangling references as diverse as Priam and Chaplin—the term, a mile wide an inch deep comes to mind—yet somehow resonant with a billionaire entrepreneur. I cite Musk here not because he is some exemplar of historical virtue; rather, I point to him as a human who has captured the popular imaginary as the incarnation of progress and futurism, who laments the contemporaneity of our existence. Simultaneously, history has never seemed more marginal in schools of education (see, for example, Christou 2010; Pitblado and Christou 2020).

History of education is not the foundation of teacher education programs (Christou and Sears 2011).5 At best, history has gone "underground" (Corbett 2013).6 As Michael Corbett demonstrates within the Canadian context, the questions asked by foundations may have merely gone *underground*, integrated across the curriculum of education programs, even as they have diminished as stand-alone offerings. While Corbett's analysis applied to sociology of education courses, its prescience should not be lost on educational historians. Perhaps we ought not to lament or decry the seeming decline of history (or any of the foundations fields examined in this series) but celebrate its influence and ability to move the needle toward a more critical disposition about schools, their history, and the contexts in which we live, work, and play. History, like any of the foundations, might be seen less as a structural foundation of concrete beneath a skyrise and more as an arterial network running through teacher education. This is a rich metaphor, which future scholarship might explore for all it enables and ignores as a heuristic for describing how history might thrive (Christou 2012; Christou and Bullock 2013).

The notion that history survives in the underground is troubling. It presumes that historians of education are comfortable with shadow. It has sinister tones. It reifies contemporaneity, which only assigns to the past instrumental value.

Why is it more relevant to develop a lesson plan than it is to understand how we came to plan lessons at all? Why is history either presented as a foundation or as a marginalized force for good relegated to the margins? There are very old ideas at play here, which relate to hypothetical orientations to change we have. Herbert Kliebard (1995) identified these orientations as "neophobia" and "neophilia." To be "phobic" of what is new is to stand by a generally established way of seeing and living in the world, fearful or hesitant of the world to come. Whereas to be "philic" of what is new is to embrace new orientations that are directly or tangentially oppositional to the established order, eager to experience change. Kliebard's distinction opens up new avenues for examining ourselves, as well as the past, yet humans operate in the spaces *between* these extremes.

Our relationship with the past can be characterized by further ambivalence. Forrest Gump, a fictional character in film, notes: "My Mama always said you've got to put the past behind you before you can move on" (*Forrest Gump* 1994).7 Gump's life becomes a lens through which ignominious moments in United States history are revealed, including the Vietnam War and the

Watergate scandal, yet Gump's words popularize a conception that history is a series of wounds we must overcome. We ought to be neither fearful of the past nor ought we to revere it.

Being historically minded—living our lives in a way that is informed by and derived by the ways we look at the past—is akin to being a Jedi attuned to the Force. T.S. Eliot ably voiced this sentiment without appeal to Star Wars:

> Time present and time past
> Are both perhaps present in time future,
> And time future contained in time past.

(Eliot 1954: 13)

We live in time. We blink and the blink is forgotten because time rolls forward and another blink is already upon us, like water lapping in a gulf. Our attention thus remains forward-looking. Unblinking, we might say. The past: it seems to get in the way.

HISTORICAL NOTES FROM THE UNDERGROUND

John Dewey, perceiving the rise of vocationalism in education, cautioned us not to conflate schools and education. Rather, he advised: "Relate the school to life, and all studies are of necessity correlated" (Dewey 1907: 107).9 The life of the learner does not begin the minute they enter a school building or, with distance learning, when the scheduled school day begins virtually. Schools, in other words, might be institutions, but education was a way of learning throughout life. At the risk of trivializing the point, a visual may be illustrative, (see Figure 0.1).

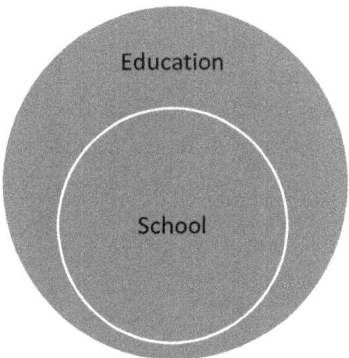

FIGURE 0.1 Education Is Bigger Than School.

Figure 0.1 is not intended to diminish the importance of schooling. If anything, I have given schooling too much real estate in the sphere of our lives. John Dewey, with unusual clarity, states the relationship as follows:

Schools are, indeed, one important method of the transmission which forms the dispositions of the immature; but here it is only one means, and, compared with other agencies, a relatively superficial means. Only as we have grasped the necessity of more fundamental and persistent modes of tuition can we make sure of placing the scholastic methods in their true context.

(Dewey 1916: 4)

Teacher education does not place schools in their context so much as elevating them to a lode star that fixes our attention. Context, in education, comes principally from history, although each of the foundations are seminal.

Why do we always begin tinkering with school curricula when we want to rebuild education? Perhaps it is because we spend many of our formative hours, days, and years within schools. Under typical circumstances, we will spend much more of our time outside of schools.[2] Yet, so many of our educational opportunities are twisted to prepare us for life *within* institutions such as schools. An education ought to liberate us from our own restraints. I am not certain that schools, even if they are educational, are liberatory. As an educational historian, I have come to doubt the foundations upon which I have stood as a teacher and a student. It is, in such plain terms, apparent that history is a foundational subject in education.

Since the 1960s, this fairly intuitive observation about the relationship of schools to life has been framed as "radical revisionism," thanks to this clever turn of phrase by Diane Ravitch (1978). While Ravitch's reproach to educational historians was explicitly directed to the conceptual tools that said radicals brought to their analyses of schools and society, her review of historiographic scholarship is comprised of as ideological as the revisionists she labels. That contemporary educational discourse is populated by invocations of the "radical left" as somehow compromised is a testament to the legacy of fault lines that emerged in the 1960s and became entrenched in the following decade.

In 1960, Bernard Bailyn published *Education in the Forming of American Society*, which explicitly defined education as a broad process of social, cultural transmission (Ravitch 1978). Bailyn was rightly critical of educational history, which, while popular in schools of education, was limited to a story of unending progress, leading to the present. Bailyn was not alone. Lawrence Cremin and scholars including Edward Krug would draw on intellectual, social, and political history to articulate broader historical examinations of the role of education in society (Cremin 1961). Ravitch acknowledged the seminal influence of this scholarship in reshaping the conversations we have about the history of education, noting: "The Bailyn-Cremin critique proved to be liberating and fruitful. It broke down the artificial barriers that had isolated educational history from the mainstream" (Ravitch 1978: 27). Bailyn and Cremin draw on the scholarship of John Dewey, echoing his thoughts about education as a process of cultural transmission "from the older to the younger. Without this communication of ideals, hopes, expectations, standards, opinions, from those members of society who are passing out of the group life to those who are coming into it, social life could not survive" (Dewey 1916: 3).

Identifying scholarship by Joel Spring, Samuel Boles, Herbert Gintis, and other contemporaries, Ravitch claims that the educational historians she identifies as radical revisionists have repudiated the liberal tradition, which underpinned the establishment of schools in society:

> Where liberals had argued that the spread of public schooling was social progress, radicals saw the public school as a weapon of social control and indoctrination; where liberals had maintained that reforms like compulsory schooling freed children from oppressive workplaces, radicals saw compulsory schooling as an expansion of the coercive power of the state; where liberals believed in the power of schooling to liberate people from their social origins, the radicals perceived the school as a social sorting device which undergirds an unjust, exploitative class system; where liberals considered the school to be an integral part of democratic society, radicals viewed it as a mechanism by which one group (an elite) exploits and manipulates another (the masses or the workers or the minorities or "the community"); where liberals had worked to insure that individual merit would be rewarded without regard to race or religion or other ascriptive factors, radicals described the outcome of this effort as meritocracy, hierarchy, and bureaucracy.
>
> (Ravitch 1978: 29)

Ravitch demands the space to describe two opposing camps in educational history, setting the tone for educational historians to take the metaphor of warring armies wrestling for control over the core narratives we tell ourselves about the relationship of schools to society over time.

I have seen two distinct pathways emerge for educational historians, which were apparent when I was a young scholar in the field. One possibility upholds Western, liberal traditions while the other questions these and seeks to undermine them. There are thus competing narratives in the history of education, only some of which might be considered a foundation for the study Western educational ideas, while others seek to question the foundation as well as its pillars. What complicates this picture is the absence of clear demarcation between these two hypothetical camps of historians of education. They are distinguished by degree, not substance. The so-called radicals are radical because they go too far, questioning the liberal order holding so many of our educational institutions together, even if their position is a logical continuation of the same line of scholarship. Bailyn and Cremin broadened the horizons of educational historians, even as their work seems to marks the borderlands between revisionist and foundational scholarship.

History is dangerous. More specifically, history has the *potential* to be dangerous. As David Tyack notes, history is also constructive and enabling, invaluable for building educational policy, not merely contextualizing:

> As contributors to the dialogue on policy, historians do not need to be wet blankets who assure the world that policies have been tried and found wanting. And certainly they should not be cheerleaders drawing happy-faced precedents for the latest reform. Like philosophers who find puzzling layers of meaning in the ordinary, or anthropologists who make the familiar strange, historians often do their best service to policy by helping people redefine both problems and solutions. Diversity flowers when people learn to think otherwise.
>
> (Tyack 2000: 19–20)

History can build up and it can tear down. It can be educative, broadening the horizons of our understanding of the human experience over time and unfolding potential. History can also contribute to what Noam Chomsky calls "mis-education," which inhibits of our capacity to know the world and act as agents of change therein (Chomsky 2000). It is little surprise, then, that history of education has been relegated to the underground in schools of education, where central control has institutional, governmental, and popular faces. History can challenge our conceptions of the extant order, sometimes radically so. One way to render history inert would be to marginalize it within a curriculum, ensuring that learners only encounter superficialities.

THE PRESSURES OF THE PRACTICAL

While opportunities for students to learn history of education are slim, the research undertaken by educational historians is immense. Larry Cuban offers a useful framing of scholarship in history of education, representing it as a continuum (Cuban 2001). For our purposes, it offers a vernacular for understanding the ways that educational history both supports and challenges policy making within a state.

There are three groups represented on Cuban's "Curriculum of Historians" (2001: 456). On the far left are "Presentists." In the center are "Policy-Sensitive Historians." On the far right of the continuum are "Non-Policy Historians."

Presentists: "ask questions anchored in the present; seek lessons for policymakers; give policy recommendations" (Cuban 2001: 456). Policy-sensitive historians: "ask questions anchored in the present; render an account of the past that raises questions about current policy without offering prescriptions" (456). Non-policy historians: "ask questions anchored in the past or present; render an account of the past with little concern for undercurrent policy." Cuban describes the center—which is where the vast majority of scholarship in educational history is best placed—as follows: "between the two groups are yet even other historians of education who see historical methods as useful tools for policy analysis and redefining a current problem by examining previous generations of reformers struggling with similar but not identical situations and the alternatives that these earlier reformers generated" (456). While there are multiple continua and dichotomies presented by scholars to define the work of educational history, lived experiences are somewhere in between, not at, the extremes. Policy-sensitive historians of education have a tremendous contribution to make to the development of historically minded education policy and governance. Such policy would, in the words of Tyack: "not only to *use a sense* of the past (which they do willy-nilly) but also to *make sense* of it" (Tyack 2000: 56 noted in Cuban 2001: 456).

In a space such as teacher education, there are other factors to consider beyond the terrain that historians of education must navigate, referred to here as the "pressures of the practical" (see, for example, Christou 2009). The first pressure relates to the accountability shift in teacher education, the need for measures of efficiency and effectiveness while increasing teacher quality. This pressure emerged, in part, as a result of shortened programs and congested curricula. The second pressure relates to the perceived theory–practice divide that perpetuates teacher education programs, miscasting history as a theoretical bit player to the real business of preparing teachers to teach. The third pressure relates to the widespread belief that classroom teaching (i.e., practicum) is the primary method for learning to teach. The fourth pressure relates to the directionality and source of teacher education reforms: from government and certifying bodies to universities and education faculty members. Teacher education programs are increasingly under pressure to add content and skills to their curricula, not to speak of other initiatives spurred on by fears and competitiveness (so often picked up as banners, then left forgotten on the field). The fifth pressure relates to the grouping together of academic disciplines under the banner of Foundations courses, blurring disciplinary lines.

Certain pressures on institutions are internal, as any school of education must contribute to the academic mission of an institution of higher learning, primarily universities. Others are external, exerted by governmental or professional institutions, which certify or represent teachers. These pressures have contributed to the marginalization of history as a foundation in teacher education, although there are certainly other formulations of the same. Educational historians would be finely depicted as pretzels by an alien in a spaceship, watching them twist one way to participate in the intellectual life of the university, particularly engaging with history departments, then another to support their students as they prepare to enter into a professional field (see Christou 2015).

There is a sixth pressure, which might be added to the non-exhaustive list above, which may be at the root of all historians of education's woes: the "apprenticeship of observation." Teacher candidates, faculty, administrators, and the public at large have already learned a great deal about history before they find their way to higher education (Lortie 1975). By virtue of having been students in history and social studies classes for most of their lives, we all have strong beliefs about what history is as a discipline and how it ought to be taught. We know this to be true in our lives. We had a mix of educative and miseducative experiences in school. Unfortunately for the educational historians, droves of students have turned away from history, as it remains one of the most despised subjects (see, for example, Perrotta and Bohan 2013).

We have very powerful images of the history classroom impressed on our minds. These images come as memories of our student years or as stories from cinema, film, and our contemporaries. Thick books stacked, teeming with content to learn. Examinations and essays, recalling details of a particular war or the sequence of events in some retelling of a dominant myth. Chalkboards, acetates, and digital slides projected onto white screens of vinyl. Lectures. War and occupation. Nationalism. So much of history is trauma.

Despite all the powerful images we have of pedagogy that treat textbooks— alongside more popular media, including film and television—as gospel, history is alive and well. Neither schools nor any institution hold monopolies over the teaching of history, let alone the history of education. Education is not a narrowing of experience, but a relational exchange between citizens, past and present. Theaters, streaming services, and the television are teeming with portrayals of the past. Bookstores, where they exist, feature complex sections on history. Streets, schools, and structures are named for historical figures and spaces. In our lives, we wrap the past around us, living as humans in time.

My first year as a professor in education, a colleague and I received an invitation to present to the history professors about the high school history curriculum preceding. These professors were concerned with meeting the students "where they were" at the beginning of their undergraduate programs. A noble aim. When we began our presentation, my colleague uttered, "Ted and I want to know why you do not actually teach history."[3] He went on to remind them of their research in archives, how nuanced and challenging the search for evidence can be, how tentatively and carefully our narratives are constructed on the basis of said evidence, and how our research often raised more questions than it answered. Yet, he cautioned, when we stand in front of a lecture hall, we pronounce that such and such an event occurred and that so and so were its causes.

We produce textbooks that by their very design must move entire movements to marginal notes and ignore others, even as we reinforce a faulty conception that all there is to know about history might be contained in a book. As if we were able to hold entireties within any pages. Even if history teacher substitute revisionist textbooks for those that "portray the past as a simple morality play," why is it colloquial to *learn* history as opposed to *doing historical work*? (Loewen 1995: 3; see also Zinn 1990).

The opposition between learning and doing is exemplified in the following narrative from Ken Osborne:

> I once visited a classroom and, not knowing what subject was due to be taught, asked a boy sitting next to me what he was learning in the class. It proved to be an interesting way to frame the question. Had I asked what subject was being taught he would have told me social studies, since that was in fact the case. But, on being asked what he was learning, he gave me an unexpected but honest answer. "To take notes off the overhead projector," he said, and that was indeed what happened for the whole period, as the students diligently copied notes from the screen.
>
> (Osborne 1991: 10)

Osborne notes that the student seemed to have a richer understanding of what history is than the teacher did. This teacher's understanding of history education is not unique, as it was based on a very powerful preconception of this discipline. We are not compelled to repeat the past unless we are entirely oblivious to its meanings and lessons.

Lortie's framing of the "apprenticeship of observation" is key to unlocking David Tyack's findings that policymakers and individuals in positions of authority think they know the past and formulate decisions on the basis of these false beliefs (Tyack 1979). To know that such and such happened in the past is not to know history. Larry Cuban succinctly referred to many of our conceptions of the past as the "blurred images" of history (Cuban 2001: 456). History of education is one of the essential tools we have to help us step back from the pressures of the practical and examine the foundation upon which we build. While the ground remains beneath our feet, it shifts relentlessly. Here is the Roman stoic Seneca:

> But those who forget the past, neglect the present, and fear for the future have a life that is very brief and troubled; when they have reached the end of

it, the poor wretches perceive too late that for such a long while they have
been busied in doing nothing.

(Seneca 1932: xiv)

Seneca reminds us that we ought to look to those who came before us as human
beings who have experienced life and sought to share their experiences with us.
We might consult with these humans who came before us as if they were our
contemporaries, learning from them and creating kinship across temporal lines.

As many historians of education are based in schools of education and
employed in some form of teacher education, it is essential to return to this
domain. While historians of education might counter preconceptions about the
foundations of our learning, Donna Kagan offers a sobering conclusion on the
basis of a comprehensive scholarly literature review:

Candidates tend to use the information provided in coursework to confirm
rather than to confront and correct their preexisting beliefs. Thus, a
candidate's personal beliefs and images determine how much knowledge the
candidate acquires from a preservice program and how it is interpreted.

(Kagan 1992: 129)

The extent to which blurred images might be at all in teacher education is
unclear. History has the potential to evoke change, but it is in the margins. That
status is largely because of blurred images about what history is. Images such
as the one Ken Osborne offers are not unique, as many of our teachers have
never experienced history, they have learned it as sets of content derived from
various sources.

Rome ne s'est pas faite en un jour. Change is not always experienced
revelation. Historians of education mine archives only to learn how little they
have been able to uncover. Beliefs are shaped over time. John Dewey's phrasing
is apt:

Old ideas give away slowly, for they are more than abstract logical forms
and categories.

They are habits, predispositions, deeply ingrained attitudes of aversion
and preference. Moreover, the conviction persists, though history shows it to
be a hallucination, that all the questions that the human mind has asked are
questions that can be answered in terms of the alternatives that the questions
themselves present. But, in fact, intellectual progress usually occurs through
sheer abandonment of questions together with both of the alternatives they
assume, an abandonment that results from their decreasing vitality and a
change of earnest interest. We do not solve them, we get over them.

(Dewey 1910: 19)

If teacher education programs only have a middling effect on changing teacher candidates' underlying beliefs, perhaps their curricula are too congested with competing demands to make this change possible, especially if the pressures of the practical determine where growth and change occur. Dewey recommends a regular spring cleaning of the questions we attend to, clearing the clutter in our minds. Policy-minded history of education is as forward-looking as the most progressive teacher education administrators, helping teacher candidates to "get over" the past, not to dwell in it.[4] The past is very much a part of our present. We live *in time*. William Faulkner's *Requiem for a Nun* stated this most laconically: "The past is never dead. It is not even past" (Faulkner 1954: 73).

As this introduction was being composed, the foundation of a Canadian national understanding of schools' role in society has been shaken by the discovery of suspected remains of more than 1,300 children buried in unmarked sites adjacent to former Residential Schools in Kamloops, Cranbrook, Penelakut Island, and Marieval. Sadly, there will be other sites found, and more remains will be brought to light. Canada's history, particularly its history of schooling, is being revealed to be less stable than presumed. A statue commemorating Egerton Ryerson, the first Superintendent of Schools in Upper Canada (now, Ontario), was toppled in front of Ryerson University (also known as X University) in Toronto because of Ryerson's known association with the Residential School System. The first Prime Minister of Canada, John A. Macdonald has had his statue in Montreal, Québec, toppled and defaced. Other statues will topple as the foundation continues to crack. History of education is thus a key instrument in the search for truth and reconciliation in a world making sense of the colonialism, white supremacy, inequity, and overt racism that have living legacies in Canadian history.

The future of educational history is bright, despite the darkness historians will uncover. Across the globe, including Canada, where this is authored, we are confronting new histories that challenge the ones we already have (Berg and Christou 2020). We cannot outrun our past any more than we can tell a story of schooling without facing the mounds of evidence brought to bear that complicate that story. History of education complicates our human existence, enriching our present interactions with each other in each present moment.

NOTES

1. Particularly as the full text of that quote is largely unavailable in the public domain beyond the Society's website (Durant 1945).

2. Teachers, administrators, and school staff may fairly refute this point.

3. This is not what I was looking to know, as I was merely a prop in this masterful lesson.

4. This is particularly essential for the complicating of "blurred images" about the
    past, as discussed earlier. See also Kliebard (1995).

REFERENCES

Berg, Christopher and Theodore Michael Christou, eds. (2020), *The Palgrave
    International Handbook of History and Social Studies Education*, London: Palgrave.
Bury, John M. (1932) *The Idea of Progress: An Inquiry into its Origin and Growth*,
    Mineola, NY: Dover Publications.
Chomsky, Noam (2000), *Chomsky on Mis-Education*, New York: Rowman &
    Littlefield.
Christou, Theodore Michael (2009), "Gone but not Forgotten: The Decline of History
    as an Educational Foundation," *Journal of Curriculum Studies*, 41 (5): 569–83.
Christou, Theodore Michael (2010), "Reflecting from the Margins: Refiguring the
    Humanist and Finding Space for Story in History," *Brock Education*, 20 (1): 49–63.
Christou, Theodore Michael (2012), *Progressive Education*, Toronto: University of
    Toronto Press.
Christou, Theodore Michael (2015), "History of Education Crossing the Street:
    Exploring the Tenuous Place of Educational History in Canadian Historiography,"
    Acadiensis, 43 (2): 157–67.
Christou, Theodore Michael and Shawn M. Bullock, eds. (2013), *Foundations
    in Teacher Education: A Canadian Perspective*, Canadian Research in Teacher
    Education: A Polygraph Series, Ottawa: Canadian Association for Teacher
    Education/Canadian Society for the Study of Education.
Christou, Theodore Michael and Alan Sears (2011), "From Neglect to Nexus:
    Examining the Place of Educational History in Teacher Education," *Encounters on
    Education*, 12 (1): 37–57.
Corbett, Michael (2013), "Where is the Sociology of Education in Canada? Boundary
    Questions, Relevance, Emerging Transdisciplinary Spaces and the Sociological
    Imagination," in Theodore Michael Christou and Shawn M. Bullock (eds.),
    Foundations in Teacher Education: A Canadian Perspective, 122–32, Canadian
    Research in Teacher Education: A Polygraph Series, Ottawa: Canadian Association
    for Teacher Education/Canadian Society for the Study of Education.
Cremin, Lawrence (1961), *The Transformation of the School: Progressivism in
    American Education, 1876–1957*, New York: Alfred A. Knopf.
Cuban, Larry (2001), "Can Historians Help School Reformers," *Curriculum Inquiry*,
    31 (4) (Winter): 453–67.
Dewey, John (1907), *The School and Society*, Chicago: University of Chicago Press.
Dewey, John (1910), "The Influence of Darwin in Philosophy," in *The Influence
    of Darwin on Philosophy and Other Essays in Contemporary Thought*, 1–19,
    New York: Henry Holt and Company.
Dewey, John (1916), *Democracy and Education*, New York: Macmillan.
Durant, Will (1945), "Invitation to History: The Map of Human Character,"
    Will Durant Foundation. Available online: https://www.will-durant.com/invitation.
    htm (accessed May 7, 2022).
Eliot, T.S. (1954), "Burnt Norton," in *Four Quartets*, London: Faber and Faber.
Faulkner, William (1954), *Requiem for a Nun*, New York: Vintage Books.
Forrest Gump (1994), Dir. Robert Zemeckis, United States: Paramount Pictures.

Government of Ontario (1931), "Inspector's Report," in *The Annual Report of the Minister of Education to the Government of Ontario*, 96.

Kagan, Donna M. (1992), "Professional Growth among Preservice and Beginning Teachers," *Review of Educational Research*, 62 (2): 129–69.

Kliebard, Herbert (1995), "Why History of Education," *Journal of Educational Research*, 88 (4): 194–9.

Loewen, James W. (1995), *Lies My Teacher Told Me*. New York: The New Press.

Lortie, Dan (1975), *Schoolteacher: A Sociological Study*, Chicago: University of Chicago Press.

Musk, Elon (2021), Twitter, November 18. Available online: https://twitter.com/elonmusk/status/1461245049585426435?lang=en (accessed May 7, 2022).

Osborne, Ken (1991), *Teaching for Democratic Citizenship*, Toronto: Our Schools Our Selves.

Perrotta, Katherine and Chara Bohan (2013), "'I Hate History': A Study on Student Engagement in Community College Undergraduate History Courses," *Journal on Excellence in College Teaching*, 24 (1): 49–75.

Pitblado, Michael and Theodore Michael Christou (2020), "Intimate Conversations: Self-Study and Educational Foundations," in Julian Kitchen, Amanda Berry, Shawn Michael Bullock, Alicia R. Crowe, Monica Taylor, Hafdís Guðjónsdóttir, and Lynn Thomas (eds), *Self-Study of Teaching and Teacher Education Practices*, 1075–1101, Singapore: Springer.

Ravitch, Diane (1978), *The Revisionists Revised: A Critique of the Radical Attack on the Schools*, New York: Basic Books.

Seneca (1932), *On the Shortness of Life*, New York: Vigeo Press.

Tyack, David (1979), "History and Policy-Making," in Herbert Walberg (ed.), *American Education: Diversity and Research*, 45–57, Washington, DC: Voice of America.

Tyack, David (2000), "Reflections on U.S. Histories of Education," *Educational Researcher*, 29 (8): 19–20.

Zinn, Howard (1990), *A People's History of the United States*, New York: Harper & Row.

CHAPTER ONE

Mapping the Field

New Foundations for Making Meaning of the Past

THEODORE MICHAEL CHRISTOU, REBECCA S. EVANS,
AND CHRISTOPHER MCCUAIG

This chapter considers history as a foundational subject. History is a means of exploring what it means to be human in context, considering those stories, sources, forces, and contexts that shape our sense of self over time. These narratives draw on the past, define the present, and orient us to the future. History tells us who we are.

Defining history is a principal challenge. While history educators variously refer to history as a field to be mastered (Wineburg 2001; Calder 2006; Diaz et al. 2008), content to be committed to memory (Ravitch and Finn 1987), and a verb (Levstik and Barton 2008; Sandwell and von Heyking 2014a; Lévesque and Zanazanian 2015), the questions posed by historians here cannot be answered easily.

Nothing is eternal, predestined, unvarying, and unalterable. Studying history as a foundation is one means of beginning to uncover why institutions, beliefs, policies, and practices are as they are. Educational structures are in continuous formation through experience, as John Dewey noted from within a pragmatist framework, history empowers the individual to be an actor in this process of change, and to act judiciously (Dewey 1938).

Our knowledge of history as a school subject has never been more detailed (Stout 2019; Miles 2021), better funded (The History Education Network 2018; Thinking Historically for Canada's Future 2021), and as far from the public knowledge of history outside of schools. History is current (Seixas, Peck, and Poyntz 2010; Clark and Sears 2020). It is international (Berg and Christou 2020). It is, sometimes, even profoundly ahistorical, propagating conspiracies of aliens in ancient Egypt constructing monuments that inspire such awe that we still cannot fathom them as testaments to collective human action.

The newness of historical thinking as an explicit element of curricula (Seixas and Morton 2013: 2; Sandwell and von Heyking 2014b: 3–4) and as a research space (Samuelsson and Wenden 2016: 479; Cutrara 2018) and hub for graduate research training may lead to a misunderstanding that history is a purely social scientific exercise belonging merely in academic spaces for teaching and learning. The meanings of history (Kovacs 1996: 291), as well as its uses (see, for example, MacMillan 2010), are legion. As are its debates, many of which have echoes that resonate well into our human past (Halvorsen 2012: 2). Those history educators who have been around the halls and virtual spaces of the academy for decades might see the present-day concern for history as an echo of Edwin Fenton's *The New Social Studies* (1967), which introduced primary sources and historical thinking before we necessarily branded them with our own contemporaneity. If they are reserved in their enthusiasm, it might be because they have seen attention to history and social studies education rise and fall before (Evans 2006: 317–19).

In this chapter, we provide an overview of history as a foundation and discuss how it relates to the broader academic discipline. First, to better understand what history as a foundational subject is, we trace the history of the foundations in a broader sense and demonstrate how the field became popular in North American faculties of education. We then showcase the history of the history foundation in an Ontario context as a case study of a wider phenomenon; we provide perspective on how it changed over time from a stand-alone foundation to its mixed present-day form. Using data from two studies on institutions that host initial teacher education, we discuss the field's contribution to teacher education in Canada as an example of the broader trend.

How history is taught in schools, just as in teacher education, has shifted on the international stage from content-based to inquiry-focused. To deepen understandings of the shift in schools of thought, we consider how historical thinking empowers students—and prospective teachers—to better appreciate the complexity of the past, while equipping them with critical thinking skills. Our discussion on the inquiry pivot reveals both the richness and challenges associated with history, when multiple, contradictory narratives are presented together. Woven into the conversation on historical thinking, is the reminder that shared narratives and stories still have much to contribute to teacher education—and as such, shared narratives, we argue, matter and should hold a firm place in the curriculum. We finish by proposing historical mindedness as the way forward. Practising such an approach promises to cultivate a more critical mindset, which will enable new teachers to deliberately reshape the future of education.

HISTORY AS A FOUNDATION IN TEACHER EDUCATION

History is an important component of teacher education. It traditionally exists in the form of a foundation, although the decline of the discipline as a foundational subject is widespread (Burbules 2018: 63). History as a foundation has the potential to cultivate critical habits of mind that are invaluable for new teachers navigating the pervasive challenges of an early teaching career (Christou and Bullock 2013b: v–vi). History as a foundation poses hard contemporary questions that challenge teacher candidates to answer for themselves. In Canada, for example, where the Indian Residential and Day Schools legacy has entered the national conversation, teachers consider their crucial role in supporting reconciliatory efforts between Indigenous and Settler peoples (National Centre for Truth and Reconciliation 2021). They are simultaneously challenged to take a critical look at the basis of reconciliation itself—a concept rooted in a Christian worldview that most Indigenous nations do not have a word for in their own languages (Madden 2019: 286). Historical inquiry invites critical thinking by asking questions, such as *how can we decolonize education? How can we dismantle systemic racism in schools?* As a foundation, history provides opportunities for teachers to analyze present circumstances, use case studies as a means of framing contemporary dilemmas, contextualize educational practice personally and collectively, and encourage historically minded dispositions (159). The foundation holds an ambitious mandate, despite its frail state.

With the provision of inquiry tools to explore the past, teacher candidates are better equipped to question the current construct of public education and see its deficiencies and shortcomings (Christou 2009: 570). As explained by historian Maxine Greene, in her article *Challenging Mystification*, teacher candidates need to develop a capacity to engage in new kinds of questioning and problem-posing in an overly authority-driven world (Greene 1976: 15). Future teachers need the foundations, with their focus on interpreting and preparing others to interpret the social, political, and economic factors that influence education (15). They must be encouraged to examine structures from the perspectives of different individual vantage points and see them as terribly flawed and unabashedly human made (15). This understanding cultivates a questioning disposition, where the prospective teacher remembers that challenging the status quo is a necessary constant.

In a system driven by the allure of discovering best practices, history as a foundation provides space to consider if these practices are the best across different educational contexts (Hlebowitsh 2012: 2). It draws awareness to the present-day fixation on evidence-based efforts, and instead invites slower and deeper reflection on what it means to be a teacher in context (2). Prospective teachers are given an opportunity to turn their search inward and consider their own educative journey (Pitblado and Christou 2009: 11). They are encouraged to engage with their own histories and think about what unique perspectives they bring to the profession (11). The foundational history course calls for thinking about one's own thinking and reflecting on one's own reflecting (Greene 1976).

An opportunity to reflect on personal experience makes the learning more individualized and moves the conversation away from considering the best methods of teaching in the present. Instead, the internal reflection invokes a search for wisdom (Christou and Bullock 2012: 14). An encounter with teaching as a historic entity requires the teacher to consider how striving for wisdom must take precedence over other teacherly pursuits that may seem important in the present moment—which we will discuss in greater detail later in this chapter. Amid an over-packed course load and a myriad of practical assignments, history as a foundation asks teacher candidates to slow down— and then pause—to think about their place in time and what they can offer to the future. It is inherently practical. And this kind of thinking needs to take place before the teacher is teaching in a classroom and struggling to respond to all its inherent demands.

In an education system where technical, outcomes-based, assessment-driven views of teaching have firmly taken hold (Burbules 2018: 64), there is an even greater need for space to slow down and question these very values. With the momentum that empirical research carries, it is increasing difficult to question educational history's place (Christou and Bullock 2013b). History as a foundation helps teacher candidates, and all educationists, frame an understanding of the current enthusiasm around twenty-first-century learning, which implies that *how* we learn must be different from previous centuries (Christou and Bullock 2013b). Prospective teachers can build confidence in their ability to question and critically engage with contemporary issues; teachers are empowered to speak authentically about the problems they face and consider how they can use their own talents to address them.

METAPHOR OF FOUNDATIONS

In teacher education, the architectural metaphor has long served to emphasize the importance of the foundational disciplines, traditionally comprising philosophy, history, and sociology (Kerr 2011: 118; Kitchen and Petrarca 2014). In the most obvious sense, the term *foundation* refers to the strong footholds that hold up a larger structure. In the history of the foundations in education, teacher education is the eye-catching bridge built on the substructures—the foundations seated in bedrock. The bridge serves a functional purpose. It gets aspiring teachers across to where they want to go. Teacher candidates cross it, often without casting an eye downwards toward what foundations are upholding the structure. They might ask questions about whether the bridge can hold them. But history invites other important questions. Is the structure solid ethically? Can it support the construction of a more just society? Teacher education would benefit from paying closer attention to the components of its substructures—the social, ethical, and moral compositions of the foundation. In what ways are the foundations deficient? What narratives do they decenter? We ought to ask such questions about the intellectual foundations of a program that has its core in educating educators.

Foundational footings act as pillars for the professional field and must stand substantially. Traditionally, what is referred to as foundations in a teacher education sense, is a curriculum that inspires deep and empowering questions, such as *what is an education for?* And *why are you doing what you are doing?* (Burbules 2018). Foundational courses give opportunities for prospective teachers to solidify their own values, accentuating a necessary support structure within themselves. Essentially, they provide the means to do what their name implies (Christou and Bullock 2013b). Without such foundations, preservice teachers are destined to merely take on a role that others have determined for them without thought, input, or agency. They remain dormant and powerless to act—instead, they aspire to merely behave (Bai 2006: 8). In the current state, foundation-building in the form of question asking is being neglected; as a result, the professional edifice of individual teachers risks crumbling.

History as a foundation has played a critical, but often neglected, role in preparing new teachers for their future careers in education, where competing demands for their time leave little room for deep questioning and critical reflection. History and social foundations—alongside the humanities in general—are in a state of crisis (Christou 2009: 570). With the shift towards accountability, disciplines need to prove their value and that they are deserving of a space in teacher education curricula (Bales 2006: 396). History as a foundation in teacher education remains elusive, although there is debate about whether the foundations should be considered marginalized or simply underground (Corbett 2013).

In a broader sense, scholars in education in North America refer to the foundations as specific interdisciplinary learning aimed at encouraging critical thinking and questioning among preservice teachers. The term foundations in teacher education programs can be traced back to George Counts's book, *The Social Foundations of Education* (1934), where he describes the conditions that shape the way teachers think about teaching. At the time, Counts was working at Columbia University Teachers College and used the term to refer to the circumstances that support educational institutions and practices (Tozer and Butts 2011). With Counts at the helm, the Foundations Division at Teachers College Columbia, which included Harold Rugg, Freeman Butts, and Kenneth Benne, among others, developed a foundations division comprised of two departments: philosophical foundations and psychological foundations. The departments set the stage for the study of mind and culture as interdisciplinary foundations of learning (Tozer and Butts 2011).

The Foundations Division went on to establish a series of required interdisciplinary foundations courses for their professional teaching program that provided prospective teachers opportunities to examine basic beliefs about the purpose and nature of education (Burbules 2018). All students in graduate programs (associated with teachers' colleges) were required to take critical, cross-disciplinary courses in educational foundations (Tozer 2017). Acknowledging that teaching practices themselves are the product of social and historical circumstances was heralded as an essential component of the foundations (Burbules 2018). The courses were considered mandatory for all prospective teachers. Educational historians, however, did not always view these interdisciplinary courses as sufficient. In a report by the Committee on Historical Foundations of the National Society of College Teachers of Education in the early 1950s, the committee recognized the significant role the foundations courses served but deemed them as inadequate substitutes for a dedicated course in history of education (McCaul 1958: 5). The Committee saw educational history as a means of helping teachers better participate in policy making in schools and community because it provided a mapping of history of the profession and education itself (5). The foundations courses, in contrast, focused on cultivating a questioning disposition and guided prospective teachers in critiquing the fundamental beliefs of education. Such tensions still exist today, where there remains a need for history as a foundation and a need for history of education. The history foundations course cannot do both. The spirit of Counts's early work on the foundations can still be traced to varying degrees across teacher education programs across North America.

With the background of the term *foundations* and its interdisciplinary inspiration in mind, we can situate our discussion on history as a foundation that holds a place within the interdisciplinary realm as well as standing on its own as a substantive pillar. The history of education has played a role in teacher education programs from the outset. In the Ontario normal school that was established by Superintendent of Education Egerton Ryerson in 1847 (Kitchen and Petrarca 2014), such historical courses were the corner stones of the preparation program (Kerr, Mandzuk, and Raptis 2011: 118). In 1906 and 1907, secondary teacher preparation was moved to be housed within universities. First a faculty was opened at University of Toronto (1906) and followed by one at Queen's University (1907). The curriculum of the three-year program comprised general courses in history and philosophy of education, psychology, school law and administration, general methods, and specialized methods in particular subjects (Kitchen and Petrarca 2014). Despite the early prominence of these offerings, history courses have long been criticized. Between 1915 and

1933, education critics claimed the courses were too theoretical and lacked the practicality needed for teacher preparation (Kerr, Mandzuk, and Raptis 2011). These early criticisms by educationists continue to be echoed today by critiques who remain distracted by the ever-present themes of efficiency, accountability, and standardization (Christou 2010a).

Beginning where we are as researchers based in the same Faculty of Education in the context of a research university in Ontario, Canada, we draw on our teacher education program as a case study of a wider phenomenon. The fluctuating prominence of history as a foundation course becomes obvious by examining the curricula over time. History of education has not always existed in the same way; historical questions have at times been embedded within other courses that populate the program. Between 1907 and 1920, the faculty at Queen's University required all prospective teachers to take a mandatory course in history of education until the teacher education program closed in 1921 as a result of political factors. The Ontario government considered the connection between teacher education and liberal arts university important, but many administrators were concerned the program did not properly prepare teachers, three-quarters of which only had secondary school education, for teaching.

When the program reopened in 1968, history became melded into the mandatory foundations courses, which were a combination of psychology, history, and philosophy (Queen's Faculty of Education 1994; Christou and Sears 2011). The foundation courses encompassed 30 percent of the program and were notably equal in weight to the observation and practice teaching component (McArthur College of Education 1968). In contrast to the prominent position, in 1995, the foundations courses were markedly absent from the curriculum, although an "Ethics in Education" course was offered that promised to critically examine human rights, equality, freedom, authority, and responsibility in relation to teaching (Queen's Faculty of Education 1995). At present, a "Historical and Philosophical Foundations of Education" course is a mandatory component of the teacher program at Queen's University, although it takes place over a three-week period and is allotted a modest total of twelve hours (Christou 2020). In its current form, the course focuses on historical thinking, questioning the education across its many forms, and self-study. Despite its limited position at Queen's University, the foundational course continues to provide space for critical inquiry and self-reflection.

FOUNDATIONS IN VARIED FORMS

History as a foundation in its varied forms serves to help prospective teacher candidates understand the complex historical, social, and philosophical roots of education so that their own practices can be enhanced (Butin 2005).

As our discussion on the history and philosophy foundations course at Queen's University revealed, these courses are aimed at cultivating a capacity for critical thinking, moral responsiveness, reflection, and social consciousness (Tozer et al. 2011). Often viewed as less practical than curriculum courses that emphasize instructional methods and outcomes, foundation courses offer opportunities to foster independent thinking and reflection on the values of education. Specifically, history as a foundation emphasizes the need to cultivate a habit of reflection and deliberative inquiry by giving prospective teachers opportunities to examine the past and consider how it continues to shape the present (Christou and Bullock 2013a). History as a foundation emphasizes a need to understand ensuing historical events that have led to teaching as a profession so new teachers enter the profession with an awareness of the past and a deepened interest in the desire to continually reflect and develop as individuals (Ediger 2018: 353).

In the present day, foundational courses continue to be organized differently across Canadian institutions and the history component varies significantly from place to place. Philosophy, history, sociology, anthropology, and sociology of education are often packaged together as a single unit, despite the diverse areas that they cover (Christou 2009). History of education and history as a foundation, as entities on their own, no longer hold prominent places in Canadian teacher education programs. In 2012, Penney Clark conducted a study of twelve Canadian universities and discovered none of them offered a compulsory history of education or history as a foundation course. She found that the University of Victoria offered an option between a history and a philosophy course for secondary school teacher candidates, and Mount Saint Vincent University also offered history of education as one elective among eight options (Clark 2013: 34). For the majority of teacher candidates, history of education was not experienced.

Two years later in 2014, Bruce Maxwell and Audrée-Anne Tremblay-Laprise conducted a large-scale survey on ethics education across ninety-six Canadian institutions that offer initial teacher education. While the survey focused on ethics education, the results provided insight on the state of history of education and social foundations offerings. After surveying heads of Canadian academic units and faculty members with experience teaching ethics-related courses in teacher education, they found 10 percent of institutions had a mandatory course in either history of education, multicultural education, or philosophy of education. These three courses are grouped together so it is difficult to ascertain how much history of education is taught. The presence in the curriculum shows that there are some institutions that continue to mandate history of education in some capacity. The same study revealed that 95 percent of academic units from institutions in the study required a minimum of one course in the social foundations. The term social foundations in this study referred to educational law (39 percent), sociology of education (30 percent), and educational foundations (28 percent). These results do not speak directly to history as a foundation, but they do suggest that history as part of a foundations grouping still has a place in teacher education (Maxwell and Tremblay-Laprise 2015). History as a foundation on its own can only be seen in traces, but its presence in various forms across the different spheres of Canadian teacher education is notable. However marginalized, it is still relevant to teacher education.

HISTORY BEYOND TEACHER EDUCATION

In the world outside of school, teachers, students, and even ministers of education draw inspiration and knowledge from the totality of their lives, not merely from the present. We stitch together the present using the fabric of our past. Our stories, which narrate our lives, draw on our pasts, even as they imagine and project our futures. We think of ourselves as beings in time until we come to school, when we somehow reimagine history and bind it between textbooks and examinations to make it most detestable for all but the most fortunate students. Or so it seems. Unfortunately, history is sometimes taught so poorly that we are often unable or unwilling to teach its manufactured narratives (Schick 1991: 331).

The distillation of history education to a set of skills or dispositions that historians do is a new syntax, which we might enforce with all the rigor of an old grammarian. These frameworks, revolutionary as they are for replacing overall objectives in history curricula that were traditionally derived from historical content to be learned with objectives based in inquiry, will be discussed further below. Yet, even as historical thinking has offered a new syntax for history education, we still bound human existence within textbooks and examinations (Berg and Christou 2020). Once a state department or ministry adopts some framework over another, it also adopts a language to mediate what it means to learn and teach. While a full history of what we are calling here the syntax of history education is beyond the scope of this chapter, a fundamental paradox in teacher education exists: we are preparing educators according to some norm, but that norm is never in itself sufficient—or appropriate.

HISTORY EDUCATION AS HABITS OF THOUGHT

The de facto foundation of teacher education programs is a collection of teaching methods courses loosely reflecting those that structure a teaching day (Christou and Bullock 2013b), and many faculty positions become available for researchers within those subject disciplines. If history of education is taught, it is often taught by the same faculty members who teach history and social studies methods courses. The state of the art of history education is undoubtedly focused on teaching history in a manner that emphasizes habits of thought and practice—often shorthanded simply as "historical thinking"—as opposed to rote memorization and drill (Berg and Christou 2020). History of education, long lamented as traditional, is thus swept up in a broader movement to cultivate historical thinking as a means of engaging students meaningfully with the world they inhabit: the present.

Because of our distance from the events of the past, most of what has transpired prior to our present experience is, in the grandest sense of knowing, unknowable. However, some occurrences leave a "material trace" that allows the event to live on in the memory of the present, and it is from this documentary evidence that we can infer both "what the event was" and "that it is a fact that the event was so and so" (Becker 1931: 1). By piecing together these stories told by this evidence we arrive at what we know as history. As a discipline, history has served many uses over the years, and has been used by nations to spread shared values, as well as by individuals and groups to question popular mythology, and make sense of life in the present. While there have been too many occasions when history has been used as tool by those looking to sow division, the subject remains an important instrument to combat ignorance and to form ways of thinking about and understanding the world today.

Traditionally, we might have imagined the role of history as central in the cultivation of like-minded citizens who can call upon the past as if with one mind. It is our position that history education serves to help fight against group think. History diversifies our perspective, adding to our own lot that of many people and contexts who came before us. History as humanism is an antidote to totalitarianism, even as history was misused in the past. A national narrative is constructed on the bases of evidence and contexts, each illuminating dimensions of all stories, including characters, settings, and plots. Chris Lorenz notes that history and story have these elements of narrative in common; however, what distinguishes history is the burden of evidence (Lorenz 1999: 583). There are many narratives and multiple histories. What is missing in the explanation, perhaps, is a frame that permits multiple, competing narratives to persist on the basis of diverse, coexisting evidence bases.

Peter N. Stearns explains how histories—in our conception, this is particularly true with national histories as a genre of all-encompassing historical narratives—are "meant to drive home an understanding of national values and a commitment to national loyalty" (Stearns 1998: 3). By focusing on national values and loyalty, history is a means of creating what Benedict Anderson refers to as an "imagined community" (Anderson 1983). In the Canadian context, famously, Jack Granatstein argued that national narratives of this type helped communities identify "who they were and who they are" while providing "newcomers with some understanding of the society in which they have chosen to live" (Granatstein 1998: 5). Granatstein is correct. National narratives are convenient tools and expedient in developing shared vision and values. However, history that simplifies, normalizes, and reduces the complexity of understanding is purposefully *miseducative* (Shelley 1989). Shared understanding serves a purpose in any community (Granatstein 1998)—when the purpose is to breed conformity, it becomes harmful. In response to "house histories," history educators in Canada and internationally have sought to refocus curricula on how we think about the past, rather than on indoctrination of singular narratives (Berg and Christou 2020).

THINKING HISTORICALLY ABOUT HISTORY AS A FOUNDATION

History is not true because it is written in a textbook. To begin with, we cannot agree what history is, although we know it is not the same as the past. Our lives are infinitely complex. History may be a disciplined approach to storytelling about the entirety of our lived experience prior to this moment although that very definition should make it clear that our understanding grows both in the particular and in the aggregate. Each history matters, but it is one story among many. To teach historical thinking is to teach students to understand how stories are made, sometimes based on learning extant stories, how we can understand the stories we tell, how to contextualize the stories we have already told, and to write stories of our own.

In the early part of the twenty-first century, there has been agreement among history education researchers internationally that the concepts associated with historical thinking should play a role in how the subject of history is approached moving forward (Seixas 2009). In terms of studying the subject in schools, this approach serves to demonstrate to students the complexity of the stories of the past and reflects Sam Wineburg's belief that "school history possesses great potential for teaching students to think and reason in sophisticated ways" (2001: 83). At its core, historical thinking is articulated in terms that empower students to question and to be critical of sources to come to a clearer understanding of history. By acquainting students with the concepts associated with historical thinking, they will gain the skills to decipher the complexity of the past and recognize the richness and challenges associated with the subject.

Historical thinking presents itself in varied forms internationally, be it in Canada, the United States, or England, but what is common is the emphasis on teaching history to the procedural or disciplinary standards of academic history (Thorp and per Persson 2019: 891). In the United States, the "five C's of historical thinking" have been adopted to teach historical inquiry—concepts of change over time, causality, context, complexity, and contingency—and are introduced in history classrooms (Andrews and Burke 2020: 19). In Canada, the pivot toward teaching through the concepts of historical thinking is articulated in classrooms across provincial and territorial jurisdictions through Seixas and Morton's (2013) six historical thinking concepts—referred to in house as the Big Six. We will expand on these concepts, which provide an indicative example of the cognitive competencies of a historian as they are presented in classrooms where historical thinking is in use (Seixas 2017: 597). The Big Six have much in common with other methods of critical assessment of historical patterns, holding that the past is qualitatively different than the present (Retz 2016: 504; Seixas 2017: 597). Complexity is centered.

Historical Significance: students gain understanding in how we decide what is important (and therefore what is not) to learn about in the past. When thinking about events, people, or developments, students learn to consider whether such elements resulted in change or are revealing in some way (Seixas and Morton 2013: 15). Historical significance is presented as constructed and variable over time.

Evidence: students gain insight into history as an interpretation based on inferences gained from primary sources. Emphasis is placed on asking good questions to help turn a source into evidence. The teacher raises questions about who created the source and for what purposes (Seixas and Morton 2013: 42). The context of the source's historical setting is presented as essential to understanding sources within the worldviews held at the time in focus.

Continuity and Change: students are invited to think about making sense of the past where so many events occur simultaneously and with overlapping complexity. Building chronologies and looking at change as a process with different turning points provides scaffolding to help students look for progress and decline, as well as organize thinking about events through periodization (Seixas and Morton 2013: 76).

Cause and Consequence: students consider the reasons events occur and what the impacts of those events are. The concept heightens awareness of change being driven by multiple actions that cause change—both intentionally and inadvertently—by historical actors.

Perspective: students consider the human, as well as the more-than-human, dimensions of historical experience. They are invited to think about how they can better understand people of the past, who held diverse perspectives and differing worldviews. The students learn to avoid presentism while still considering how universal human experiences can help us relate to people in the past through inferences based on evidence (Seixas and Morton 2013: 138).

Ethical Dimensions: students are invited to be critical of the past without necessarily being critical of the past. Historical actions become reflected in present actions and contexts. Students can examine human actions framed as historical contexts, problems, articulations, or artifacts as reflections of our humanity.

With an understanding that lessons from the past come with limitations, history is presented as a way of helping make informed judgments about present-day issues (Seixas and Morton 2013: 170). These concepts provide a way of developing students' ability to think individually and infer soundly (Thorp and per Persson 2019). The conceptions alone, however, do not constitute the full study of history in schools, nor should they. Much is lost when history is boiled down to a scientific method.

While historical thinking concepts were introduced to combat the passive study of a single narrative approach to the past, we acknowledge that the study of history must be more than simply a set of skills to be employed. Further, it is never possible to fully remove ourselves from the interpretations we make of the past. Our stories about the past are still essential, but they are one dimension of a robust pedagogy for history of education and history as a foundation that is rooted in engagement with the present. We have many histories, but they are not all equal in impact or reception. Some of our stories have special relevance, weaving together the present, the past, and some imagined futures. These histories are hard to shake, as their roots are long. Their foundations, to return to one of the predominate metaphors for the term in engineering and structural design, are strong.

HISTORICAL KNOWLEDGE AND THE FOUNDATION OF KNOWLEDGE IN HISTORY

Earlier we discussed the foundations in teacher education as being rooted in multidisciplinary courses meant to question the purpose of education (Burbules 2018). We presented history as a foundation holding up a footbridge for prospective teachers—in a very practical sense—to walk across as they prepare for a career in teaching. History as a foundation, we proposed, was comprised of critical questions about the education system and its structure. This time, we use the bridge metaphor to explain historical knowledge and the foundation of knowledge in history—which differs from the instrumental form of questioning that we discussed earlier. Consider the 2,000-year-old Pont du Gard aqueduct bridge in southern France. The ancient Roman bridge boasts of being the highest bridge in the first century CE—to maintain such status, it required particularly sound foundations (Pont du Gard n.d.). Pont du Gard was instrumental in bringing water to the Roman colony Nemausus, known today as Nîmes (History of Bridges 2022). The 275-meter limestone structure has fared well over time due to its powerful foundations. This prominent example of an early aqueduct—later turned footbridge—sits firmly on six foundational arches, 6.3 meters wide, that are designed to support the all-important water channel on the uppermost level, which is but 3 meters wide (Pont du Gard n.d.). Its foundations—three tiers of arches held together without mortar—are durable and have withstood periods of great neglect and misuse.

While the broader field of teacher education continues to lay claim to the metaphor, here, we present the metaphor with a different purpose, inviting consideration of how history of education—with its chronologies and contradictory stories, its topical-problem thematic pursuits, and perhaps even in a small and contextualized way, its narrow and ill-conceived house history—can support the development of a questioning disposition, while also providing some common ground (McCaul 1958). The aqueduct's arches are comprised of different stories—overlapping, unifying, and opposing ones. History, aside from its disciplinary or inquiry role, serves a foundational purpose in creating shared history and memory in a profession as it does in society—even if such history is insufficient in and of itself (Christou and Sears 2011). The need for these shared stories cannot be disregarded, just as the need for strong foundations is hard to dispute.

Having a durable foundation in the form of shared narratives and stories has much to offer the teaching profession in terms of shared bonds. Such stories and narratives must be told with caution and treated with transparency (Christou 2010a). The historians and their worldviews matter. Narratives—built on the interpretation of evidence—can provide insight into some of the past forces driving and shaping the profession, such as industrialization and the feminization of teaching (Seixas 2012). These narratives are neither neutral nor objective (Barton 2006: 53). But they allow prospective teachers to explore their current educational and social contexts in relation to the educational and social contexts that existed in the past (Christou 2010a). They build a shared understanding and a sense of connection to those who have come to the profession before them.

Stories of the past from voices beyond Western European educationists must also be included (Christou 2010a: 54). Knowing diverse stories allows teacher candidates to reach beyond their own individual experiences and inhabit the world of someone beyond themselves (Christou 2010b: 170). Textbooks have a place too—despite their "superficial and sometimes banal treatment of educational history" (Pitblado and Christou 2019: 3). Providing some hope that better resources will come that facilitate access to primary sources, stories, and other artifacts, making the doing of educational history more accessible and perhaps, even, more engaging (see the interactive map on Indian Day Schools as an example: Indian Day Schools n.d.). An educative history must empower teachers to retell these stories in their own way, within their context, adding new evidence (Krasner 2021: 14).

We should not be surprised by history changing our perceptions of the past or even the way we tell stories. Changing our perceptions of the past is how history works. As we discover new evidence and add new traces to the storyline, we are connected and recentered all at once (Ehrmann 1999: 217). Our perspectives of the present change too. Teachers can benefit deeply from having a sense of connection to the histories and traditions of their profession (Christou 2009). Even though these histories and traditions are sometimes laced with controversies.

Historical Mindedness: An Old Idea with New Relevance

We opened this chapter by problematizing history education. We presented three different definitions of history: a field to be mastered (Calder 2006; Diaz et al. 2008), content to be committed to memory (Ravitch and Finn 1987), and a verb (Levstik and Barton 2008; Sandwell and von Heyking 2014a; Lévesque and Zanazanian 2015). We offered an overview of the substantive features of historical thinking, an innovation in the teaching of historical foundations associated with a larger pivot in history education internationally. We emphasized that narratives must be provided with care, showing multiple interpretations, and allowing room for contradictory storylines. Now we will consider the future of the field of history in education and history as a foundation and suggest that we look toward historical mindedness, which is a centering concept that invites us to synthesize both knowledge and thinking while living in the present.

Historical mindedness carries with it definitions of history in many forms. It is more than a combination of historical knowledge and historical thinking in some contextually appropriate measure. At the end of the nineteenth century, the American Historical Association highlighted the connection between the past and present by stating that "no conscious advance, no worthy reform, can be secured without both a knowledge of the present and an appreciation of how forces have worked in the social and political organization of former times," and therefore students "should be introduced to the past which has created the present" (McLaughlin et al. 1898: 2). Ken Osborne adds that the idea of historical mindedness has been understood to relate to the idea "that history was more than a collection of facts and skills" and "that it was an 'educational' and not merely an 'informational' subject" (2000: 70). Through its combination of stories, historical analysis, and connection to life in the present, historical mindedness can be viewed as an overall framework for the study of history. It is a valuable goal to provide students with a way of approaching the past and their lives.

Despite these aims for history educationists—we include students as stakeholders in learning here and use the term broadly—history is seen to be stale, full of anecdotes, facts, and examinations (Wineburg 2004: 1402). To be fair, many of these impressions of the study of history were formed through mandatory history courses taken in schools, where content was all too often presented as being important in and of itself, with little attempt for students to actively engage with the subject-matter. In 1898, George M. Wrong, a professor of history at the University of Toronto, reported that, for the most part, the quality of history teaching in Canadian schools was so poor that "pupils came to regard history as a dreary and painful study" (1898: 2). While Wrong was hopeful that the situation would soon improve, over a century later, reports indicate that many students do not equate what they study in high school as meaningful history (Sandwell 2006: 6), and often view the subject as little more than "one more hurdle to be cleared on the way to graduation" (Osborne 2006: 120). If the intention of studying history in school is for students to see relevance in their own lives, then more work is required.

At various times, history has been used as an instrument to actively exclude certain members of society in favor of the dominant ruling class. At other times, history has suppressed and elevated, marginalized and featured on center stage. When multicultural societies, such as those across North America, focus on a narrative of the past that does not reflect the lived realities of large parts of its population, it reflects the practice of what Edward W. Said (1978) terms Orientalism within its own country, pitting the dominant, familiar "us" against a strange "them." When the subject is politicized in this way, the study of history can lead to feelings of not only disinterest but also distrust and fear (Weintraub 2000). In Canada, many Indigenous, Black, and racialized students recognize that the history curriculum has been used as a tool of exclusion by a lack of representation in course material, or worse, of active discrimination by characterizing certain groups as forces of disruption standing in the way of the country's progress (Stanley 2006). Equally disturbing is the acknowledgment that many teachers are uncomfortable with teaching students how relevant issues of history can be to today's world for fear that students might "draw their own conclusions, conclusions that might challenge the status quo" (Barton 2006: 68). By demonstrating that history includes and affects everyone, the subject's relevance will become more apparent to all. However, to achieve this, thorough debate on a range of topics from "nation, race, gender, culture, and identity" are required so the subject can move from being one of distrust and fear to one that presents opportunities of empowerment to all members of society (Stearns, Seixas, and Wineburg 2000: 4).

Indeed, it is because of a continued misuse of the subject as a tool for division, that it is so important for all members of society to understand history so as not to fall victim of its abuse. Kieran Egan highlights the importance of teaching children to think critically about the past, and to "teach understanding of history as one of the most important defenses against (the current epidemics of) provincialism and myth" (Egan 2002: 131). The inclusion of multiple viewpoints and perspectives allows students to evaluate sources, come to their own conclusions, and "begin to distinguish what should be remembered, memorialized, or celebrated" and "to judge what is an appropriate response in the present" (Seixas and Morton 2013: 171). So, although Peter N. Stearns acknowledges that "the products of historical study are less tangible, sometimes less immediate, than those that stem from some other disciplines" (1998: 1), the tools that it provides in terms of thinking about a wide range of topics including use of evidence, responding to change, and understanding other people and societies, makes history both extremely useful and relevant.

History is made most effective when all teachers, students, and citizens can see the ways that it has a direct effect on their lives. In this sense, educators should demonstrate how history affects what we know of the world, how we think about the past, and how this knowledge and thinking affects the way that we live in the present. So long as we guard against the single narrative, there are still significant stories that are important to be aware of that assist with understanding news reports in a variety of media, comprehending the reasoning behind political decisions, and how to be an informed citizen in general (Granatstein 1998). Certainly, the call for greater perspectives on the past means that we must become familiar with more history, not less. This added complexity of multiple accounts creates rich problems requiring critical thought to interpret the evidence for ourselves (Wineburg 2001). Through the process of analysis and reflection, history allows us the opportunity to understand not only the past but also how society functions in general (Stearns, Seixas, and Wineburg 2000). When the knowledge and thinking of the past are applied to living in the present, we are presented with an historically minded approach: "the way of viewing the world that the study of history produces" (Osborne 2006: 125).

NEW FOUNDATIONS FOR HISTORICAL FOUNDATIONS

A new foundation for history as human inquiry has emerged. We must accept that the traditional multi-disciplinary approach to the foundations, rooted in the early teacher college tradition founded at Columbia University, can no longer hold (Burbules 2018). We call the foundations metaphor into question and claim that it has lost its meaning (Christou 2010a: 50). In its present diminished form, history as a foundation boils the field down to an instrumental purpose, thus missing its rich and textured potential of educating prospective teachers to the fullest through human inquiry. It does not make sense to call such an insubstantial structure a foundation as it is narrower and feebler than the edifice it supports (51). It makes a mockery of the term.

We considered how the foundation metaphor might serve to represent shared history of the profession—the complicated, disruptive, and contradictory stories based on evidence that make up the tapestry of teachers' past educational and social contexts. But this, too, does not represent history in its fullest form. On its own, as we saw, neither can it bear the weight of educating prospective teachers. Educational historians must reconceptualize history as a foundation—its purposes, methods, position, and content (Christou 2010a: 51).

How do we envision the history as a foundation of education in the future? As we introduced earlier, history education might borrow an old idea and offer it new relevance. Historical mindedness is the synthesis between knowledge and thinking. We conclude that if history as a foundation is to live into the future of teacher education—historical mindedness might light the way.

Nothing is eternal. As the Romantic poet Percy Shelley noted: "Man's [*sic*] yesterday may ne'er be like his morrow; / Nought may endure but Mutability" (2003). History as a foundation needs to be reimagined if it is to survive. We exist in an academic context concerned primarily with measurement and application of best practices. The teaching context mirrors the same obsession, focusing on measuring outputs and comparing them in ranking exercises. In a profession quick to worship false deities named after the various efficiencies, historical mindedness might best be proposed to teacher education gatekeepers through assessable competencies (Greene 1976: 13). Competency-based education has emerged in various domains including education, but especially medicine, as a means of focusing on higher order cognitive processes of competence (Lawrence et al. 2011: 373). The approach has its flaws. In medicine, despite the widespread agreement that competency-based education is important, dependable assessment tools have yet to be generated and fully agreed upon (Lurie 2011). For historical mindedness to be accepted within education's accountability frameworks, it might be best to package it as a series of competencies holding measurable aims.

It is unlikely that history will ever have the opportunity in teacher education to fulfill all its varied definitions: a field to be mastered (Wineburg 2001; Diaz et al. 2008), content to be committed to memory (Ravitch and Finn 1987), and a verb (Levstik and Barton 2008; Sandwell and von Heyking 2014a; Lévesque and Zanazanian 2015), but there is potential for the future of the teaching profession to include a deeper emphasis on human inquiry. Historical mindedness offers a pathway toward more educated and critical teachers—ones that dare to question present-day practices and speak authentically inside and outside their classrooms (Greene 1976: 17), while grounding themselves in awareness of the stories and histories of those who have gone before. This agency needs to be developed in preservice teachers to deliberately shape the future of education.

REFERENCES

Anderson, Benedict (1983), *Imagined Communities*, New York: Verso.
Andrews, Thomas and Flannery Burke (2020), "Historical Thinking Must Address Change, Causality, Context, Complexity, and Contingency," in Barbara Krasner (ed.), *Historical Revisionism*, 19–26, New York: Gravenhaven Publishing.

Bai, Heeson (2006), "Philosophy for Education: Towards Human Agency," *Paideusis*, 15 (1): 7–19. https://doi.org/10.7202/1072/1072690ar.

Bales, Barbara L. (2006), "Teacher Education Policies in the United States: The Accountability Shift Since 1980," *Teaching and Teacher Education*, 22 (4): 395–407. https://doi.org/10.1016/j.tate.2005.11.009.

Barton, Keith (2006), "History, Humanistic Education, and Participatory Democracy," in Ruth Sandwell (ed.), *To the Past: History Education, Public Memory, and Citizenship in Canada*, 50–69, Toronto: University of Toronto Press.

Becker, Carl L. (1931) "Everyman His Own Historian," *American Historical Review*, 37 (2): 221–36.

Berg, Christopher W. and Theodore M. Christou (2020), *The Palgrave Handbook of History and Social Studies Education*, New York: Palgrave Macmillan.

Burbules, Nicholas C. (2018), "The Limits of the 'Foundations' Metaphor in Education," *Educational Foundations*, 31 (3–4): 63–73.

Butin, Dan W. (2005), "How Social Foundations of Education Matters to Teacher Preparation: A Policy Brief," *Educational Studies*, 38 (3): 214–29.

Calder, Lendol (2006), "Uncoverage: Toward a Signature Pedagogy for the History Survey," *Journal of American History*, 92: 1358–70.

Christou, Theodore M. (2009), "Gone but Not Forgotten: The Decline of History as an Educational Foundation," *Journal of Curriculum Studies*, 41 (5): 569–583. https://doi.org/10.1080/00220270902875197.

Christou, Theodore M. (2010a), "Reflecting From the Margins of Education Faculties: Refiguring the Humanist and Finding a Space for Story in History," *Brock Education*, 20 (1): 49–63.

Christou, Theodore M. (2010b), "That Which Has Been Bequeathed to Us," *Tawarikh: International Journal for Historical Studies*, 1 (2): 169–78.

Christou, Theodore M. (2020), *FOUN 102 Historical and Philosophical Foundations of Education Syllabus*, Queen's University, Faculty of Education.

Christou, Theodore M. and Shawn M. Bullock (2012), "The Case for Philosophical Mindedness," *Paideusis*, 20 (1): 14–23.

Christou, Theodore M. and Shawn M. Bullock (2013a), "The History of Education as a Frame for Teacher Education," in Theodore M. Christou and Shawn. M. Bullock (eds.), *Foundations in Teacher Education: A Canadian Perspective*, 19–29, Ottowa: Canadian Association of Teacher Education. Available online: http://cate-acfe.ca/wp-content/uploads/2019/05/Foundations-in-Teacher-Education-A-Canadian-Perspective.pdf (accessed May 7, 2022).

Christou, Theodore M. and Shawn M. Bullock (2013b), "Introduction: A Timely Examination of a Rather Old Set of Ideas," in Theodore M. Christou and Shawn M. Bullock (eds.), *Foundations in Teacher Education: A Canadian Perspective*, v–vi, Ottowa: Canadian Association of Teacher Education. Available online: http://cate-acfe.ca/wp-content/uploads/2019/05/Foundations-in-Teacher-Education-A-Canadian-Perspective.pdf (accessed May 7, 2022).

Christou, Theodore and Alan Sears (2011), "From Neglect to Nexus: Examining the Place of Educational History in Teacher Education," *Encounters on Education*, 12: 37–57.

Clark, Penney (2013), "History of Education and Passages to the Future," in Theodore Christou and Michael Bullock (eds.), *Foundations in Teacher Education: A Canadian Perspective*, 30–7, Ottawa: Canadian Association of Teacher Education.

Clark, Penney and Alan Sears (2020), *The Arts and the Teaching of History*, New York: Palgrave Macmillan. https://doi.org/10.1007/978-3-030-51513-3_7.

Corbett, Michael (2013), "Where is the Sociology of Education in Canada? Boundary Questions, Relevance, Emerging Transdisciplinary Spaces and the Sociological Imagination," in Theodore M. Christou and Shawn M. Bullock (eds.), *Foundations in Teacher Education: A Canadian Perspective*, 133–43, Ottowa: Canadian Association of Teacher Education.

Counts, George S. (1934), *The Social Foundations of Education*, New York: Charles Scribner's Sons.

Cutrara, Samantha (2018), "The Settler Grammar of Canadian History Curriculum: Why Historical Thinking is Unable to Respond to the TRC's Calls to Action," *Canadian Journal of Education*, 41 (1) (July): 250–75.

Diaz, Aelene, Joan Middendorf, David Pace, and Leah Shopkow (2008), "The History Learning Project: A Department 'Decodes' its Students," *Journal of American History*, 94: 1211–24.

Dewey, John (1938), *Experience and Education*, New York: Macmillan.

Ediger, Marlow (2018), "The Case for History of Education in Teacher Education," *Education*, 138 (4): 353–5.

Egan, Keiran (2002), *Getting it Wrong from the Beginning*, New Haven, CT: Yale University Press.

Ehrmann, Jacques and Jay Caplan (1999), "The Tragic/Utopian Meaning of History," *Yale French Studies*, (96): 217–31. https://doi.org/10.2307/3040724.

Evans, Ronald (2006), "The Social Studies Wars, Now and Then," *Social Education*, 70 (5) (September): 317–21. Available online: https://www.socialstudies.org/system/files/publications/articles/se_700506317.pdf (accessed May 7, 2022).

Fenton, Edwin (1967), *The New Social Studies*, New York: Holt, Rinehart and Winston.

Granatstein, Jack L. (1998), *Who Killed Canadian History?* Toronto: Harper Perennial.

Greene, Maxine (1976), "Challenging Mystification: Educational Foundations in Dark Times," *Educational Studies*, 7 (1): 9–29. https://doi.org/10.1207/s15326993es0701_2.

Halvorsen, Anne-Lise (2012), "'Don't Know Much About History': The New York Times 1943 Survey of U.S. History and the Controversy It Generated," *Teachers College Record*, 114 (1) (January): 1–32. http://dx.doi.org/10.1177/016146811211400101.

History of Bridges (2022), "Pont du Gard – Ancient Roman Bridge," last modified January 2022. Available online: http://www.historyofbridges.com/famous-bridges/pont-du-gard/ (accessed May 7, 2022).

The History Education Network/History et éducation en réseau (2018). Available online: http://thenhier.ca/en.1.html (accessed May 7, 2022).

Hlebowitsh, Peter (2012), "When Best Practices Aren't: A Schwabian Perspective on Teaching," *Curriculum Studies*, 44 (1): 1–12.

Indian Day Schools (n.d.). Available online: http://indiandayschools.org (accessed May 7, 2022).

Kerr, Donald, David Mandzuk, and Helen Raptis (2011), "The Role of the Social Foundations of Education in Programs of Teacher Preparation in Canada," *Canadian Journal of Education*, 34 (4): 118–34.

Kitchen, Julian and Diana Petrarca (2014), "Teacher Preparation in Ontario: A History," *Teaching & Learning*, 8 (1): 56–71.

Kovacs, G. (1996), "The Meaning of History: A Further Contribution to URAM Buber Studies (Ultimate Reality and Meaning 17: 33–49)," *Ultimate Reality and Meaning*, 19 (4): 285–91.

Krasner, Barbara (2020), *Historical Revisionism*, New York: Gravenhaven Publishing.

Lawrence, Katherine, Tim Allen, Carlos Brailovsky, Tom Crichton, Cheri Bethune, Michel Donoff, Tom Laughlin, Stephen Wetmore, Marie-Pierre Carpentier, and Shaun Visser (2011), "Defining Competency-Based Evaluation Objectives in Family Medicine," *Journal of the College of Family Physicians of Canada*, 57 (10): 373–80.

Lévesque, Stéphane and Paul Zanazanian (2015), "'History Is a Verb: We Learn It Best When We Are Doing It!': French and English Canadian Prospective Teachers and History," *Revista de Estudios Sociales*, 52 (1): 32–51.

Levstik, Linda S. and Keith C. Barton (2008), *Researching History Education: Theory, Method and Context*, New York: Routledge.

Lorenz, Chris (1999), "You Got Your History, I Got Mine: Some Reflections on the Possibility of Truth and Objectivity in History," *Österreichische Zeitschrift für Geschichtswissenschaft*, 10 (4): 563–84.

Lurie, Stephen (2011), "History and Practice of Competency-Based Assessment," *Medical Education*, 46 (1): 49–57. https://doi.org/10.1111/j.1365-2923.2011.04142.x

Madden, Brooke (2019), "A De/Colonizing Theory of Truth and Reconciliation Education," *Curriculum Inquiry*, 49 (3): 284–312. https://doi.org/10.1080/036267 84.2019.1624478.

Maxwell, Bruce and Audrée-Anne Tremblay-Laprise (2015), "A Survey of Ethics Curriculum in Canadian Initial Teacher Education," *Revue des Sciences de L'Education de McGill*, 50 (1): 15–38.

McArthur College of Education, Queen's University at Kingston (1968), Faculty of Education Calendar First Session.

McCaul, Robert (1958), "Historical and Philosophical Foundations of Education," *Review of Educational Research*, 28 (1): 5–15.

McLaughlin, Andrew C., Herbert B. Adams, George L. Fox, Albert Bushnell Hart, Charles H. Haskins, Lucy M. Salmon, and H. Morse Stephens (1898), "Value of Historical Study," in *The Study of History in Schools*, Report to the American Historical Association by the Committee of Seven. Available online: https://www. historians.org/about-aha-and-membership/aha-history-and-archives/historical-archives/the-study-of-history-in-schools-(1898)/value-of-historical-study (accessed May 7, 2022).

MacMillan, Margaret (2010), *The Uses and Abuses of History*, New York: Penguin.

Miles, James (2021), "Teaching and Learning for Historical Justice: A Comparative Case Study of Four Sites of History Education in Canada," Ph.D. Diss., University of Toronto.

National Centre for Truth and Reconciliation (NCTR) (2021), "Reconciliation Through Education," University of Manitoba. Available online: https://nctr.ca/education/ (accessed May 7, 2022).

Osborne, Ken (2000), "Historical Mindedness and Historical Thinking," *Canadian Social Studies*, 34 (4): 70.

Osborne, Ken (2006), "'To the Past': Why We Need to Teach and Study History," in Ruth Sandwell (ed.), *To the Past: History Education, Public Memory, and Citizenship in Canada*, 103–31, Toronto: University of Toronto Press.

Pitblado, Michael and Theodore Christou (2019), "Intimate Conversations: Self-Study
    and Educational Foundations," in Julian Kitchen (ed.), *2nd International Handbook
    of Self-Study of Teaching and Teacher Education*, 1–24, Singapore: Springer Nature.
Pont du Gard (n.d.), "An Ancient Work of Art." Available online: https://www.
    pontdugard.fr/en/ancient-work-art (accessed December 20, 2021).
Queen's Faculty of Education, Queen's University at Kingston (1994), Faculty of
    Education Calendar 1994–1995.
Queen's Faculty of Education, Queen's University at Kingston (1995), Faculty of
    Education Calendar 1995–1996.
Ravitch, Diane and Chester E. Finn Jr. (1987), "Measuring Mediocrity: Statistics on a
    Generation's Cultural Chasm," *The Washington Post*, November 3.
Retz, Tyson (2016), "At the Interface: Academic History, School History and the
    Philosophy of History," *Journal of Curriculum Studies*, 48 (4): 503–17. https://doi.
    org/10.1080/00220220272.2015.1114151.
Said, Edward (1978), *Orientalism*, New York: Random House.
Samuelsson, Johan and Joakim Wendell (2016), "Historical Thinking About Sources
    in the Context of a Standards-Based Curriculum: A Swedish Case," *Curriculum
    Journal*, 27 (4) (October): 479–99. https://doi.org/10.13039/501100004359.
Sandwell, Ruth (2006), *To the Past: History Education, Public Memory, and
    Citizenship in Canada*, Toronto: University of Toronto Press.
Sandwell, Ruth and Amy von Heyking (2014a), *Becoming a History Teacher:
    Sustaining Practices in Historical Thinking and Knowing*, Toronto: University of
    Toronto Press.
Sandwell, Ruth and Amy von Heyking (2014b), "Introduction," in Amy von Heyking
    and Ruth Sandwell (eds.), *Becoming a History Teacher: Sustaining Practices in
    Historical Thinking and Knowing*, 3–10, Toronto: University of Toronto Press.
Schick, James B.M. (1991), "What Do Students Really Think of History?" *The History
    Teacher*, 24 (3) (May): 331–42. https://doi.org/10.2307/494622.
Seixas, Peter (2009), "A Modest Proposal for Change in Canadian History Education,"
    Teaching History, 137: 26–30.
Seixas, Peter (2012), "Progress, Presence and Historical Consciousness: Confronting
    Past, Present and Future in Postmodern Time," *Paedagogica Historica*, 48 (6)
    (December): 859–72. https://doi.org/10.1080/00309230.2012.709524.
Seixas, Peter (2017), "A Model of Historical Thinking," *Educational Philosophy and
    Theory*, 49 (6): 593–605. https://doi.org/10.1080/00131857.2015.1101363.
Seixas, Peter and Tom Morton (2013), *The Big Six: Historical Thinking Concepts*,
    Toronto: Nelson Education.
Seixas, Peter, Carla Peck, and Stuart Poyntz (2010), "'But We Didn't Live in Those
    Times': Canadian Students Negotiate Past and Present in a Time of War," *Education
    as Change*, 15 (1): 47–62. https://doi.org/10.1080/16823206.2010.543089.
Shelley, Percy Bysshe (1989), "Mutability," in *The Poems of Shelley*, vol. 1, edited by
    Geoffrey Matthews and Kelvin Everest, 456–7, London: Longman.
Shelley, Percy Bysshe (2003), "Mutability," in Thomas Hutchinson (ed.), *The
    Complete Poetical Works of Percy Bysshe Shelley*, Project Gutenberg. Available
    online: https://www.gutenberg.org/cache/epub/4800/pg4800.html (accessed
    May 7, 2022).
Stanley, Timothy (2006), "Whose Public? Whose Memory? Racism, Grand Narratives
    and Canadian History," in Ruth Sandwell (ed.), *To the Past: History Education,
    Public Memory, and Citizenship in Canada*, 32–49, Toronto: University of Toronto
    Press.

Stearns, Peter (1998), "Why Study History?" American Historical Association. Available online: https://www.historians.org/about-aha-and-membership/aha-history-and-archives/historical-archives/why-study-history-(1998) (accessed May 7, 2022).

Stearns, Peter, Peter Seixas, and Sam Wineburg (2000), *Knowing, Teaching & Learning History: National and International Perspectives*, New York: New York University Press.

Stout, Aaron P. (2019), "The Purpose and Practice of History Education: Can a Humanist Approach to Teaching History Facilitate Citizenship Education?" MA thesis, University of Lethbridge.

Thinking Historically for Canada's Future (2021). Available online: https://thinking-historically.ca/ (accessed May 7, 2022).

Thorp, Robert and Anders per Persson (2019), "On Historical Thinking and the History Educational Challenge," *Educational Philosophy and Theory*, 52 (8): 891–901. https://doi.org/10.1080/00131857.2020.1712550.

Tozer, Steven (2017), "Social Foundations of Education as an Unwelcome Counter-Narrative and as Educational Praxis," *Journal of the American Educational Studies Association*, 54 (1): 89–98.

Tozer, Steven E. and R. Freeman Butts (2011), "The Evolution of Social Foundations of Education," in Steven Tozer, Bernardo P. Gallegos, Annette Henry, Mary Bushnell Greiner, and Paula Groves Price (eds.), *Handbook of Research in the Social Foundations of Education*, 4–14, New York: Routledge.

Tozer, Steven, Bernardo P. Gallegos, Annette Henry, Mary Bushnell Greiner, and Paula Groves Price (2011), *Handbook of Research in the Social Foundations of Education*, New York: Routledge.

Weintraub, Shelly (2000), "'What's This New Crap? What's Wrong with the Old Crap?' Changing History Teaching in Oakland, California," in Peter Stearns, Peter Seixas, and Sam Wineburg (eds.), *Knowing, Teaching & Learning History: National and International Perspectives*, 178–93, New York: New York University Press.

Wineburg, Sam (2001), *Historical Thinking and Other Unnatural Acts*, Philadelphia: Temple University Press.

Wineburg, Sam (2004), "Crazy for History," *Journal of American History*, 90 (4) (March): 1401–14. https:///doi.org.proxy.queensu.ca/10.2307/3660360.

Wrong, George M. (1898), "History in Canadian Secondary Schools," in *The Study of History in Schools*, Report to the American Historical Association by the Committee of Seven. Available online: https://www.historians.org/about-aha-and-membership/aha-history-and-archives/historical-archives/the-study-of-history-in-schools-(1898)/apppendix-vi-history-in-canadian-secondary-schools (accessed May 7, 2022).

CHAPTER TWO

Purposes of Education

Unsettling Historical Accounts of Settler Colonial Public Education

NICHOLAS NG-A-FOOK, PATRICK PHILLIPS,
MARK T.S. CURRIE, AND JACKSON PIND

What are the purposes of settler-colonial, nation-state-sponsored public education? What have they been? What might they be? Of course, answers to any of these questions depends on who you ask, and/or who is doing the asking. In *Schooling in Transition*, Burke and Milewski (2012) outline the different political, epistemological, cultural, and historical perspectives and debates that have framed different historians' interpretive historiographic responses to such curricular and pedagogical questions. "Education history of the past fifty years can be conceptualized," as Burke and Milewski suggest, "in terms of four broadly but overlapping stages: the traditional progressive approach of the 1950s and 1960s; the revisionism of the 1970s; the emphasis on factors of race, class, and gender of the 1980s, and by the 1990s, the turn toward diversity and multidisciplinarity" (2012: 3). In their introduction, Burke and Milewski stress, "since the 1990s, education history in Canada has been characterized by diversity, and historians have continued to broaden their field of inquiry to include formal and informal types of education" (6). Educational historians in the United States have addressed similar historical debates about school reform.

Today many teachers and students can access Google, TikTok, YouTube, and several other search engines and social media platforms for their information. Moreover, the recent global COVID-19 pandemic, international conflict, and populist movements have framed current debates on the purpose of public education. Within technoeconomic stories of progress, the school curriculum must now be retrofitted for smartphones, iPads, iPods, and digital literacies (Smith, Ng-A-Fook, Radford, Pratt 2018). Teachers and students are now plugged into multinational, socially mediated platforms with their powers of data mining, advertising, and commercializing our virtual realities (Ng-A-Fook 2016). To ensure the national security of future capital, public education is called upon to create more "effective" approaches by securing edubusiness partnerships with multinational companies such as Apple, Google, and Microsoft. Together we will develop the next generation of technolaborers, experiment with social innovation, and establish cutting-edge incubators within the elementary and high school, and university schooling systems that promise to nurture entrepreneurialism as exit "outcomes" for global citizenship.

This chapter, then, seeks to situate and unsettle past historical interpretations about the purposes of public education in relation to settler colonialism and strategic anti-racist readings of educational history. We also seek to illustrate how the settler colonial purposes of schooling are intractably linked with our political and interpretive readings of history education. We have sought to demonstrate how the building of nation-states in North America relied on a public education system and respective curricular that continues to "fuel" the notion of progress connected to unfettered technoeconomic growth and the ongoing extractive devastation of the more-than-human world. To do so, we draw on the scholarship of different Indigenous, Black, and racialized scholars who have and continue to call on different educational stakeholders to re-story the purposes of public education in ways that seek to sustain the livelihood of our relations with each other, the land, and its kin. We seek to unlearn and learn from different scholarship that is often relegated to the historical margins of public education's center curricular stage.

And yet, has history of education as a field continued to diversify itself in terms of its central actors inside and outside of faculties of education, its purpose as a field of study, and in turn the respective historical accounts put forth in its associated professional journals and research writ large? Such diversification has implications for how the ongoing historical accounts of, for example, the "settler colonial" purposes of schooling have been revised and narrated as an educational story of great forgetting. Settler colonial imaginaries, as Donald (2019) reminds us, have seeped into the curricular purposes of public education where ideologies of the market inform our understandings of, and relations with, all forms of human living. In turn, drawing on *The Story of B*, Donald emphasizes that one of the primary purposes of settler colonial public education and curricula is to teach the next generation how to forget and remember certain national narrative mythologies. "By the time history began to be written down, and the Enlightenment process was well underway, it was assumed that human beings really only began to live as they were meant to during this time" (Donald 2019: 114). Moreover, as Smith makes clear, the European concepts of Indigenous histories, within and in relation to the settler colonial purposes of public education, have generally been theorized as "a progression from: (1) initial discovery and contact, (2) population decline, (3) acculturation, (4) assimilation, (5) reinvention as a hybrid, ethic culture" (1999: 88). In turn, as Smith stresses, Indigenous nations, communities, and scholars, are more likely to articulate their lived experiences and histories as: "(1) contact and invasion, (2) genocide and destruction, (3) resistance and survival, (4) recovery as Indigenous peoples" (88). Such great forgetting within the field of history education, the purposes of settler colonial public education systems, and their respective curricula, have also worked in turn to exclude other communities.

The purposes of settler colonial schooling have also been stamped, as Kendi affirms, from the beginning for Black communities:

> When we look back on our histories we often wonder why so many Americans did not resist slave trading, enslaving, segregating, or now mass incarcerating ... Consumers of these racist ideas have been led to believe there is something wrong with Black people, and not the policies that have enslaved, oppressed and confined so many Black people.
>
> (2016: 11)

The purposes of public schooling then, as we know it in North America, have been shaped by the intergenerational racist and segregation eugenic "progressive" philosophies that emerged during the "Age of Enlightenment." For example, in *Engendering Curriculum History*, Hendry writes:

> The Age of Enlightenment can be credited with the emergence of modern schooling as a right of all "citizens." Thus the idea of schooling (rather than family, church, or community) as a primary apparatus for shaping cultural norms and ideologies of morality and civic knowledge emerged in this time period. While the liberating effects of this expansion of education cannot be underestimated, when we look more closely at the emergence of "schooling" and its corollary discourses of "rationality," it had profound colonizing effects.
>
> (2011: 109)

But freedom and liberating effects for whom? And, in relation to what "democratic" purposes of public schooling? Walcott suggests "that the conditions of a potential Black freedom remain outside of modernity's imagining" (2021: 2–3). In turn, as he points out, "there is within the logic of modernist freedom, which assumes a linearity—that one perfects *what it means to be human* in a linear fashion" (3). Such concepts of "democratic" freedom, within a "linear progressive narrative, actually prohibit," as Walcott maintains, "Black subjects' [and others] access to that very same linear modernist freedom" (3). Consequently, the purposes of schooling as a form of democratic emancipation, one imagined and tied to a white settler colonial judicial and legislative narrative status of Black and/or Indigenous nonbeing, and imagined as a progressive becoming toward freedom, remain, for Walcott, an extension of the social relations and status of being emancipated from the "former conditions of enslavement" and/or colonization (3). In response, he calls for a break, a freedom not yet realized, from the ideological apparatus that made such forms of enslaved, segregated, and/or emancipated public schooling possible in the name of white settler colonial Judeo-Christian historical narratives of modernity, citizenship, and nation-state democracy.

In a recent article published in *Forbes* magazine, thirty-eight of the fifty states in the United States have introduced, if not passed, bills that seek to ban specific curricula, pedagogies, and resources that would be used to take up issues of racism and anti-racism; Two-Spirit, lesbian, gay, bisexual, transgender, queer or questioning, and intersex (2SLGBTQI+); and non-/anti-capitalist ideologies such as communism, Marxism, or Maoism (Greene 2022). Primarily political conservatives, white members of the American public and political representatives have strongly focused on holding the line in relation to the teachings of critical race theory (CRT), histories of enslavement, systemic racisms, and/or other forms of violence perpetuated in the name of democracy and cultural practices of whiteness. For politicians, and certain citizens, such a civic education is not consistent with the purpose of public schooling or the history or social studies curricula.

Florida in the United States introduced a bill that would ban the use of CRT in schools, along with most critical (re)membering of the past to ensure that certain teachers and students do not have to feel any "discomfort" when learning and teaching history (Alfonseca 2022). Holding the curricular line against rewriting (re-righting) a grand national (white) narrative and the discomfort with addressing uncomfortable topics betrays a desire for education to (re)produce an unquestioned historical singularity of the purposes of "modern" schooling among citizens in the United States and in Canada (Stanley 2006). "The anxiety over the loss of manliness and racial superiority found its corollary," as Hendry reminds us, "in the increased need for social control and regulation. Education (in fact schooling became its mandatory name during this time) was a primary avenue through which this control and regulation of identity was exercised" (2011: 139). It is toward such purposeful need for social control and regulation that we now turn our historical attention.

A BRIEF HISTORY OF THE PURPOSES OF SETTLER COLONIAL PUBLIC EDUCATION

Histories of forgetting, their discursive regimes, teach us that the purpose of schooling cannot be divided from the westernizing macro and micro contexts of its experience. In his narration of the history of the Western educational experience, Gerald L. Gutek (1987) consciously sets out to avoid obfuscating generalizations, the conflation of education and schooling, and the tendency of educational historians to analyze past events primarily through a progressive-traditionalist dualism. At the same time, however, Gutek's own definition of education suggests that Western experiences of learning, whether formal or informal, are part of a larger project of colonization:

> Education is a process that attempts to ensure the cultural continuation of the group, race, or nation. ... [It] transmits skills, knowledge, modes of inquiry, and values from the mature to the immature, either informally through the milieu or formally through the school. ... [The] school's task is to transmit the dominant aspects of the cultural heritage by emphasis on cultural continuity.
>
> (1987: 11)

The corollary of such a process is that education and schooling can also attempt to erase, sever, limit, devalue, colonize, and dominate. In this section, we attend to a partial historical account of North American schooling and its settler colonial purposes, beginning with early colonization through to the so-called ongoing political and ideological culture wars.

Gutek's (1987) earliest accounts of rupture and change within Western education are moments of invasion and colonization—in this case, the colonizing tides of ancient Greek city-states. While we lack the space to systematically survey thousands of years of written educational histories, it is worth noting that schooling, as a "Western" experience, has often been deployed academically to solidify a collective (national) identity, whether it was the classic Greek polis or a frontier ripe for settler colonial expansion. Axelrod's account of nineteenth-to twentieth-century Canadian schooling begins as a narrative of settler colonialism: "The territory now known as Canada was occupied in the 1600s by some 300,000 Native people" (1997: 4). Indigenous Peoples, diverse and numerous nations with distinct languages, cultures, and ways of educating their young, were met with the French and British economic settler colonial purposes of "territorial expansion and commercial success" through a "combination of violence, alliance, and appeasement" (4). While Indigenous Peoples and their knowledge systems recede into the background early into Axelrod's historical account, his words nevertheless foreshadow the lasting settler colonial legacy of Canada's Residential Schooling and Day Schooling systems (Joseph 2018).

Although settler colonies had long attempted to forcibly coerce Indigenous Peoples into adopting European life ways, it was through the passing of the Indian Act in 1876 that the Canadian government adopted the industrial school system of the United States. These schools were run by different white Judeo-Christian religious organizations (Ng-A-Fook 2007; Carleton 2017; Milloy 2017). The colonial purpose and effect of these schools cannot be overstated. With federally enforced mandatory attendance by 1894, these schools were organized not only to force assimilation of First Nations students by preventing them from learning their languages and cultures, but also to subjugate and extinguish Indigenous lives and futures. Indeed, what Milloy (2017) has aptly called *A National Crime*. As Barman writes, "By taking children away from the old ways and 'civilizing' them into European ways, so the argument ran, 'the Indian problem' would be solved in a single generation" (2012: 255–6). In the final report of Canada's Truth and Reconciliation Commission (TRC 2015), the commissioners called for an investigation into the thousands of First Nations students who died and never came home from these schools (Quon 2021; Piapot 2022). Survivors and their families continue to experience intergenerational trauma. And yet, despite such settler colonial purposes of schooling, several First Nations individuals and communities have resisted, survived, and renewed their respective politics of self-determination, and in turn, are controlling the present and future purposes of education for their communities (see Haig-Brown 1988; Battiste 2013; Raptis 2016; McDermott et al. 2021).

Settler colonial schooling in North America from its inception was a project of colonization and nation-building. Between the 1790s and 1850s, nearly a million British immigrants settled what is now a confederated nation-state called Canada. Along the way, the purposes of education often sought to keep pace with settler needs: first and foremost, survival, and later to establish and maintain religious, cultural, and national continuity (Axelrod 1997). "For all their cultural and linguistic differences," Axelrod attests, English and French colonists shared two traits in common: "their fate on the North American continent had been shaped by war, and they lived in a world in which religion and schooling were deeply intertwined" (1997: 6). From frontier survival through to the establishment of common schools, schooling was very much about maintaining loyalties to one's religious faith and colony, as well as teaching certain "normalized" racialized, gendered, and class roles. In turn, students often read Christian Eurocentric doctrine as part of the school curriculum while also learning how to contribute to the prosperity of a growing colony (Ng-A-Fook, Ingham, and Burrows 2018). Today, these educational purposes remain entwined in schooling's contemporary arrangements, from the constitutionally enshrined rights for separate Francophone and Anglophone Catholic and Protestant (now primarily secular public) provincialized and territorial education systems in Canada to the economically motivated, globalizing standardized testing culture shared across today's "commonwealth" borders from coast, to coast, to coast (Tomkins 2008).

Schooling as a regime of social and economic progress—and by extension a force of creating certain kinds of settler colonial democracy—fueled the purposes and demands of the industrial revolution. In the United States, early reform movements followed "the course of development into an industrial nation" where public schooling became about transforming an influx of mixed European heritage into a sweeping, egalitarian "democratic frontier" (Gutek 1987: 359). State and local government control of schooling gradually replaced denominational religious control, brought about the "common school," or public school, movements on both sides of the border. These political educational movements were predicated on the belief that schooling could not only make society productive and governable but also serve a progressive aim to improve future conditions and overcome the challenges of rapid change. Such an "age of improvement," as Tomkins (2008: 26) calls it, was marked by rapid emergence of public institutions such as the common school as a stabilizer of colonial order. By the mid-1800s, the province of Ontario became increasingly connected by roads, its population burgeoning with waves of immigration, while radio and print became the media of Canadian culture. This expansion was, however, feared to be unequal and destabilizing. As Tomkins notes: "Urban growth was seen ... as a serious menace to the future of the nation, even as cities were paradoxically regarded as the physical embodiment of progress and culture" (29). Cities were magnets for a diversifying immigrant population, whom for Egerton Ryerson, an appointed Chief Superintendent of Schools for Upper Canada in 1846, were linked to the spread of not only physical disease but also to the "worse pestilence of social insubordination and disorder" (29). Public schooling was, for settler colonial leaders such as Ryerson, a solution for sanitizing and moralizing children toward becoming "proper" citizens within the growing settler colonial nation-state called Canada.

By the turn of the twentieth century, part of the purposes of public schooling had thus become linked to a nation's future as much as the continuance of its past. Practically, this meant schooling should segregate children from the present within a programmatic preparation for a future, taught by prepared and certified teachers. Theoretically, this meant that schooling could be understood, pursued, and promoted as an educational science. This programmatic life emerged at the intersection of John Dewey's (1916) philosophy and the reality of George Counts's (1932) reconstructionism as the architecture of economy-focused, postwar education reform. Pared down to a paradigmatic history, Dewey's theories maintain that education is a democratizing activity, and that this activity should be operationalized on an experiential level in schools (Christou 2012). However, Dewey and other early reformists do not specify for whom such experiences are created, or who might benefit from such future democratic rights. Dewey in 1916 championed a humanistic naturalism that reconciled and retained the then-burgeoning bio-psychological essentialism. For Dewey, schooling should facilitate a "native mechanism" of learning in a child, whose immaturity is in fact an "absolute" "power to grow" that needs no extrinsic source (1916: 52). As Gidney and Millar (1990) suggest in their account of the rise of secondary education in the province of Ontario, these democratic futures were largely for a middle-class, or at very least "respectably poor," population. During the nineteenth century, "the working classes benefited most from the extension of government into social, economic, and educational affairs" (Gutek 1987: 420). The twentieth century, however, saw the rise of the laissez-faire state and its simultaneous alignment of schooling with nationalistic identity while discounting differences among students in favor of universal potential through controlling curriculum policies and their reforms. Whether Deweyan naturalism or Counts's embrace of schooling as a pragmatic means to address rapid change in science, industry, and technology, the purpose of schooling that emerged out of the twentieth century assumes— and increasingly so today—particularly neocolonial, neoliberal, and capitalist imaginings of individuals and communities in relation to the profitability of an *Age of Technoeconomic Labor and Progress.*

It is not a historiographic leap, then, to turn to the reform movements and debates of the present and recent past as a shared settler colonial project. As the history of schooling became and arguably continues as a history of contested educational policy reforms, the work of historians and critics of education suggests divergent and clashing purposes. However, rereading with a settler colonial lens, such purposes become less distinct. While we lack the space to address each debate and movement in North American school reform and their local expressions, Ackerman suggests that contentions of school reform—top-down policy control of what should be taught and how—are "manifestations of a [centuries-long] fundamental debate between progressive educators and traditionalists" (2003: 345). This scale of tension appears to be evidenced by influential historians and critics of these debates; their words, meanwhile, suggest that this tension belies a shared interest in the maintenance of political and cultural institutional practices of whiteness and settler colonial power (Sharma 2020).

Hirsch's (1999) critique of progressive education begins in opposition to an ostensibly different aim: schools shall achieve economic and social justice through furnishing students with an "extensive body of school-based background knowledge as a necessary foundation for communication and participation in society," in contrast to a "widespread" progressivist doctrine of skills- and student-centered learning (1999: 14). Yet, Hirsch's own critique suggests that a traditionalist (or core knowledge-based) approach to schooling is not exactly the solution, calling for "transformation" on a deeper level. "It is the enemy within that needs to be defeated," declares Hirsch (15). This enemy is the "controlling system of ideas" of schooling, maintained by "schools and their allies in state departments" (63). In other words, it is the control of students' futures as a kind of *capital* that interests Hirsch. Similarly, central to Ravitch's critique of the history of American school reform is her claim that progressivism forged and worsened "profoundly undemocratic" socioeconomic stratification, usually based on race and class, abrogating the school's "primary responsibility for the development of young people's intelligence and character" (2000: 15–17). This was achieved not through progressive educational theory. Here Ravitch notes the following key systemic shift in power and its control:

> The invention of the scientific curriculum expert represented an extraordinary shift of power away from teachers, parents, and local communities to professional experts. The most vital educational decisions would in the future be made by experts who spoke an arcane language of their own, incomprehensible to laymen. This shift redefined the meaning of democratic control of education.
>
> (2000: 164)

Ravitch's conclusion stresses that "if there is a lesson to be learned in the river of ink that was spilled in education disputes of the twentieth century, it is that anything in education that is labeled a 'movement' should be avoided like the plague" (Ravitch 2000: 453). For Ravitch, all reforms have somehow benefited and failed students. Schools have a deeper, if unspecified, purpose beyond surface politics, Ravitch suggests, and "must concentrate on their fundamental mission of teaching and learning" (467). The question that remains amidst such a broad sense of purpose is yet: for whom?

In a sense, Ravitch's and Hirsch's critiques of school reform are not incompatible with a settler colonial analysis. For Willinsky (1998), the legacy of imperialism, Western schooling's purpose, has remained inextricably colonial. Schools teach, as Willinsky (1998) reminds us, writing that conquers, mathematics that extracts from land, and geography that divides peoples. Through this lens, the so-called culture wars of North American education take on a deeper meaning. Whether it is sex education, school choice, or the inclusion of anti-racism curricula, schooling "is a key institutional context through which a society tells itself a story about itself. Modern pluralism makes conflict in educational processes inevitable, and schools unavoidably become places where competing conceptions of the good are contested" (Dill and Hunter 2010: 275). Today, amidst even sharper contention of what counts as the "good," or of most worth, is what we assume as uncontested. How might we contest a "good" life based on globalized technoeconomic neoliberalism and maintenance of colonial boundaries as a purpose of schooling? It is such imperial habits of mind and how they continue to inform our educational imaginary that we should seek to unsettle.

UNSETTLING SETTLER COLONIAL PURPOSES OF SCHOOLING

Canada is presently at a crucial crossroads between its settler colonial history, colonizing present, and calls to foster a more just future as the purposes of public education. This so-called era of reconciliation is unfolding within a wider global context of resurgent Indigenous voice and scholarship in education, politics, law, science, and ecology (cf. Cajete 1994; Battiste 2000; Battiste and Youngblood Henderson 2000; Lightfoot 2016; Smith, Tuck, and Yang 2018; Donald 2019). Schooling in a Western Eurocentric context has for centuries reproduced concepts of history, worldviews, and a settler historical consciousness without which past and present colonization could not operate (Willinsky 1998; Carleton 2011; Tupper 2020). "Coming to know the past has been," as Smith writes:

> part of the critical pedagogy of decolonization. To hold alternative histories is to hold knowledges. The pedagogical implication of this access to alternative knowledges is that they can form the basis of alternative ways of doing things. Transforming our colonized views of our own history (as written by the West), however, requires us to revisit, site by site, our history under Western eyes.
>
> (1999: 34)

Moreover, it has been deployed post-contact with Indigenous peoples as a political and military tool for assimilating and eradicating Indigenous ways of being, knowing, and living.

For thousands of years before European settlement, several Indigenous peoples educated their children through not only communal, land-based, and experiential modes of learning, but also through holistic worldviews that did not necessarily divide our onto-epistemological relations as human/non-human, public/private, rich/poor, and other forms of settler colonial dichotomies (Donald 2012; Brant-Birioukov 2021). This creates an education system that has been obscured by an anthropocentric, homogenizing, and "overwhelmingly abstract linear temporal conception of history that infuses current Western thinking with deadly consequences" (Wildcat 2005: 431). Consequently, colonization continues to "affect all of us in nearly every facet of our lives," and as a result, "schooling is a place where understanding of the particular history of colonization of what has come to be called Canada can and should be taken up" (Haig-Brown 2018: 320). It also means that schooling and its respective settler colonial purposes must somehow come to terms with the reality that Indigenous and non-Indigenous peoples need to learn how to think and "live together in the same place" when our educational "tipis are held down by the same peg. Neither is going anywhere" (Chambers and Blood 2012: 50).

Dwayne Donald (2009, 2019), a curriculum scholar of Indigenous and non-Indigenous educational systems, philosophies, and histories, inspires us to realize that a questioning of education's history would be incomplete without an address of ontological-epistemological meanings embedded in its conception and practice. Donald foregrounds not only the social but also spatial geographies of education as a foundation to how Indigenous and non-Indigenous Canadians might learn to relate to one another and the more-than-human world. Drawing on Donald's curricular and theoretical lenses, we suggest that purposes of public education can be understood as built and maintained according to the same colonial frontier logics that naturalized the historical and ongoing harms of colonization.

Central to this perspective is the mythology of "forts," which are both literal representations of colonial power and metaphorical restrictions that prioritize Eurocentric education as a means of protecting itself. Certain knowledge and purposes of education, namely Eurocentric settler colonial approaches, were spread and defended by hundreds of forts on the Canadian frontier, while seeking to exclude certain (his)stories beyond those walls. "Canadians have given themselves so deeply to this mythic national narrative that the story has come to own the ways in which they," as Donald cautions us, "conceptualize their past and present relationships with Aboriginal peoples" (2009: 3). Therefore, settler nationalizing mythologies have real and ongoing impacts within our current education system. Donald reminds us that it is an "ethical imperative" to acknowledge that "the past occurs simultaneously in the present and influences how we conceptualize the future. It requires that we see ourselves related to, and implicated in, the lives of those who have gone before us and those yet to come" (7). Such purposes of education call on us to "live in the world together with others and must constantly think and act with reference to these relationships" (7). In this sense, Donald (2012, 2019) seeks to trouble the metaphorical and sometimes literal divisive curricular and pedagogical walls that are constructed and act as systemic barriers, for example, between people and the purposes of settler colonial public education.

Drawing on Indigenous Métissage, Donald seeks to disrupt how Indigenous or non-Indigenous (his)stories are often recounted as an oversimplified binary, on education's center stage. Rather, Donald invites us to weave a variety of texts together, which provides "a means for métissage researchers to express the interconnectedness of wide and diverse influences in an ethically relational manner" (2009: 8). By doing so, we might offer a situated account of purposes of education that "does not deny difference, but rather seeks to understand more deeply how our different histories and experiences position us in relation to each other" (Donald 2012: 535):

> Métissage, as research praxis, is about relationality and the desire to treat texts—and lives—as relational and braided rather than isolated and independent. I explicitly connect métissage to the legacies of colonialism and the need for recognition of the mutual vulnerability and dependency of colonizer and colonized, insider and outsider, as well as the presumed primacy of "literate" societies over repressed oral traditions and storytelling.
> (2012: 537–8)

And yet, the walls of the educational fort have not come down. Rather they have shifted to incorporate concepts and perspectives that were always present but that were commonly left outside the curricular discursive regimes, or at the margins of the Eurocentric settler colonial curriculum and its historical and contemporary accounts of what and whose knowledge was and is of most worth toward sustaining our individual and collective livelihoods. Moreover, the challenge to these discursive and material shifts is that efforts must be more than just "add-n-stir," tackling issues of racism, gender, sexuality, and other onto-epistemological relational inclusions and exclusions.

Adding more space within the walls of history and creating a different shape to the fort are important steps, but the walls and their settler colonial structures and systems must also be addressed. Focusing on the juxtaposition and relations among different historical narratives can create more doors in the walls of the educational fort, affording us pedagogical and curricular opportunities for a critical analysis and synthesis of the purposes of public schooling, while recognizing and utilizing the active links between education and wider society. The relationships through which people live and learn are numerous and multifaceted. They are also ongoing and unsettled. How might our understandings of education reflect this, rather than attempting to impose visions of purposeful fixity? Below, we bring attention to a variety of scholars whose work offers new coordinates for understanding the future of schooling through history as a case study, and so pushing against the fortified purposes of settler colonial technoeconomic conceptions of public schooling.

(RE)PURPOSING HISTORY EDUCATION: UNSETTLING FRAMEWORKS AND HISTORIES

In this section, we look to voices and communities that have largely been excluded from what counts as (settler colonial) history and history education. We propose (re)purposing history education toward (re)writing and (re)righting a different history that yet engenders and articulates shared goals of citizenship, democracy, and sustaining collective human prosperity with each other and the more-than-human world. That curricular and pedagogical endeavor in and of itself could be viewed as a purpose of education. In examining these voices and communities, we see that different pedagogical and curricular discursive governmental regimes work as interlocking systems that support each other and need to be recognized as such, rather than as separate and/or disconnected from one another (e.g., teacher education, government policy, K-12 education, postsecondary education, curriculum-as-lived) (Willinsky 1998; Smith 1999; Stanley 2006). Our proposed (re)purposing does not aim to conflate different forms of curricula. Our proposal has precedent, linking to early articulations of history education's purpose. Bestor's (1953) condemnation of the American schooling system implicated history education as failing to meet the needs of current and future students, prompting historians of education to revise history as integral to teacher preparation (e.g., Cremin 1955, 1956; Anderson 1956), continuity and enfranchisement of a unique national, cultural identity (Butts and Cremin 1953), and even an earlier address of the history of racism and education (Harlan 1958). (Re)purposing history education thus affords us opportunities to reconsider schooling that addresses settler colonial education but without repeating its history of complicity in assimilation, appropriation, individual, systemic, and societal racisms, as well as other historical and contemporary harms.

Brant-Birioukov, Ng-A-Fook, and Kane (2020) examine what has been and could be done to reconceptualize teacher education in relation to reconciliation after generations of atrocities against Indigenous peoples by Canadian governmental systems. As these authors indicate, faculties of education in Ontario universities are now expected to address Indigenous histories, issues, and perspectives. However, in too many cases such topics are added to curricula out of obligation rather than a sustained interest in de-marginalizing such knowledge. Brant-Birioukov, Ng-A-Fook, and Kane conclude that "[overcoming] the existing tensions surrounding an inherited Eurocentric curriculum cannot be reduced to best practices but involves an honest engagement with the historical particulars that came before" (2020: 56). While they are focused specifically on the place of Indigenous histories and issues within teacher education, their point can be taken up in relation to how the purposes of education continue to silence and marginalize different communities. For example, the lived experiences and perspectives of Black scholars and other racialized scholars whose contributions have yet to be recognized by and within the teacher education, the public schooling system, and their respective curricula (Fanon 1963; Cooper 2007; Kendi 2016; hampton 2020; Walcott 2021). Brant-Birioukov, Ng-A-Fook, and Kane call on us "to foster a teacher education agenda that destabilizes Settler-dominant narratives ... at the forefront of teacher education curricula" (2020: 56). This is not a call to remove the scholarship of scholars who self-identify as anglophone, white, European, American, and/or Canadian from our teacher education courses. Rather, we seek to unsettle dominant settler colonial scholarship from its canonical pedestal, and acknowledge the pedagogies, curricula, and content from racialized and Indigenous scholars, its excellence, toward juxtaposing, deconstructing, reconstructing, and restorying such historical accounts about the purposes of public schooling in relation to each other (Henry et al. 2017). How might we then draw on such scholarship to unsettle the settler colonial purposes of public schooling?

Black, Indigenous, and other non-white racialized scholars have sought to situate concepts of racialization, racism, and anti-racism, and the respective roles they play in various facets of life, including education in all forms. W.E.B. DuBois ([1903] 1994) introduced the concept of *double consciousness*. He expressed how Black people in the United States live both as Black and American, and how the two conflict with each other within a nation and nationality built on political systems of racial oppression and segregation. When we reconsider this doubleness in relation to educational purposes, we can see assimilationist attitudes, simultaneously praising Black, Indigenous, and other racialized students for their successes in school and postsecondary institutions, while also marginalizing these students from the very settler colonial segregated and racists schooling systems in which they negotiated and survived toward becoming "successful." These students become at once *good learners and citizens* in their alignment with the dominant, market-focused views of education (Donald 2019), while also *excluded* from the national fabric of what constitutes being (or not) a "Canadian," and/or "American" citizen. Conceptualizing the process of racialization, Franz Fanon ([1952] 2008) looked at the ways Black bodies are ascribed racialized labels and meanings. In the context of K-12 and postsecondary schools, such creation of racialized categories and meanings can work to essentialize and marginalize certain identities. Here we are reminded of Edward Said's (1978) theorizing of *Orientalism*, which seeks to illustrate the ways that certain racialized subjectivities are formalized through the perceptions of Europeans, and not through how that "othered" person self-identifies. Historical narrative put forth in a settler colonial school curriculum has often worked as a discursive regime to racialize and other non-white European identities (Ng-A-Fook, Ingham, and Burrows 2018).

Postcolonial theorist Gayatri Spivak (1988) asks, "Can the subaltern speak?", sparking debates about whether colonized, marginalized voices can ever truly be heard. Are they forever filtered through colonial systems and discourse? From here, questions may arise about how government policy and education's turn to diversity in the 1990s worked, and what education looks like today, with a wider range of histories and communities' lived experiences being addressed but with the purposes of *preparing* students for citizenship and the workforce. Kimberlé

Crenshaw (1991) gave rise to initial discussions of *intersectionality*, which, put simply, is the concept that people do not live with a single identity and rather exist with multiple intersecting identities and lived experiences. In different contexts, one or several identities—gendered, racialized, cultural, sexual, religious, national, and so on—can play prominent and/or minor roles in relation to how a person presents themselves and is read by others, and/or is represented (or not) within curricula. Such intersecting differences challenge the settler colonial purpose of schooling in relation to creating *good citizens* who contribute toward the cohesive prosperity of a technoeconomic society.

The examples above are not exhaustive, but they are indicative that such educational conversations are not new. Drawing on postcolonial, Indigenous, Black, anti-racist, and/or anti-colonial interpretative frameworks, they provoke us to reexamine our human relations with each other and the more-than-human world. Such scholars have made significant contributions to restorying and restoring racialized and "othered" histories and lived experiences. While these examples are not from the field of educational studies, per se, if a purpose of formal education is to learn to critically examine and engage that which exists in the world, should the field of education and history education and their respective systemic and discursive regimes not also include and be informed by ideas brought forth from a range of lived experiences who are often part of a global majority but not yet represented as excellence, or with purpose, within a settler colonial curriculum?

Although a settler colonial framework has sought to become more inclusive of anti-colonial and anti-racist ideas, concepts, and texts, it fails to unsettle the structures and systems that support the ongoing reproduction of settler colonial dominance. Schooling as a settler curriculum, Tuck and Gaztambide-Fernández (2013) argue, is designed to ensure the futurity of settler colonizers by continuously replacing all that is Indigenous, leaving *rematriation* and *refusal* as the only recourse. Tuck and Gaztambide-Fernández (2013) contend that approaches such as multiculturalism and critical race theory have become thwarted in terms of their educational purposes. "One of the core reasons that each of the interventions [...] has failed to interrupt settler colonialism and settler colonial replacement," they posit, "is that each has tried to make powerful shifts without alienating white settlers" (Tuck and Gaztambide-Fernández 2013: 85). Rematriation, as they describe, is about rethinking for what purposes different people do curriculum research, development, and practice, "so that Indigenous communities and other over-researched but invisibilized communities can reject narratives and theories that have been used against [them], and re-story knowledge and research to forward [their] own sovereignty and wellbeing" (85). Such rethinking, however, continues to be constrained by the existing settler colonial disciplinary and discursive regimes that continue to dominate educational institutions, including teacher education programs and the field of history education itself. In Gaztambide-Fernández's entry into the *SAGE Guide to Curriculum in Education* (2015), he notes that his project of "Browning" the curriculum describes an "impossible" task. For him, the walls of the academy will always push back from existing settler colonial purposes of educational research and/or public education. Here Gaztambide-Fernández reminds us to recursively question "how White supremacy has shaped and continues to manifest in curriculum studies," as the building blocks of a Western technoeconomic empire (2015: 421).

To examine the repurposing of public education and its relations to/ with teacher and postsecondary education requires operationalizing and understanding differences. Ibrahim (2014) argues that the categories and labels we use for identities—particularly the racialization of Blackness—are (re)created within what he calls the social imaginary—an assemblage of ideas, a discursive or symbolic space in which identities are already constructed, imagined, assembled, and positioned. Carl James describes how such processes manifest in the concrete experiences of everyday Canadian school life, noting that, in Canada, "racism, if at all acknowledged [in the curriculum], is commonly thought to be an individual's shortcoming based predominantly on cultural differences and lack of exposure to those considered different" (2008: 102). Canadian education, therefore, tends to dress the walls of schools with celebrations of "cultural difference," working to mask "power differentials based on race and the normalized white cultural identity, [...] the notion of color blindness" (102). Racializing representations thus stand in for meaningful anti-racist discourse in schools, hiding and reinforcing the structural fortifications of racism in settler colonial education. Following Ibrahim and James, to see the purposes of education as fixed—maintaining and (re)producing settler colonial systems—is to understand people, their communities, and identities as also static. Doing so draws lines that lead to exclusions and failed attempts at inclusions.

Drawing on Stanley's (2014) anti-essentialist anti-racist approach, racisms and anti-racisms are understood as plural. As he outlines it, different racisms work in differing ways, but the common element between them is the effect of exclusion. The exclusionary effects vary with context, which supports yet again Donald's position that people exist and operate in relational ways. Because of the complexities of racism(s), Stanley criticizes official anti-racist stances, such as those taken in schools, for continued focus on prejudice reduction and single-focus strategies. While educators should intervene if single, targeted acts of racism occur, these efforts alone do not end exclusions. Stanley points out that within schools, "antiracist understanding necessarily starts with seeking out and bringing into knowledge the self-representations of the excluded" (2014: 13). While no "classroom can ever represent all of the meanings of all of the people of the world," it is possible to move beyond the Eurocentric limitations of the government public schooling curriculum (13). Stanley is calling for efforts to not only recognize and stop perpetuating exclusions and divisions, but also to build bridges by helping all students to seek out interconnections amidst their complex local, national, and international relationships. His proposed strategy seeks to offer some guidance for "the long and difficult work of rethinking racisms and our own teaching practices" (14). However, his strategy does not come with guarantees, but rather, spaces where formal education seeks to ensure all students feel that they have a place and a purpose in our shared world.

Battiste (2013), Brant-Birioukov (2021), Kovach (2010), and Wilson (2008) seek to decolonize education and its settler colonial purposes by examining and presenting Indigenous histories, ways of knowing, ways of researching, and ways of teaching. Aladejebi (2021), Dei (2014), Este, Lorenzetti, and Sato (2018), and Walcott (2021) take up historical and contemporary views and efforts toward anti-Black racisms, anti-racist education, and intergenerational legacies of colonialism here in Canada and elsewhere. These scholars do not merely represent recent scholarship that can support our collective restorying of the settler colonial purposes of education and its respective histories. Rather, their historical and philosophical works are also crucial toward *understanding*, *doing*, and *unsettling* settler colonial accounts of the history of education and its purposes. While this scholarship incorporates the worldviews, lived experiences, and contributions of Indigenous, Black, and other racialized communities, their ideas and the stories of the past that are connected to and have shaped public schooling are still largely absent in the future preparation of those who will lead and teach the next generation of children and youth within the public schooling system (Currie, Ng-A-Fook, and Drake 2021).

Illustrating how minimally histories of Black people and communities in Canada are taught, in 2020 the Ontario Black History Society (OBHS) introduced #BlackedOutHistory (OBHS 2020). The OBHS provides a variety of educational opportunities for learning about Black history in Canada, such as speaking and facilitating workshops in classrooms, and offering tours of Toronto to highlight the markers and spaces of Black history in the city. The #BlackedOutHistory initiative looked at the *Nelson 8 History* textbook—a commonly used Canadian history textbook in Ontario Grade 8 classrooms—and redacted all textbook content that was not about Black history. After the redactions, only thirteen of the textbook's 255 pages remained with content still legible. Only 5 percent of the textbook gives any attention to a racialized group that has been present in what is now Canada for over 400 years. Although highlighting the lack of Black history presented in the textbook may not on its own be providing specific pedagogies or content, it does indicate where changes need to be made and the ways that community efforts can actively inform where research and teaching should attend.

We recognize that there are more initiatives being taken than just the OBHS efforts, and what we present here are strong endeavors but far from the only ways to bolster anti-racism and decolonization as purposes of education, particularly history education. However, in relation to scholarship calling for de-centering Euro- and white-centric curricula and pedagogy, the example shows that education is actively shaped, not inevitable. Additionally, we acknowledge that while our discussion focuses on possibilities for repurposing the educational disciplinary forts along anti-racist and decolonizing lines, there are numerous other identities and experiences that connect with but differ from racism and colonization. These too can contribute to troubling and reimagining the purposes of education. While we cannot provide an extensive discussion of all these experiences of the past in relation to the settler colonial purposes of schooling, we do want to mention a few of them. Recalling Blount's (2006) historical accounting of schools as "institutions of promise" in which educators have embodied societal tensions and futures of gender and sexuality, histories of desire are also part of the history of education and the purposes of public schooling. Gender and sexuality education scholar Lee Airton (2018) suggests that Canadian social and cultural concepts of gender and sexuality, via a "new gender culture," are arguably evolving faster than the curricula designed to teach them. Consequently, a fixed sense of government curriculum policy presupposes what its students will appear as, or what their overall expectations should be, and so risks excluding the particular and fluid identities that are in classrooms. A primary motivation across Airton's scholarship and teaching is thus to materialize the ostensible purposes of social justice teacher education (SJTE) without foreclosing the classroom identities—students—who are yet unknown.

Like Hendry's intermediating of history and curriculum as a nonlinear and gendered narrative, we ask again, "In the case of the tale of schooling, what identities/subjects are made possible or impossible when curriculum history presents itself as an apparently unified, linear story" (2011: 16)? Each approach we engaged with above offers new directions by departing from strictly an *Age of Enlightenment*, neoliberal, settler colonial, progressive historical narrative. Our situated knowledge, experience, and existence itself is a relational flux that is contextualized by the interpretive lenses of our times. Perhaps it is less important to squabble over which content is right or wrong than it is to understand the effects and affects of where we choose to stand in our relations, mindful of the walls that fortify these positions in relation to the historical and contemporary purposes of public education. Thus, we are, by our different positionalities, constrained in our methodological *métissage*, its situated historical accounts, about the (re)purposing of public schooling. Our gestures toward revisiting the different historical purposes of education and role(s) of history education are to emphasize different relational interconnections.

Education repurposed through such *métissage* is therefore mindful of its own navigation of our fortified discursive interpretations, social imaginaries, and historical consciousness, while carrying hope for the creation of educational communities built on equitable, ethical, caring, and life-sustaining relations.

ONGOING CHALLENGES TO UNSETTLING THE PURPOSES OF SCHOOLING

The combined crises of climate change, a worldwide pandemic, and the ongoing discovery of First Nation children in unmarked graves in Canada have left both historians and students of the history of education with significant questions about the purpose of school. The Truth and Reconciliation Commission's (TRC) *Calls to Action* were created by Residential School Survivors to address the ongoing impacts of intergenerational trauma by demanding that major institutions including education, health care, child welfare, and the justice system radically change their approaches towards Indigenous people. In the six years since the publication of the Truth and Reconciliation (TRC) reports, only eleven of the ninety-four *Calls to Action* have been achieved (Jewell and Mosby 2021). Not heeding these calls is a refusal to listen to survivors of genocide that happened in Canada. Although Canadian educators have embraced a call for the greater inclusion of Indigenous perspectives, cultures, and histories in the public curriculum, the progress on the calls specifically aligned with education have been met with both resistance and incremental changes to the history of education. As evidenced throughout this chapter, the purposes of education, as they are understood during any age, are directly linked into the period they were produced. For John Dewey and George Counts this meant a pragmatic focus on reality based on postwar economic and social conditions in the United States, just as scholars in the 1960s and 1970s were impacted by the criticisms of Western democracy by civil rights movements. In the 2000s, scholars such as Ibrahim (2014), Aladejebi (2021), Brant-Birioukov (2021), and others have critically responded to the intergenerational impacts of colonialism and implemented forms of anti-racism in response. These examples demonstrate the link between the educational foundations and our current sociopolitical and economic contexts. As a result, we argue that the purpose of education must be remade to meet the concerns of our present needs.

Donald reminds us that, to break away from the dominant segregated historical narratives of the fort, we must "remember other ways to be human" (2019: 103). As the climate crisis is created, controlled, and maintained by humans—we have the agency and understanding to imagine new ways of relating to the world. According to Donald, the dominant curriculum ideology currently "promotes the market as a concept through which all forms of human living can and should be understood" (2019: 104). Predicated on this myth are the themes of settler colonialism, including individualism, anthropocentrism, and progress with which the curriculum is imbued, either explicitly or implicitly. Therefore, Donald reminds us what it means to be human, or even what it means to be educated in our society, "is directly connected to the market and the benefits that accrue from it" (111). As a result of this ontological perspective, both the curriculum and purpose of education begin only at the start of settler colonialism when new markets were first exploited. Donald explains: "The central message, then, is that before the current era nothing of significance happened" (114). The purpose of education neglects thousands of years of history and knowledge that was gathered on Turtle Island before contact.[1] As put forth in this chapter, educational histories have neglected the lived experiences, histories, and stories of Indigenous, Black, and other racialized minority, and gendered communities in Canada. In turn, education has negatively impacted these voices and contributed to "ontological violence that has direct impacts on the well-being of youth" (113). These factors are starting to be addressed by the work of Brant-Birioukov, Ng-A-Fook, and Kane (2020). Yet it also requires support across the country. Despite this movement towards the inclusion of Indigenous knowledge, Brant-Birioukov has argued that a "settler historical consciousness continues to permeate our curricular conversations in Canada" (2021: 252). To this curricular end, she reminds us,

> Despite the perceived irrelevance of Indigenous knowledge in our modern, fast-paced world, Indigenous knowledge has proven to be responsive to crises, grief, and renewal. Indigenous cultures, languages, governance, and teachings have survived—not despite colonization but due to complex and responsive knowledge systems that dared to innovate in the face of colonization.
>
> (Brant-Birioukov 2021: 248)

Moreover, instead of providing room within our education systems to legitimize the value of Indigenous knowledge toward our current crisis, the common trope of the "vanishing Indian" dominates our discussions and is disconnected from Indigenous realities today. Therefore, as Brant-Birioukov makes clear, "the foremost threat to Indigeneity is not modernity but epistemological hegemony" (2021: 253). Education then promises to play a crucial role toward unsettling such hegemony within our past and current curricular conversations.

As knowledge is always in a relational flux, our current circumstances urgently require us to respond with both old and new educational purposes, histories, and perspectives. To meet these challenges, the purpose of education can be transformed to fit into interdisciplinary, place-based, and experiential learning activities that are informed by the past to prepare for the uncertain future. In some regards, we do not have time to lament on the state of purposes of schooling. Instead, we should focus our energy on building relationships across different fields and responding to the climate crisis while centering the voices that have been impacted the most by this change. As the impacts of climate change affect future generations, how will the purpose of education address (redress) past, present, and future individual, systemic, and societal challenges created by the ongoing cultural practices of settler colonialism? Steeves (2015: 62) defined the term "pryto-epistemology" as a form of academic renewal based on the environmental management tradition of Indigenous people who used fire to renew forest ecosystems. This type of regenerative practice affords opportunities to purposefully sustain our relations and life-sustaining sustenance with, and as, interconnected forest communities.

Heather Davis and Zoe Todd (2017) stress that colonialism started the climate crisis with the genocide of Indigenous peoples. They write:

> What is truly terrifying about the times we live in is not only the cyclical recurrence of climate change. It is not the fact that white people and people with power are now having to face what Indigenous peoples, Black people whose ancestors experienced the horrors of slavery, and others have faced for the past five hundred years – that could be considered some kind of perverted justice. But the scale of the destruction has increased exponentially, while our governance systems often work against efforts to sustain livable climates and the abilities of people to adapt.
>
> (Davis and Todd 2017: 775)

Climate change is a symptom of a much larger problem relating to the land and how its economic structures have been supported by the settler colonial purposes of public education. In response, how might the purpose of education encourage the ability of people to adapt and change over time to meet this horrifying reality while prioritizing the voices of those who have already faced the horrors of government policies supporting land dispossession, genocide, and enslavement?

Recently, McGregor, Pind, and Karn have encouraged the field of history education to use our current geological epoch (the Anthropocene) "as a theoretical tool to analyze change over time, cause and consequence, and the ethical implications of human-environment relationships" (2021: 493). They also suggest that we need to foster interdisciplinary and collaborative relationships with diverse knowledge holders as no single program, educator, or individual can confront these challenges alone. And most importantly, to "find creative ways to present materials that teach students how to think rather than what to think" (502). In direct connection with these ideas was the term developed by Brant-Birioukov (2021) called "In(di)genuity," which refers to the resilience, adaptation, and innovations that Indigenous educators and teachers deployed in the face of the pandemic. Brant-Birioukov writes, "Since time immemorial, our medicines became refined, alliances and treaties were broken and solidified, and the complexities of educating our youth were in constant flux to respond to the changing needs of our communities. Reconciling the old with the new was a valuable Indigenous asset" (2021: 250). How might the purposes of public education focus on learning from those who have already faced impossible challenges and kept their sustainable knowledge systems intact? That is our hope in relation to the past, present, and future challenges we are yet to face, and the renewed (re)purposing of public education we need to create and sustain together.

NOTE

1.   Turtle Island refers to the original name given to the place we are writing from, as both the Anishinaabe and Haudenosaunee have origin stories about a turtle forming their homelands on its back. Within writing by Indigenous peoples, this is the common terminology provided to the lands also known as North America. Please see Weaver (2016: 197).

REFERENCES

Ackerman, David B. (2003), "Taproots for a New Century: Tapping the Best of Traditional and Progressive Education," *Phi Delta Kappa*, 84 (5): 344–9.

Airton, Lee (2018), *Gender: Your Guide: A Gender-Friendly Primer on What to Know, What to Say, and What to Do in the New Gender Culture*, New York: Simon and Schuster.

Aladejebi, Funké (2021), *Schooling the System: A History of Black Women Teachers*, Montreal and Kingston: McGill-Queen's University Press.

Alfonseca, Kiara (2022), "New Florida Bill Would Ban Feelings of 'discomfort' in Teachings About Racism in US History," *ABC 7 News*, January 20. Available online: https://abc7news.com/critical-race-theory-florida-bill-discomfort-ron-desantis-what-is-crt-in-schools/11491558/ (accessed May 7, 2022).

Anderson, Archibald W. (1956), "Bases of Proposals Concerning the History of Education," *History of Education Journal*, 7 (2): 37–98.

Axelrod, Paul (1997), *The Promise of Schooling*, Toronto: University of Toronto Press.

Barman, Jean (2012), "Schooled for Inequality: The Education of British Columbia Aboriginal Children," in Sara Z. Burke and Patrice Milewski (eds.), *Schooling in Transition: Readings in Canadian History of Education*, 255–76, Toronto: University of Toronto Press.

Battiste, Marie (2000), *Reclaiming Indigenous Voice and Vision*, Vancouver: UBC Press.

Battiste, Marie (2013), *Decolonizing Education: Nourishing the Learning Spirit*, Saskatoon, SK: Purich Publishing.

Battiste, Marie and James Youngblood Henderson (2000), *Protecting Indigenous Knowledge and Heritage: A Global Challenge*, Vancouver: UBC Press.

Bestor, Arthur Eugene (1953), *Educational Wastelands: The Retreat from Learning in Our Public Schools*, Urbana: University of Illinois Press.

Blount, Jackie M. (2006), *Fit to Teach: Same-Sex Desire, Gender, and School Work in the Twentieth Century*, Albany: University of New York Press.

Brant-Birioukov, Kiera (2021), "Covid-19 and In(di)genuity: Lessons from Indigenous Resilience, Adaptation, and Innovation in Times of Crisis," *Prospects*, 51 (1): 247–59.

Brant-Birioukov, Kiera, Nicholas Ng-A-Fook, and Ruth Kane (2020), "Reconceptualizing Teacher Education in Ontario: Civic Particularity, Ethical Engagement, and Reconciliation," in Anne M. Phelan, William F. Pinar, Nicholas Ng-A-Fook, and Ruth Kane (eds.), *Reconceptualizing Teacher Education: A Canadian Contribution to a Global Challenge*, 39–65, Ottawa: University of Ottawa Press.

Burke, Sara Z. and Patrice Milewski, eds. (2012), *Schooling in Transition: Readings in Canadian History of Education*, Toronto: University of Toronto Press.

Butts, R. Freeman and Lawrence A. Cremin (1953), *A History of Education in American Culture*, New York: Holt.

Cajete, Gregory (1994), *Look to the Mountain: An Ecology of Indigenous Education*, Rio Rancho, NM: Kivaki Press.

Carleton, Sean F.P. (2011), "Colonizing Minds: Public Education, the 'Textbook Indian', and Settler Colonialism in British Columbia, 1920–1970," *BC Studies: The British Columbian Quarterly*, 169 (Spring): 101–30.

Carleton, Sean (2017), "Settler Anxiety and State Support for Missionary Schooling in Colonial British Columbia, 1849–1871," *Historical Studies in Education/Revue d'histoire de l'éducation*, 29 (1): 57–76.

Chambers, C. and N. Blood (2012), "Love thy Neighbour: Repatriating Precious Blackfoot Sites," *One World in Dialogue Journal*, 2 (1): 38–51.

Christou, Theodore M. (2012), *Progressive Education: Revisioning and Reframing Ontario's Public Schools, 1919–1942*, Toronto: University of Toronto Press.

Cooper, Afua (2007), "Unsilencing the Past: Memorializing Four Hundred Years of African Canadian History," in David Divine (ed.), *Multiple Lenses: Voices from the Diaspora Located in Canada*, 11–22, Newcastle upon Tyne: Cambridge Scholars.

Counts, George S. (1932), *Dare the School Build a New Social Order?* Carbondale: Southern Illinois University Press.

Cremin, Lawrence A. (1955), "The Recent Development of the History of Education as a Field of Study in the United States," *History of Education Journal*, 7 (1): 1–35.

Cremin, Lawrence A. (1956), "The Role of the History of Education in the Professional Preparation of Teachers: Recommendations of the Committee," *History of Education Journal*, 7 (3): 99–132.

Crenshaw, Kimberle Williams (1991), "Mapping the Margins: Intersectionality, Identity Politics, and Violence Against Women of Color," *Stanford Law Review*, 43 (6): 1241–99.

Currie, Mark T.S., Nicholas Ng-A-Fook, and Aaron Sardinha Drake (2021), "Is CRRP Enough?: Addressing Antiracism(s) in Teacher Education," *Journal for the American Advancement of Curriculum Studies*, 14 (2): 1–28.

Davis, Heather and Zoe Todd (2017), "On the Importance of a Date, or, Decolonizing the Anthropocene," *ACME: An International Journal for Critical Geographies*, 16 (4): 761–80.

Dei, G.J.S. (2014), "Personal Reflections on Anti-racism Education for a Global Context," *Encounters in Theory and History of Education*, 15: 239–49.

Dewey, John (1916), *Democracy and Education: An Introduction to the Philosophy of Education*, New York: Macmillan.

Dill, Jeffrey S. and James Davidson Hunter (2010), "Education and the Culture Wars," in S. Hitlin and S. Vaisey (eds.), *Handbook of the Sociology of Morality*, 275–91, New York: Springer.

Donald, Dwayne T. (2009), "Forts, Curriculum, and Indigenous Métissage: Imagining Decolonization of Aboriginal-Canadian Relations in Educational Contexts," *First Nations Perspectives*, 2 (1): 1–24.

Donald, Dwayne (2012), "Indigenous Métissage: A Decolonizing Research Sensibility," *International Journal of Qualitative Studies in Education*, 25 (5): 535–55.

Donald, Dwayne (2019), "Homo economicus and Forgetful Curriculum," in Huia Tomlins-Jahnke, Sandra D. Styres, Spencer Lilley, and Dawn Zinga (eds.), *Indigenous Education: New Directions in Theory and Practice*, 103–25, Alberta: University of Alberta Press.

Du Bois, W.E.B. ([1903] 1994), *The Souls of Black Folk*, New York: Dover Publications.

Este, David, Liza Lorenzetti, and Christa Sato (2018), *Racism and Anti-racism in Canada*, Halifax, NS: Fernwood Publishing.

Fanon, Frantz ([1952] 2008), *Black Skin, White Masks*, New York: Grove Press.

Fanon, Frantz (1963), *The Wretched of the Earth*, trans. Constance Farrington, New York: Grove Press.

Gaztambide-Fernández, Rubén (2015), "Browning the Curriculum: A Project of Unsettlement," in Ming Fang He, Brian D. Schultz, and William H. Schubert (eds.), *The SAGE Guide to Curriculum in Education*, 416–23, Los Angeles: Sage Publications.

Gidney, R.D. and W.P.J. Millar (1990), *Inventing Secondary Education: The Rise of the High School in Nineteenth-Century Ontario*, Montreal: McGill-Queen's University Press.

Greene, Peter (2022), "Teacher Anti-CRT Bills Coast To Coast: A State By State Guide," *Forbes*, February 16. Available online: https://www.forbes.com/sites/petergreene/2022/02/16/teacher-anti-crt-bills-coast-to-coast-a-state-by-state-guide/?sh=658a36064ff6 (accessed May 7, 2022).

Gutek, Gerald L. (1987), *A History of the Western Educational Experience*, Prospect Heights, IL: Waveland Press.

Haig-Brown, Celia (1988), *Resistance and Renewal*, Vancouver: Arsenal Pulp Press.

Haig-Brown, Celia (2018), "Working to Reconcile: Truth, Action, and Indigenous Education in Canada," in Tania Das Gupta, Carl E. James, Chris Andersen, Grace-Edward Galabuzi, and Roger C.A. Maaka (eds.), *Race and Racialization: Essential Readings*, 318–37, Toronto: Canadian Scholars Press.

hampton, rosalind (2020), *Black Racialization and Resistance at an Elite University*, Toronto: University of Toronto Press.

Harlan, Louis R. (1958), *Separate and Unequal: Public School Campaigns and Racism in the Southern Seaboard States, 1900–1915*, Chapel Hill: University of North Carolina Press.

Hendry, Petra (2011), *Engendering Curriculum History*, New York: Routledge.

Henry, Frances, Enakshi Dua, Carl E. James, Audrey Kobayashi, Peter Li, Howard Ramos, and Malinda S. Smith (2017), *The Equity Myth: Racialization and Indigeneity at Canadian Universities*, Vancouver: UBC Press.

Hirsch, E.D. (1999), *The Schools We Need: And Why We Don't Have Them*, New York: Anchor Books.

Ibrahim, Awad (2014), *The Rhizome of Blackness: A Critical Ethnography of Hip-Hop Culture, Language, Identity, and the Politics of Becoming*, New York: Peter Lang.

James, Carl (2008), "Re/presentation of Race and Racism in the Multicultural Discourse of Canada," in Ali A. Abdi and Lynette Shultz (eds.), *Education for Human Rights and Global Citizenship*, 97–112, Albany: State University of New York Press.

Jewell, Eva and Ian Mosby (2021), "Calls to Action Accountability: A 2021 Status Update on Reconciliation," Yellowhead Institute, December 11. Available online: https://yellowheadinstitute.org/trc/ (accessed May 7, 2022).

Joseph, R.P. (2018), *21 Things You May Not Know About the Indian Sct*, Port Coquitlam: Indigenous Relations Press.

Kendi, Ibram X. (2016), *Stamped from the Beginning: The Definitive History of Racist Ideas in America*, London: Hachette UK.

Kovach, Margaret (2010), *Indigenous Methodologies: Characteristics, Conversations, and Contexts*, Toronto: University of Toronto Press.

Lightfoot, Sheryl R. (2016), *Global Indigenous Politics: A Subtle Revolution*, London: Routledge.

McDermott, Mairi, Jennifer MacDonald, Jennifer Markides, and Mike Holden (2021), "Uncovering the Experiences of Engaging Indigenous Knowledges in Colonial Structures of Schooling and Research," *Engaged Scholar Journal: Community-Engaged Research, Teaching and Learning*, 7 (1): 25–44.

McGregor, Heather E., Jackson Pind, and Sara Karn (2021), "A 'wicked problem': Rethinking History Education in the Anthropocene," *Rethinking History: The Journal of Theory and Practice*, 25 (4): 483–507.

Milloy, John S. (2017), *A National Crime: The Canadian Government and the Residential School System*, Manitoba Studies in Native History Book 11, Winnipeg: University of Manitoba Press.

Ng-A-Fook, Nicholas (2007), *An Indigenous Curriculum of Place: The United Houma Nation's Contentious Relationship with Louisiana's Educational Institutions*, New York: Peter Lang.

Ng-A-Fook, Nicholas (2016), "Storying Curriculum as Technoeconomic Progress: A Lament!," *Antistasism*, 6 (1). Available online: https://journals.lib.unb.ca/index.php/antistasis/article/view/24506 (accessed May 7, 2022).

Ng-A-Fook, Nicholas, Mark Ingham, and Tylor Burrows (2018), "Reconciling 170 Years of Settler Curriculum Policies: Teacher Education in Ontario," in Theodore Christou (ed.), *Curriculum History of Teacher Education*, 125–44, New York: Routledge.

Ontario Black History Society (OBHS) (2020), *#BlackedOutHistory. Ontario Black History Society*. Available online: https://blackhistorysociety.ca/ (accessed May 7, 2022).

Piapot, Ntawnis (2022), "Kapawe'no First Nation Discovers 169 Potential Unmarked Graves on Alberta Residential School Site," *The Globe and Mail*, March 2. Available online: https://www.theglobeandmail.com/canada/article-alberta-first-nation-discovers-169-potential-unmarked-graves-on/ (accessed May 7, 2022).

Quon, Alexander (2021), "What the TRC Report Tells Us About the Marieval Indian Residential School," *CBC News*, June 25. Available online: https://www.cbc.ca/news/canada/saskatchewan/history-of-marieval-indian-residential-school-1.6078473 (accessed May 7, 2022).

Raptis, Helen (2016), *What We Learned: Two Generations Reflect on Tsimshian Education and the Day Schools*, Vancouver: University of British Columbia Press.

Ravitch, Diane (2000), *Left Back: A Century of Battles over School Reform*, New York: Simon and Schuster.

Said, Edward W. (1978), *Orientalism*, New York: Pantheon Books.

Sharma, Nandita (2020), *Home Rule: National Sovereignty and the Separation of Natives and Migrants*, Durham, NC: Duke University Press.

Smith, Andrea (2016), "Heteropatriarchy and the Three Pillars of White Supremacy," in The INCITE! Anthology (eds.), *Color of Violence*, 66–73, Durham, NC: Duke University Press.

Smith, Linda T. (1999), *Decolonizing Methodologies: Research and Indigenous Peoples*, London: Zed Books.

Smith, Bryan, Nicholas Ng-A-Fook, Linda Radford, and Sarah Smitherman Pratt, eds. (2018), *Hacking Education in a Digital Age: Teacher Education, Curriculum, and Literacies*, i–202, Charlotte, NC: Information Age Publishing.

Spivak, Gayatri Chakravorty (1988), "Can the Subaltern Speak?" in Cary Nelson and Lawrence Grossberg (eds.), *Marxism and the Interpretation of Culture*, 271–313, Urbana: University of Illinois Press.

Stanley, Timothy J. (2014), "Antiracism Without Guarantees: A Framework for Rethinking Racisms in Schools," *Critical Literacy: Theories and Practices*, 8 (3): 4–19.

Stanley, Timothy J. (2006), "Whose Public? Whose Memory? Racisms, Grand Narratives and Canadian History," in Ruth Sandwell (ed.), *To the Past: History Education, Public Memory, and Citizenship in Canada*, 32–50, Toronto: University of Toronto Press.

Steeves, Paulette F. (2015), "Decolonizing the Past and Present of the Western Hemisphere (the Americas)," *Archaeologies*, 11 (1): 42–69.

Tomkins, George S. (2008), *A Common Countenance: Stability and Change in the Canadian Curriculum*, Vancouver: Pacific Educational Press.

Truth and Reconciliation Commission of Canada (2015), *Canada's Residential Schools: The Legacy*, Montreal: McGill-Queen's University Press.

Tuck, Eve and Rubén A. Gaztambide-Fernández (2013), "Curriculum, Replacement, and Settler Futurity," *Journal of Curriculum Theorizing*, 29 (1): 72–89.

Tupper, Jennifer A. (2020), "Cracks in the foundations: (Re)storying Settler Colonialism," in Kristina R. Llewellyn and Nicholas Ng-A-Fook (eds.), *Oral History, Education, and Justice*, 88–104, New York: Routledge.

Walcott, Rinaldo (2021), *The Long Emancipation: Moving toward Black Freedom*, Durham, NC: Duke University Press.

Weaver, Hilary N., ed. (2016), *Social Issues in Contemporary Native America: Reflections from Turtle Island*, Abingdon: Routledge.

Wildcat, Daniel R. (2005), "Indigenizing the Future: Why We Must Think Spatially in the Twenty-First Century," *American Studies*, 46 (3/4): 417–40.

Willinsky, John (1998), *Learning to Divide the World: Education at Empire's End*, Minneapolis: University of Minnesota Press.

Wilson, Shawn (2008), *Research Is Ceremony: Indigenous Research Methods*, Black Point, NS: Fernwood Publishing.

CHAPTER THREE

Curriculum

The Educational Experience in the School Curriculum

PETER HLEBOWITSH

The school curriculum is, in effect, a blueprint for educational action. It aims to organize a special educational environment, one that is moved by a normative mandate that underscores the things, institutionally speaking, that all children need to learn. This obviously includes, most fundamentally, teaching children to read and to be widely literate, but it also includes a long list of other vital undertakings. In North America, the curriculum commonly allies itself with a set of comprehensive learning pursuits that target individual-personal, socio-civic, academic-intellectual, and vocation-career goals (Goodlad 1984). Individual-personal goals encompass a range of concerns pertaining to the emotional and physical well-being of students, the pursuit of student interests and aptitudes, and ultimately the construction of a self-identity. Socio-civic goals speak to citizenship, social consciousness, the appreciation of cultural differences, and various matters related to moral judgment and moral behavior. Academic-intellectual goals involve establishing the fundamentals of literacy and numeracy, together with the cultivation of thinking and evaluation skills and the engagement of knowledge and insight embedded in the subject disciplines. And career-vocational goals promote specialized skills, as well as habits and outlooks that cast an eye on the world of work while also shaping career choices.

In this way, it is useful to understand that the design of the school curriculum is always a boundary setting exercise (Hlebowitsh 2005a). Everything that might be worthy of inclusion cannot possibly be accommodated in the school experience. Critical choices, dictated by time and resource constraints, must always be made. Teachers and others will inevitably be involved in deciding what to include in the curriculum, and by effect, what to exclude. So how does such a process work? How can anyone make a claim on what is most educational?

Fortunately, this question has been targeted historically by scholars in the curriculum field who have worked to identify a general normative or institutional strategy for the education of youth in school settings. Much of this work was originally influenced by John Dewey's effort to describe the nature of an educational experience. Dewey put his finger on a number of factors that proved to be useful for curriculum scholars trying to understand how to design educational experiences. As we shall see, the factors identified by Dewey were rooted in his theory of experience and in an effort to distinguish between educational and mis-educational experiences. The effect for curriculum scholars was a kind of model that offered a concrete way to think about the educational value of a school experience. It gave scholars in the field a way to help design and implement educational experiences at the local level and to evaluate the educational worth of larger scale educational reforms. In this way, Dewey's work enabled a community of scholars to assist practitioners directly and to raise cautions against the emergence of vogue or misguided educational reforms.

I will start with a discussion of Dewey's theory of experience and follow it with an effort to understand the macro-reforms that the school have faced in North America against the criteria that Dewey fashioned in defining an educational experience.

WHAT IS AN EDUCATIONAL EXPERIENCE?

The question of what constitutes an educational experience is naturally tied to the result one expects to witness from an educational experience. John Dewey took this question on directly by first characterizing the conditions of an educational experience as foundationally tied to the cultivation of behaviors and discernments that could help individuals create a better future for themselves and for those around them (Dewey 1938). To Dewey, to be educated meant to be able to control one's own fate intelligently and ethically—an effect that could span out in a way that could positively influence a broadly conceived common good. In this way, he saw educational experiences as building blocks for the creation of a better future. To think about an educational experience inevitably meant thinking about, to use Dewey's descriptor, the cultivation of "desirable habits that live fruitfully and creatively in future experiences" (Dewey 1938: 28). For those interested in the design of the school curriculum, the question then became, how does one gain such an effect? Dewey provided an answer to this question that laid important groundwork for the school curriculum.

The Experiential Continuum

Dewey's effort to shape the character of an educational experience starts with his idea for what he referred to as an experiential continuum. Dewey dedicated quite a bit of thought to the task of demonstrating how an experience can, on the one hand, be educational and lead to the profitable development of the individual or, on the other, be mis-educational and lead to arrested or some distorted form of development.

To Dewey, an educational experience was necessarily connected to the practical matters of living, which were inevitably mediated by important normative factors. The issue of normative purpose is important. Dewey understood that the idea of educational growth was in effect without any moral valance. One can become well educated in the work of, say, crime and some other form of social deviancy. As Dewey stated it, "that a man may grow efficiency as a burglar, as a gangster or as a corrupt politician, cannot be doubted" (Dewey 1938: 36). True educational growth, to Dewey, had to move in a special axiological direction. Dewey was not bashful in saying that the best option in this respect was associated with outcomes tied to the values and aims of living in a democracy. He believed growth that opened the door to new possibilities, that equipped the learner with ways to independently pursue knowledge, and that vested the learner in experiences that were enlarging and cosmopolitan in nature were key. These were the kinds of educational experiences that empowered individuals to create better futures for themselves—experiences that cultivated a habit to learn more, or that opened a door to new possibilities for continued inquiry and understanding, precisely the kind of experiences that lived fruitfully, to use Dewey's apt descriptor, in subsequent experiences.

But the experiential continuum required something more than normative influences. It also required learner-centered ones. The continuum was, in effect, a two factor design, accounting for the nature of the child's own lived experience, which Dewey described as internal factors, as well as for what it meant to be an educated person in a good society, which Dewey saw as objective factors, or what I have already described as normative ones. Taken together these two conditions formed the educational situation. Thus, when objective (or normative) factors interacted with internal ones (with the talents, desire, needs, and unique history of the individual) in the form of an experience (or in our case, a school experience), whatever ensued from such an interaction was likely to invest itself constructively in subsequent experiences. Dewey called these two factors the longitudinal and latitudinal aspects of experience (Dewey 1938: 44).

In this way, the work of the educator is directly related to making pedagogical decisions inclusive of internal factors within the range of a child's life and development. This means that the educator must account for the experiences, aptitudes, development characteristics, personality traits, and personal interests of the child. Interestingly, Dewey's main critique against traditional education, as he called it, was tied to the fact that traditional education had little regard for internal factors. The form of traditional education that was the target of Dewey's criticism was marked by an instructional doctrine that elevated the importance of abstraction over physical activity—that had, in effect, very little residency in the life of the learner. The distinguishing feature of traditional education disavowed physical activity in the school, leaving objective factors without their energizing life engagements. "In schools," noted Dewey, "those under instruction are too customarily looked upon as acquiring knowledge as theoretical spectators, minds which appropriate knowledge by direct energy of intellect" (Dewey 1916: 164). The mentalistic biases of traditional education served to privilege a view of learning that was mainly cognitive in nature, giving the act of knowing a higher standing than the act of doing and effectively removing itself from internal factors.

So, the first emerging insight from the experiential continuum is that it cannot function educationally without accounting for internal objectives. This, in fact, has become a tenet for the design of the curriculum (Tanner and Tanner 1980).

Dewey makes it clear, however, that the educational embrace of internal factors should not be strictly child centered. In the experiential continuum, the educator needs to think about internal factors as they interact with key objective factors, especially as they relate to normative concerns that speak to the selection and organization of subject matter, and various other factors tied to teaching decisions. "No experience," declared, "is educative that does not lead to knowledge of more facts and entertaining of more ideas and to a better and more orderly arrangement of them" (Dewey 1938: 55). Thus, the organization of subject matter and other objective concerns related to, say, living an informed life in a democracy, such as the cultivation of key reasoning skills, communication skills, inquiry skills, and social skills, become fundamental factors in the building of an educational experience. The teacher must know the nature of the child from the position of the life experience, inclusive of developmental concerns, levels of aptitude, cultural and linguistic matters, familial prejudices, and more, while also having at her disposal a full understanding of the objective factors needed to activate an educational experience.

So, what is an educational experience? It starts with an understanding that experience can only be educational if it enlists the nature and life of the child, responding to internal factors related to interest, aptitudes, developmental concerns, and a raft of psycho-social influences. Such a position, however, is mediated by objective factors related to subject matter, civic values, and normative standards of purpose as well as professional standards of practice. Dewey made this claim directly in the *Child and the Curriculum*, which was written in context for the laboratory school that he and his wife had opened at the University of Chicago in 1894:

> The fundamental factors in the educative process are an immature underdeveloped being; and certain social aims, meanings, values incarnate in the matured experience of the adult. The educative process is the due interaction of these forces.
>
> (Dewey 1902: 40)

Dewey went on to stress the organic consideration of the internal with the objective, noting also that their separate consideration would lead the school to embrace an unbalanced educational approach that could set the conditions for pendulum-like changes in school reform, swinging from child-centered to subject-centered perspectives. In this way, Dewey's idea on the experiential continuum makes the case for a theory of experience that could serve as a tool to assist with the work of selecting and organizing educational materials and methods. This is a defining design for the school curriculum, which is the concern of the next section.

THE EXPERIENTIAL CONTINUUM AS A PSYCHO-SOCIAL SCREEN FOR THE CURRICULUM

The historical design of the curriculum is very much dependent on the application of a psycho-social screen that helps it deal with questions related to the selection of goals, the organization and implementation of instruction, the selection of content, and the use of various evaluation tools. Such a screen, as we shall see, is largely fashioned out of Dewey's experiential continuum. The key sources to the screen include, not surprisingly: (1) a commitment to the nature of the learner (the internal factors in Dewey's experiential continuum); (2) an account of the chief values and aims guiding the normative conduct of society, and (3) the embrace of subject matter that is responsive to the learner and critical to the healthy development of the individual in the context of society.

Tanner and Tanner have argued that such a triad of concerns has paradigmatic standing in the curriculum field, representing a consensus view on how a curriculum can begin to operate as a school-based plan for the education of all youth (Tanner and Tanner 1980). The Tanners demonstrated the centrality of these three sources by documenting their visibility in the work of curriculum thinkers throughout the twentieth century (Tanner and Tanner 1980). In this way, the three sources (or influences) on the curriculum have served the field very well and continue to have good standing as a useful mechanism for the development of the school curriculum.

The three factors, in fact, found their most public expression in ralph Tyler's well-known rationale for curriculum development, a point that we will discuss in more detail below (Tyler 1949). Tyler gave the three factors metaphorical life by referring to them as screens in the design of the curriculum. The basic idea was that, regardless of how the curriculum might be designed, the educator would be required, one way or another, to attend to the role that the nature of the learner, the values and aims of society, and subject matter choices play in shaping the curriculum, even as these factors might be differently conceived across philosophical orientations by educators with differing outlooks on teaching and learning (Hlebowitsh 2012).

The character of Tyler's rationale was best revealed in its early development, when Tyler used it as a study guide for his graduate students. The course guide highlighted a list of reading references that outlined how studies of children, youth, and adults could inform and shape important objectives in the curriculum. As Wraga put it, the readings reflected a "range of perspectives on personal-social development within each age group and included psychological, educational and social issues" (Wraga 2017: 237). Similar lists of references, pertaining to the use of subject matter and social (life experience) sources, were also furnished. One can see that Dewey's educational continuum was alive in the development of the rationale and in the manner in which Tyler was positioning the teaching/learning experience as a framework, not as an ideology, with the effect of compelling educators to weigh their decisions in light of the learner's interests and developmental needs, in the spirit of the ethical foundations of democratic living, and in the context of socially and intellectually worthwhile knowledge. Let's take a closer look at how this might be done.

The Nature of the Learner

The first factor is what I already introduced as internal factors rooted in the nature of the learner. Other educational thinkers, of course, even before Dewey, also recognized the importance of considering the nature of the learner in the conduct of the school. In many cases, however, the embrace of the learner was wholly child centered. Among the earliest and most noteworthy examples of this can be found in the work of the eighteenth-century thinker Jean-Jacques Rousseau, who orchestrated a view of childhood that was equivalent to what we might refer to as a doctrine of original goodness. To Rousseau, children were born good and innocent, but made sinful and depraved by their interactions with the adult world and its institutions (Rousseau 1911). Rousseau detailed a classically child-centered position dedicated to a view of learning that advised teachers to step back and take a more limited interactive role with children in the interest of honoring their spontaneity and emergent wishes. And while the unrestricted embrace of the child's wishes and needs made Rousseau's idea difficult to translate into bounded normative practice, it nonetheless opened the door to several creative practitioners who began to rethink the act of teaching in the new light cast by the presence of the learner.

Following Rousseau's lead, several child-centered initiatives began to emerge in Europe during the mid and latter parts of the nineteenth century, each offering up inventive perspectives on how teaching can be conducted with the full view of the learner in mind. These initiatives included: the work of Pestalozzi (1894), who gave the curriculum new vitality by elevating the role of activity in the school experience; the work of Herbart (1901), who rethought the organization of subject matter in the school to reflect the social environment of the child; the work of Froebel (1887), who designed instructional materials that he believed brought out the inner powers of children in school; and the work of Montessori, who empowered the idea of sensory learning for very young learners and who otherwise worked to bring more social interaction into the school (Tanner and Tanner 1980).

In North America, the child-centered response has its own unique expression. It included the awakening of a child study movement led by the psychologist G. Stanley Hall (1901), the rise of normal schools as a site for teacher education, the development of the American kindergarten, and vital experimentation with child-centered schools (Tanner and Tanner 1980). Rugg and Shumaker (1928) documented the popularity of the child-centered perspective in the American schools during the early decades of the twentieth century. These movements, with few exceptions, were defined by their commitment to bringing the internal factors of the experiential continuum to the fore, without much regard for an accompanying social or normative theory of education.

Dewey was quite critical of such child-centered responses, noting that a purely child-centered approach was basically directionless because it started and stopped with the learner and had no guiding normative authority. "Nothing can be developed from nothing," declared Dewey, "nothing but the crude can be developed out of the crude – and this is what surely happens when we throw the child back upon his achieved self as a finality and invite him to spin the truths of nature or of conduct out to that" (1902: 282). This early flirtation with child-centered views would dog the progressive educational movement for decades, giving its critics a way to accuse educational progressives of advancing an anti-intellectual school experience.

Today, of course, the foundation of the curriculum is partly built on the learner. Most educators understand the need for the school experience to attend to the life experiences of learners and to account for developmental factors related to what, when, and how certain skills should be taught. Factors related to learners give us developmental insight on readiness and pacing, and they open our eyes to individual aptitudes and individual weaknesses. They underscore a basic principle of good instruction by emphasizing the need to fashion individualized and differentiated forms of instruction.

Just how one navigates through the nature of the learner is influenced by one's philosophical orientation. A behaviorist's view of the learner, with its focus on stimulus–response connections, is obviously one that differs significantly from that of, say, a Piagetian view and its focus on developmental stage theory. Dewey's experiential continuum does provide some educational direction on this count by insisting that any calculation of the learner must account for societal norms and subject matter obligations. This helps to constrain the range of educational possibilities.

The Values and Aims of Society

The school, as indicated above, is a functionally normative institution that carries a public mandate to educate the upcoming generation of youth into the ways and mores of society: to learn what it means to be a good person living a good life in a good society. The family, of course, plays the same role, but unlike the family, the school is deliberately conceived to fulfill a societal mandate that aims to amplify the key skills, subject matter, and dispositions needed for engaging in civic life. The health of the commonweal is always dependent on the role of the school to advance key normative concerns, including teaching children how to read, think, communicate, inquire, study, and behave in a manner that is within the range of reasoned action, as dictated by the values and aims of the society.

In North America at least, the public school can be viewed as an agent of democracy. Dewey, in fact, referred to the school as an embryonic democracy—a scaled down and simplified unit of democracy that offers a formative understanding of democratic processes. As such, the curriculum is expected to create opportunities for children to work together and to engage in circles of social interaction that produce a shared sense of identity, marked by trust, reasoned respect for differences, and cooperation, while still maintaining a sense of discipline and social order without resorting to authoritarian methods.

One can start to organize the curriculum in this direction by detailing the skills needed to effectively live under the conditions of life in a democratic society, at a level that might befit the age and development of the child. Such skills have a pervasive status in the curriculum, meaning that they do not necessarily belong to any one discipline but are otherwise widely distributed in the organization of a school-based experience. These skills could include thinking and problem-solving skills, ones that can be further broken down into logical, scientific, and even artistic forms of thinking. In the same way, a range of communication skills can be pervasively structured into the curriculum. One can easily imagine, for instance, how thinking and writing clearly, as well as varied forms of thinking and writing, can serve to develop strong citizenship skills. One can appreciate how speaking well and demonstrating skills at argumentation or how the ability to use different forms of communication (including technological, musical, visual, and mathematical forms) can go a long way toward supplying objective material for the curriculum, as conceived in Dewey's original articulation of his experiential continuum. Along these same lines, a curriculum that encourages children to seek reliable sources of evidence, to understand the relation between cause and effect, and that cultivates skills of persuasion, as well as skills of detecting and avoiding deceptive forms of persuasion, all fit the bill.

Of course, there are also instructional issues here that are processual in nature. The design of the school curriculum is not exclusively a matter of what is taught. It also helps to shape the conduct of the teacher who, by taking account of democratic values and aims, should strive to employ methods of teaching that encourage conversation, get children to work together, reinforce civility, and ultimately produce a diverse discourse community. All of this is a reminder that schooling is fundamentally moved by a social theory and by some expression of hope for the kind of society that the school aims to build.

Subject Matter

The school curriculum inevitably advances the study of a selected body of knowledge or subject matter. The question of what knowledge is most worthy has, in fact, been an enduring one for educators (Spencer 1860). When we say that x is worthy of inclusion in the curriculum, we are sending a clear signal about valuing x, believing that school children will be served by knowing it. This gives subject matter normative stature.

The state commonly plays a key role in determining the nature of the subject matter that makes its way into the school curriculum. It does this by developing content standards representative of what all youth are expected to know. Such standards typically aim to cover the facts, ideas, concepts, and thinking modes present in the various subject areas that every student should know. In the United States, these standards vary from state to state. Irrespective of such differences, however, standard setting is a way to shape the discourse community of a school in the interests of forging a common and shared basis of understanding—what some might call the basis for cultural literacy. Forging a common language is one of the more basic expressions of such an effort. But building a common cultural vocabulary through idioms, shared cultural stories, shared histories, and shared values is part of the action as well.

The old-world view of subject matter that Dewey criticized was connected to a learning doctrine known as mental discipline, which upheld the view that the intellectual faculties of students could be best developed and improved by exercising certain "mind muscles" that only a certain number of subject areas were uniquely able to activate. The thinking was that certain subjects were, in effect, intrinsically endowed with the capacity to cultivate the mind's intellectual faculties and that the study of such subjects represented the best preparation for the education of all youth. Under these conditions, the main function of the elementary school curriculum was to build up the fundamental skills needed to access the subject areas while at the secondary school level the focus was to organize the subject areas in a way that gave children an exposure to their mind training possibilities.

Subject matter choices are of course mediated by the age and maturity of the child, as a well as by different curricular functions. Specialized subject matter, for instance, plays an important role in developing certain career ambitions and in satisfying certain individual intellectual/academic interests. In the final analysis, however, the instructional role of subject matter in the curriculum requires us to return to Dewey's construction of the experiential continuum and think about how the logical organization of the subject matter (the manner in which key principles, propositions fact, and concerts are laid out) articulate with the psycho-social organization of the subject matter.

THE HISTORICAL FORMATION OF THE EDUCATIONAL EXPERIENCE IN THE SCHOOL CURRICULUM

The design of the school curriculum carries, at a minimum, three basic obligations. It first serves to identify the chief purposes to be undertaken by the school. It sets the light, as it were, that stands at the end of the tunnel. Second, it lays out the rough experiential landscape of the school by framing and organizing the subject matter, skills, and dispositions that will shape and direct instructional judgments. And finally, it offers a way to evaluate its own effectiveness by making itself accountable to its original purposes. It should be noted that these present-day demands on the curriculum have taken some time to fully materialize in the schools. The insertion of an evaluation mechanism in the curriculum, for instance, is a relatively recent phenomenon, as is the idea of casting the action of the school in relation to something more than subject matter. As we shall see, the historical formation of the school curriculum is tied to an evolving idea on what constitutes an educational experience and to the role that the experiential continuum plays in affecting the conduct of the school.

Social Efficiency and the Particularizing of the School Experience

The formalization of curriculum development as a practice in North American public schools can be traced to the early twentieth century and to the methodology propounded by John Franklin Bobbitt (Kliebard 1986). Using a technique known as activity analysis, Bobbitt sought to identify activities in the school that he believed prepared learners for specific tasks in life—among them vocational, socio-civic, familial, and intellectual tasks. His effort to connect the main activities of life to the actual conduct of the school represented an early methodical approach to organizing what got taught in schools and became the driving force behind the rise of the field of curriculum studies and the valorization of a process that we now call curriculum development (Hlebowitsh 2010).

Bobbitt's early idea for the design of a curriculum was relatively straightforward. He believed that the main building blocks for the curriculum were to be found by inventorying the specific nature of activities that went into being an adjusted and high-functioning adult, including activities related to the role of citizen, family member, and worker. Bobbitt felt he could identify the activities that were key to leading a good life, codify them, and then embed them into subject areas. His view was that this approach would prepare children to become successful adults.

Bobbitt confronted the task of identifying activities of the school curriculum at the local level and aimed to construct them at a high degree of detail and specificity. "The most significant feature of the work of practical curriculum making today," stated Bobbitt, "is the tendency first to particularize with definiteness and in detail the objectives" (1921: 607). Bobbitt's curriculum reports, which were often conducted in large-scale school settings, were filled with thousands of skills and behaviors that were, by the function of their specificity, often fixed at rather low, mechanistic levels (Bobbitt 1915, 1922).

For the advocates of Bobbitt's method, the approach had clear educational benefits. It was not difficult to see why Bobbitt's work garnered so much support. To start, his method made the school curriculum more closely connected to everyday life and enlivened the school experience with activity. This was a significant strength of Bobbitt's approach because it connected well with an emerging regard for the progressive principle of "learning as doing." Bobbitt also felt that activity analysis presented an important alternative to the mentalistic tradition of learning that dominated the schools at the time. Bobbitt, not surprisingly, was a critic of schooling that emphasized "the memory reservoir" of students, to use his phrase. With activity analysis, Bobbitt could assert that his system of learning was interested in conduct, action, behavior, and the learner as a doer (Hlebowitsh 2007).

Although Bobbitt's efforts to encourage activity in the curriculum had a progressive bent, the activities introduced into the curriculum were almost exclusively taken from adult life concerns that had little association with the internal factors in Dewey's experiential continuum. The fact that such activities were not relevant to the lives of children was only one of its problems. There was also the issue of only appropriating current or present-day activities in the curriculum, which resulted in a curriculum designed to educate youth for the status quo—for things as they already existed. Bobbitt assumed that the school experience was little more than training for adjustment to existing social conditions. Bode (1927) and others criticized Bobbitt on the grounds that individuals needed generalizable skills such as problem-solving, that could empower judgment and equip young people with ways to deal with emergent problems and issues, not just activities that were isomorphic with existing conditions. To look at present-day conditions as the answer to the curriculum was to promote an outdated training experience not likely to have much currency beyond the present. By failing to show much regard for the learner and for democratic values and aims, such a view stood in contradiction to both the internal and objective (qua, normative) features of Dewey's experiential continuum.

The Tyler Rationale and the Role of the Objective

The criticism directed at activity analysis inevitably raised a new prospect for the design of the curriculum. Because the passion for specificity in the curriculum was beginning to wane, a new approach began to take shape that looked in an entirely different direction. If specificity was the problem, then perhaps a solution could be found in reconceiving the curriculum to target levels of general training that transcended particular conditions. This, in fact, became the driving idea behind a new way to conduct the curriculum, yielding a more sophisticated approach that focused less on activities and more on objectives, less on specific skills to inculcate and more on generalizable traits and skills and dispositions to be developed (Hlebowitsh 2021).

The conceptual break from Bobbitt's embrace of particularity was precipitated by an emerging literature on learning transfer. A body of scholarship coming from the work of Charles Judd (1908, 1939) asserted that learning was transferred best via general principles applicable to individual situations. In practice, this meant that learning was best served when experiences were moved by learning traits and behaviors that had wide applicability and generalizability, or as Mayer and Wittrock (1996) characterized it, by the specific transfer of general skill, as opposed to the specific transfer of specific behavior (Hlebowitsh 2021).

Ralph Tyler (1949), who studied under Charles Judd, took this idea quite seriously and formulated a rationale for curriculum development based on four key undertakings: (1) the articulation of the school's purposes, (2) the selection of experiences used to fulfill those purposes, (3) the design of a framework for the organization of the experiences, and (4) the identification of the evaluative tools used to determine whether the experiences fulfilled the school's expressed purposes. These four functions would become known as the Tyler Rationale.

Tyler firmly believed that that the formulation of objectives was key to the school development process, but only if the focus was on the generalizability of the objectives. "I tend to view objectives as general modes of reaction to be developed rather than highly specific habits to be acquired," Tyler (1949: 43) remarked. Under these conditions, teachers would be able to exercise their own intelligence and creativity in fashioning responsive and more fully expressed school experiences. The objectives were there to guide and direct teacher judgment, not to dictate it. In this way, the Tyler Rationale moved the curriculum development process away from Bobbitt's preoccupation with particularity and toward general modes of understanding and development.

Tyler also understood that the act of curriculum development had to be guided by some managing direction. Simply teaching to a purpose did not provide enough guidance. Teaching also had to be shaped simultaneously by factors that would ensure that the act of teaching was itself professionally grounded or, for our purposes, embedded in Dewey's theory of an educational experience. To this end, Tyler (1949) outlined the need for the curriculum development process to be filtered through factors that resembled Dewey's experiential continuum: (1) studies of the learner; (2) studies of contemporary life outside of school, and (3) suggestions from subject specialists. Tyler called them screens and argued that, when taken together, the screens represented a framework for decision-making in the curriculum. Tyler, in effect, was compelling educators to weigh their decisions in the light of the learner's interests and developmental needs, in the spirit of the ethical foundations of democratic living, and in the context of socially and intellectually worthwhile knowledge. The movement from Bobbitt to Tyler was a tectonic change for the curriculum field that brought about a new way to organize the school experience, complete with a new reference vocabulary including something quite novel: the evaluation of experience.

Because the act of evaluation was one of the four questions listed in his rationale, it had to be dealt with directly. In fact, for Tyler, the concept of evaluation was systemic to the curriculum development process. Clearly, this meant that the curriculum had to have an appraisal system in place that accounted for a fully articulated expression of what students were expected to learn in school. If an objective related to, say, the development of inquiry skills was elevated in the curriculum, some effort had to be made to evaluate it. This meant that the evaluation system itself had to be dynamic. Tyler, in fact, recommended a wide range of appraisal options, including the use of interviews, student products, questionnaires, specially designed surveys, and more. Tyler swung the evaluation door wide open and proffered innovative ways to examine school effects, and by doing so, he strengthened the role of objectives in the curriculum.

Under Tyler's influence, the curriculum seemed to have righted itself by becoming aligned with Dewey's experiential continuum. The alignment was not perfect, however, because Tyler's rationale did not fully exploit the sources that were needed to be responsive to both internal and objective factors. The insertion of an evaluation mechanism did help, but problems surfaced in relation to the rationale's heavy reliance on the formation of objectives, which themselves represented a kind of separation from life experience.

Tyler's new approach, in fact, had its fair share of critics who were quick to point out, first, that what Tyler counseled was not especially different from what Bobbitt had advocated a generation earlier and, second, that despite his best intentions, Tyler had simply orchestrated a production model of teaching and learning that resulted in organizing the school experience along narrow and disintegrating lines. Indeed, this was the main point of a critique advanced by Herbert Kliebard in 1970. Kliebard (1970) endeavored to link Tyler's work to the social efficiency traditions that first arose in the early parts of the twentieth century. He believed that the rationale promoted a behavioristic view of teaching and learning that generated an unhealthy passion for narrowly constructed curriculum objectives that, in the end, dragged the school experience down to its least complex activities. Debate over Kliebard's (1995) criticism continued over the course of several decades, often without any real resolution.

Instructional Models and the Rise of the Content Standard

Part of the problem in resolving the debate around the Tyler Rationale was related to the well-meaning interpreters of Tyler who had found his framework to be amenable to the design of instructional devices that favored hyper-specific objectives and highly atomized classroom applications (Mager 1962; Popham 1972). In North America, this resulted in a movement that promulgated the use of behavioristically driven instructional models designed to ensure the mastery of learning. The work was heavily influenced by the emergence of a behaviorist psychology whose principles helped to rationalize the use of these closed systems of instruction.

In the United States, the high-water mark for the use of behavioristically driven instructional models was set in the late 1970s. They were promoted under different labels, including "competency-based instruction," "mastery learning," and "programmed instruction," but what they all had in common was a sequential and hierarchical pattern of highly specific learning objectives. The purpose of these models was to offer a tightly designed sequence of objectives integrated into predesigned instructional exercises (often workbook exercises), which if followed properly, guaranteed student mastery. The assumption was that anything worth knowing was measurable and reducible to a working sequence of objectives. Such a view, however, could not be easily reconciled with Dewey's experiential continuum because it limited the expression of experiences in the classroom to only those that can be measured easily. For instance, under the demands of competency-based strategies, the curriculum itemized exactly what needed to be taught and how it could be evaluated for mastery. The curriculum, in effect, directed the teacher to teach to each competency directly and regulated each student's movement through the curriculum with mastery tests for each competency. The result was a highly skill-based school experience commonly marked by lower cognitive activities. This movement was, in many respects, a return to the work of Franklin Bobbitt. In fact, it was arguably even less progressive and less aligned to Dewey's experiential continuum than Bobbitt's method of activity analysis, mostly because of its weak connection to internal factors. As a popular advocate for these mastery learning forms, James Popham echoed an early twentieth-century sentiment when he noted the need to "divert some of our national resources into constructing lists of potential objectives in precise form from which the teachers can choose" (1969: 60).

Although the predilection to mark out the curriculum with hyper-specified objectives eventually faded, the idea of using objectives to organize the curriculum remained, this time directed mostly as subject matter requirements or what we might today view as content standards in the curriculum. And again the shift was not without its share of useful progressive ideas and practices.

A content standard is little more than a goal that stipulates what should be taught. While content standards can help to standardize *what* is taught, they do not speak to *how* things should be taught. Such standardization has its attractions. For instance, standardization can act as a quality control measure for the school experience, ensuring that whatever a school deems to be most worthy of being taught is distributed fairly and equitably to all its charges. The presence of a content standard in the curriculum makes it difficult for the school to differentiate instruction in a way that results in an inequitable exposure to the knowledge and skills that the state normatively upholds. Thus, with standards in place, we can have some confidence that achievement differences between individuals or subgroups will not be the by-product of some misdistribution of what is taught, at least as it is set out in the curriculum. In this sense, standards can be seen as investments in equitable opportunities to learn (Hlebowitsh 2009). In the late 1980s and 1990s, the major professional teaching organizations in the United States went so far as to develop their own national standards, including the National Science Teachers Association, the National Council of Teachers of Mathematics, the National Council of Teachers of English, and the National Council of Teachers of Social Studies. The states followed suit and by the late 1990s, almost every state had adopted some version of national standards in mathematics and reading. State governors and national legislators jumped in too, setting national content standards for the school curriculum to mark out what every American child needed to know.

But content standards are more complicated (and more controversial) than they might appear. They can and have been politicized, especially in domains such as history, and they can be organized at different levels of specificity as well as within different forms of subject matter organization. Also, content standards have a way of getting tied to testing programs and if such tests take on a high-stakes character, the school curriculum can have the effect of having marginalized anything that is not fashioned as a content standard. In other words, when we link tests to standards alone, we run the risk of creating a school experience that is not fully attentive to the widest purposes of the school and this, in turn, may lead to a failure to take into account both the internal and objective features of experience.

Rethinking the Curriculum in the Deliberative Tradition

From 1969 to 1978, Joseph Schwab published a series of essays, known as the practical essays, that very much altered the way scholars thought about the design of the school curriculum (Westbury and Wilkof 1978). Schwab, it should be said, was a curriculum scholar whose early experience with science education reforms tilted his thinking in the direction of valorizing local school-based judgments over theoretical ones or ones brought to the school from external sources. To Schwab, the idea that there could be universally applicable ways of successfully conducting instruction, even if sanctioned by research, was simply a chimera. He carried a deep skepticism toward any school reforms efforts that were pitched as valid for all educational situations. His practical essays served to reconceive what it meant to do curriculum work in the schools by highlighting the necessity of shaping the curriculum through the judgment of those working on the local school ground. As a first step, Schwab wanted to make it clear that abstract ideas about the school or the classroom were not especially useful tools for anyone involved in curriculum work largely because, as Schwab put it, they could never be equal, in substance or relevance, to their real counterparts. "Theories," he said, "could not be mistaken for real things – real acts, real children, things richer than and different from their theoretic representations" (Schwab 1969: 12). This admonition was a reminder that the curriculum resided with its participants and with the exercise of situational judgment done in the living context of the classroom: with people. He made this especially clear by declaring that the development of the curriculum should not be dictated from sources removed from the school because "it arises at home, seeded, watered, and cultivated by some or all of the teachers who might be involved in its institution" (Schwab 1983: 258). The statement was, in part, Schwab's way of underscoring the role of internal factors in the curriculum.

Schwab's point spoke to a common misperception among scholars who are apt to believe that theory can drive judgment. The educational situation was too particularized, he said, and too resistant to an abstracted view of action to allow theory to have its way in practice. And if we did allow it to have its way, the result would inevitably lead to the pursuit of overreaching principles and procedures in the conduct of the school, including superficial formulations of universal teaching methods and models, which by their very nature would prove to be less than useful in the local setting. One contemporary example of such overreaching principles can be found in the rise of the "best practices" movement, which presumed to certify the worth of teaching practices entirely from the standpoint of central tendencies in research. Another is that of teacher-effects researchers who used metrics to declare what could be judged as good or bad teaching. Yet another is the growing tendency among scholars to base their work on rigid ideological and politicized pledges (Hlebowitsh 2012). In each of these examples, local conditions were confronted with a uniform or singular solution, usually construed from afar by individuals with no local or situational knowledge. Schwab was insistent on saying that schools and classrooms were *sui generis,* and not easily managed with approaches that had no sanction from or ownership in the local situation.

The curriculum approach that Schwab was encouraging lived on the ground of the school and represented a method of practice that aimed to bring a wide group of participants into the curriculum planning process, while still holding its participants to a logical and moral framework for practical action (Reid 2006). Such a problem-focused method moved it away from the embrace of generalities, in favor of locally bound particularities, especially those framed as problematic and in need of an intervention. Consequently, the starting point for curriculum development shifted away from the use of universal methods and instead organized responses embedded in the local flavor and needs of the school. Westbury characterized the change as one that reshaped the role of the teacher from an implementer to one that held the teacher up as a reflective professional who was expected to make independent professional judgments (Westbury 2000). The question for teachers under these conditions was not simply "what is effective," but rather, more broadly, "what is appropriate for these children in these circumstances." Here, in fact, we find that the internal and the objective features of the experiential continuum can lock together on the school site, empowered by the judgment of the teacher, who instead of following the directions or instructions of some best method or universally applicable approach, is required to think reflectively.

Schwab aimed to use the curriculum to compel school leaders and educators to see their professional problems as opportunities for improvement and to leverage their own resources and expertise in the interests of seeking solutions to problems instead of relying on the counsel of outside sources. The guideposts for these deliberations were influenced by what Schwab referred to as the commonplaces of the curriculum. And more than anything, Schwab's critique moved the field of the curriculum away from its preoccupation with organization, a habit that was encouraged by the popularity of the Tyler Rationale and by the need to give normative form to the complex undertakings of the school. It was the perfect critique against the Tyler Rationale because it laid down an analytical marker that Tyler took for granted—what we might now call reflective practice or what Westbury called forms of reasoning about teaching (Westbury 2000).

This new perspective, it should be said, also opened the door to a sympathetic European tradition rooted in the idea of the *didaktik*, which aimed to make the variable of content taught in the action of the school more dynamic and better connected to the lived experience of the individual, presenting yet another good Deweyan connection. Such a person-centered focus, as it were, conceived at both the individual (internal) and collective (objective) level, was also at the very center of the German concept known as *bildung*, which prioritized individual growth, focusing on moral development and self-understanding, as well as collective social responsibility. The triangulation of the deliberative tradition with the idea of the *didaktik* and the conceptual features of *bildung* certainly had its day in the North American curriculum literature.

Unfortunately, the deliberative tradition that was advanced by Schwab never gained much traction in the schools, a victim perhaps of its own rarified approach and by the arrival of a new wave of scholars who looked askance at research that focused on institutional concerns. Many of these new curriculum scholars no longer regarded curriculum development as a worthy intellectual pursuit and felt it should be replaced by a view of curriculum scholarship that was marked by deep ideological and political quests. The hoped-for extension of curriculum work as an institutional undertaking itself became little more than a theoretic undertaking in North America, making its way onto the pages of the *Journal of Curriculum Studies* and resulting in several important works dedicated to what was an emerging deliberative tradition, but not having any working relevance in the work in schools.

CONCLUSIONS

The educational experience in the context of the school is borne from an interplay between inner child-centered factors and objective normative ones that Dewey originally outlined. The result is three sources of support for the design and implementation of the school experience, sources designed to enliven teacher judgment on matters of instruction and pedagogy in ways that allow for some divergence of response tied to philosophical and social dispositions. The formation of the educational experience in the formal development of the curriculum started as an activity that was relevant to key life roles and eventually turned to the creation of objectives and standards that could better capture generalizable skills. The Tyler Rationale set the stage for a new progressive way to organize the curriculum. But the embrace of objectives in the rationale proved to be better suited to an emerging behavioristic tradition than anything else. And the general construction of objectives in the curriculum faced criticism by getting tied into testing protocols that ironically and unintentionally led to a narrowed and impoverished school experience. The Tyler Rationale put the curriculum on the right track. It just needed a better way to articulate with local school conditions to ensure that local voices were being heard and local problems were being tackled. Schwab's emphasis on working with people represented a complementary development for the Tyler Rationale and raised the real possibility of a kind of singularity or unified approach toward curriculum work (Hlebowitsh 2005b). But the deliberative school of curriculum development did not scale widely in the schools of North America and the reality we face today is that the educational experience in the context of the school curriculum, as articulated by Dewey in his orchestration of the educational continuum, still awaits its full and complete embrace.

REFERENCES

Bobbitt, John F. (1915), *The San Antonio Public School System: A Survey Conducted by J.F. Bobbitt*, San Antonio, TX: The San Antonio School Board.

Bobbitt, John F. (1921), "A Significant Trend in Curriculum-Making," *Elementary School Journal*, 12 (April): 607–15.

Bobbitt, John F. (1922), *Curriculum Making in Los Angeles*, Chicago: University of Chicago Press.

Bode, Boyd (1927), *Modern Educational Theories*, New York: Macmillan.

Dewey, John (1902), *The Child and the Curriculum*, Chicago: University of Chicago Press.

Dewey, John (1916), *Democracy and Education*, New York: Macmillan.

Dewey, John (1938), *Experience and Education*, New York: Macmillan.

Froebel, Friedrich (1887), *The Education of Man*, New York: Appleton.

Goodlad, John (1984), *A Place Called School*, New York: McGraw-Hill.

Hall, G. Stanley (1901), "The Ideal School as Based on Child Study," in D.H. Calhoun (ed.), *Educating of Americans*, New York: Houghton-Mifflin.

Herbart, Johann Friedrich (1901), *Outlines of Educational Doctrine*, New York: Macmillan.

Hlebowitsh, Peter S. (2005a), *Designing the School Curriculum*, Boston: Pearson Education.

Hlebowitsh, Peter S. (2005b), "Generational Ideas in Curriculum: A Historical Triangulation," *Curriculum Inquiry*, 35 (1): 73–87.

Hlebowitsh, Peter S. (2007), *Foundations of American Education*, Dubuque, IA: Kendall/Hunt Publishing.

Hlebowitsh, Peter S. (2009), "The Criteria of Good Aims and the Idea of the Curriculum Standard," in Patrick Jenlick (ed.), *Dewey's Democracy and Education Revisited: Contemporary Discourses for Democratic Education and Leadership*, 78–96, New York: Rowman and Littlefield.

Hlebowitsh, Peter S. (2010), "Curriculum Development," in Craig Kridel (ed.), *The Encyclopedia of Curriculum Studies*, 202–5, Los Angeles: Sage.

Hlebowitsh, Peter S. (2012), "When Best Practices Aren't," *Journal of Curriculum Studies*, 44 (1): 1–12.

Hlebowitsh, Peter (2021), "Ralph Tyler, the Tyler Rationale and the Idea of Educational Evaluation," *The Oxford Research Encyclopedia of Curriculum Studies*. https://doi.org/10.1093/acrefore/9780190264093.013.1036.

Judd, Charles Hubbard (1908), "The Relation of Special Training to General Intelligence," *Educational Review*, 36: 28–42.

Judd, Charles Hubbard (1939), *Educational Psychology*, New York: Houghton Mifflin.

Kliebard, Herbert M. (1970), "Reappraisal: The Tyler Rationale," *School Review*, 78: 259–72.

Kliebard, Herbert M. (1986), *The Struggle for the American Curriculum*, Boston: Routledge.

Kliebard, Herbert M. (1995), "The Tyler Rationale Revisited," *Journal of Curriculum Studies*, 27 (1): 81–8.

Mager, Robert F. (1962), *Preparing Instructional Objectives*, Palo Alto, CA: Fearon Publishers.

Mayer, R.E. and M.C. Wittrock (1996), "Problem-Solving Transfer," in D.C. Berliner and R.C. Calfree (eds.), *Handbook of Educational Psychology*, 47–62, New York: MacMillan Library Reference USA.

Pestalozzi, Johann Heinrich (1894), *How Gertrude Teaches Her Children*, Syracuse, NY: Bardeen.

Popham, W. James (1969), *Instructional Objectives*, New York: Rand McNally.

Popham, W. James (1972), "Objectives '72." *PDK* (March): 432–5.

Reid, William A. (2006), *The Pursuit of Curriculum*, Greenwich, CN: IAP.

Rousseau, Jean-Jacques (1911), *Emile*, London: Dent.

Rugg, Harold and Ann Shumaker (1928), *The Child-Centered School: An Appraisal of the New Education*, New York: World Book Company.

Schwab, Joseph J. (1969), "The Practical: A Language for Curriculum," *The School Review*, 78 (1): 1–23.

Schwab, Joseph J. (1983), "The Practical 4: Something for Curriculum Professors to Do," *Curriculum Inquiry*, 13 (Fall): 239–65.

Spencer, Herbert (1860), *Education: Intellectual, Moral and Physical*, New York: Appleton.

Tanner, Daniel and Laurel Tanner (1980), *Curriculum Development: Theory into Practice*, New York: Macmillan.

Tanner, Daniel and Laurel N. Tanner (1988), "The Emergence of a Paradigm in the Curriculum Field: A Reply to Jickling," *Interchange*, 19 (Summer): 50–8.

Tyler, Ralph W. (1949), *Basic Principles of Curriculum and Instruction*, Chicago: University of Chicago Press.

Westbury, Ian (2000), "Teaching As a Reflective Practice: What Might Didaktik Teach Curriculum," in Ian Westbury, Stefan Hopmann, and Kurt Riquarts (eds.), *Teaching as a Reflective Practice: The German Didaktik Tradition*, 15–39, New York: L. Erlbaum Associates.

Westbury, Ian and Neil J. Wilkof (1978), "Introduction," in Ian Westbury and Neil J. Wilkof (eds.), *Science, Curriculum, and Liberal Education: Selected Essays*, 1–42, Chicago: University of Chicago Press.

Wraga, William G. (2017), "Understanding the Tyler Rationale: Basic Principles of Curriculum and Instruction in Historical Context," *Espacio, Tiempo y Educación*, 4 (2): 227–52.

CHAPTER FOUR

Schools and Education Systems

Oscillating between a Force for Change and an Agent of Social Stagnation

RYAN W. COUGHLAN

Throughout history, schools have been both products of institutionalized norms as well as tools for shaping societal practices. Education systems around the world take on myriad responsibilities.[1] Most notably, schools deliver a curriculum that strives to provide children with the skills and knowledge they will need for adulthood. Chapter 3 of this volume underscored the complexity and fraught nature of school curricula and emphasized the ways in which the curriculum has sat at the core of the work of schooling throughout history. But our schools do much more than deliver a curriculum—they are a place for children to develop social skills, explore extracurricular interests, model and act out politics, and be subject to structured rules and norms.

In some education systems, schools provide more far-reaching services, including medical care, counseling services, legal services, adult education, and food and housing assistance, to name just a few. Regardless of the specific manifestation of education systems, John Dewey argued that schools should be a place to both prepare children to be active members of their communities and to experiment with and imagine a more perfect society (Dewey 1900). Aligned with Dewey's vision, countless education reformers have sought to bring about changes in our education system with the twin hopes of improving students' lives and advancing society as a whole. As much as policymakers, activists, academics, and others bemoan education systems' slow pace of change and advancement, education systems have shifted in dramatic ways throughout modern history (Tyack and Cuban 1995). Despite marked progress, education systems remain riddled with inequities and injustices.

In this chapter, I explore the historical transformation of the US education system while underscoring the ways in which schools have oscillated between passively upholding conventions and actively facilitating change. There is no better way to illustrate the movement between these two roles than by looking at who has been able to access the US education system and what quality of education different groups of people have been able to access. Educational access has been a direct product of a collection of institutional factors that have shaped schools throughout time. First, I trace the history of educational access in the United States. Then I consider how specific factors—including school oversight, school funding, school attendance areas, and internal school structures—have helped determine who gets what kind of education in our society. More often than not, those in power have used these institutional factors to build schools that attempt to maintain the status quo. However, the actions of some teachers, students, parents, educational leaders, and advocates have occasionally altered these institutional factors to transform not only schools but also society at large. I contend that the historical foundations of education provide us with a framework for understanding both what shapes schools and education systems as well as how to use schools and education systems to transform society.

HISTORICAL INTERPRETATIONS OF EDUCATION

In many ways, historical interpretations of education align with political perspectives. The democratic-liberal school of historians of education—characterized by the work of Lawrence Cremin (1970, 1980, 1988)—focuses on the ebbs and flows of the expansion of equality of opportunity throughout time. Leading conservative perspectives—characterized by E.D. Hirsch (1988, 2016), Allan Bloom (1987), and Chester Finn Jr. (1991)—emphasize educational excellence and highlight changes in educational standards and the curriculum throughout time. Finally, the rapidly expanding radical-revisionist school—including a wide range of scholars such as Joel Spring (2002, 2004, 2018) and Vanessa Siddle Walker (2000, 2018)—critiques the history of education and emphasizes the ways in which identity and power have shaped schools to privilege some and trammel others. Historical evidence as well as the present reality necessitate that I use a radical-revisionist lens for this chapter. If we are to look at the history of education with clarity and use the past to illuminate a more just future, it is critical to present an honest and direct account of how education systems have alternately constrained and expanded access to people based on their identities.

EDUCATIONAL ACCESS TODAY

Setting aside inequities and injustices for a moment, it is worth recognizing that access to a high school education in the United States is ubiquitous today. High school graduation rates are at an all-time high (McFarland et al. 2018), high school dropout rates are at an all-time low (McFarland et al. 2018), and college attendance rates have steadily risen for decades (U.S. Department of Education 2020). For over a century, children across the United States have had universal access to elementary and secondary schooling; however, universal access has not been a guarantee of equitable access. Still, the Supreme Court outlawed school segregation with the 1954 *Brown v. Board of Education* decision, Congress began prompting instruction for English Language Learners through the 1968 Bilingual Education Act, and Congress assured access to schooling for students with disabilities through the 1975 Education for All Handicapped Children Act. As a whole, the US education system has made undeniable progress in advancing educational access.

Despite marked progress in regard to educational access, there are persistent inequities in the quality of education available to different groups of children. Some of these inequities even show signs of worsening. In the decades following the *Brown v. Board of Education* Supreme Court decision, many school districts across the country desegregated. During this period of time, racial achievement gaps shrank dramatically (Johnson 2018). Unfortunately courts began to halt their oversight of desegregation efforts in the 1990s, and achievement gaps once again widened as schools resegregated (Frankenberg et al. 2019). In addition to the fact that racial segregation is worsening in many US schools, there is a persistent gap in educational resources across the country (U.S. Department of Education 2020). School spending levels correlate with the racial demographics of school districts and precipitate gaps in educational outcomes (Shores and Ejdemyr 2017).

There are countless other measures that underscore persistent gaps in educational access. Far too often, wealth, race, disability status, and language proficiency status correlate with access to high-quality teachers, welcoming learning spaces, advanced coursework, innovative extracurricular activities, and appropriate forms of school discipline (Darling-Hammond 2015). Children in the US do not have equitable access to educational opportunities. In turn, there is a persistent and abhorrent gap in educational achievement and life outcomes that this country must address if it hopes to achieve its promises of equality and justice. In the following sections, I explore the history of schools and education systems that has brought us to this point where inequality is rampant despite the fact that there is greater access to education than ever before.

TRACING THE HISTORY OF EDUCATIONAL ACCESS IN THE UNITED STATES

Throughout the past four centuries, formal schooling in the United States has changed dramatically; yet the power structures shaping educational access have remained quite consistent. From the outset, education in what would eventually become the United States privileged a specific group of people and beliefs. The first formal educational institution in the "New World," Harvard College, trained clergymen for the colonies. In a similar vein, the first public schools in the colonies aimed to provide children with the literary skills to read the Bible. The 1642 and 1647 *Old Deluder Laws* established the first public schools in Massachusetts and required that all towns with fifty or more households appoint a teacher to provide reading and writing instruction to children (Cremin 1970). The education system born from the *Old Deluder Laws* taught Protestant beliefs to Protestant children. Much of the history of education in the United States that followed fits a similar mold in which education systems privilege those in power and uphold their culture and ideals.

Following the American Revolution, some key figures in the fledgling American democracy made impassioned arguments about the need for an educated citizenry to maintain a healthy democracy. Perhaps most notably, Thomas Jefferson argued for a system of public schooling in Virginia to ensure a literate population that could help advance the new nation. Even though Jefferson's view of universal public schooling was primarily limited to white men, most in power still thought Jefferson's idea was too radical and costly (Meacham 2012). Here, as throughout much of the history of education in the United States, one can clearly observe the complex interplay between schools as tools for upholding norms and schools as mechanisms for advancing society. Most members of the governing class saw no reason for government-funded schools since their own children had access to private tutors and a growing network of independent schools. It took well over a century after the American Revolution for the entire United States to adopt the system of universal public schooling that Jefferson believed would help advance society. Universal public schooling prevailed only when the governing class saw how they could benefit from such a system (Cremin 1980).

In the decades before and after the Civil War, an ever-growing proportion of children attended school as formal education became more readily available. It was during what historians dub the Common School era that Horace Mann

(1848) famously declared that public schooling would be "the great equalizer of the conditions of men." With the Industrial Revolution reshaping the economy and immigration changing the social fabric of the United States, reformers such as Mann forcefully and convincingly argued for free and universal schooling. The expanding education system of the Common School era brought opportunities for social mobility to some. However, access to public education often grew at the behest of factory owners seeking to prepare children for the labor force. One account notes that the common school was "a pernicious device for teaching skills such as hygiene, punctuality, and rudimentary skills that would create docile, willing workers" (Sadovnik et al. 2018: 74).

Radical revisionist historians of education view Horace Mann's optimistic vision of universal public schooling as foundational to the meritocratic myth. As in the Common School era, there continues to be a tension between social reformers who look to the education system as a tool for equality and advancement and conservative elites who use schools to reinforce power structures. Nearly two centuries have passed since Horace Mann declared that schools would be a fountain of equality, yet America's caste system persists unrelentingly (Wilkerson 2020).

Following the successful expansion of public education during the Common School era, educational leaders in the Progressive era of the early twentieth century sought to reinvent the function of schools and the delivery of curriculum. John Dewey, the most famous Progressive era education reformer, maintained Horace Mann's optimism that schools could advance equality and society's collective advancement as he developed a philosophy of education centering on the personal growth of each individual pupil.[2] Prior to the Progressive era, education was mostly teacher-centered and focused on academic knowledge and skills. Dewey's efforts expanded the scope of schooling to try to meet the holistic needs of children and support the development of social and vocational skills. During the Progressive era, a wave of immigration from Eastern Europe compelled urban education systems to find ways to address the needs of increasingly diverse student bodies. Schools shifted in two notable ways to meet this moment. First, schools began offering a wider range of services to provide for the essential needs of their students. As Dewey (1902) noted in one speech, "What we want is to see the school, every public school, doing something of the same sort of work that is now done by a settlement [house]." During the Progressive era, schools began offering access to medical care, food, and other services that are now part of the fabric of most education systems. Second, schools took advantage of their expanded role in teaching social skills to promote assimilation. By assimilating newcomers through the education system, the dominant white, Protestant culture and ideals persisted. Despite growing demand for culturally responsive teaching (Ladson-Billings 1997), public schools in the United States continue to anchor around white, middle-class ideals in much the same way as they did during the Progressive era's wave of immigration.

Throughout the century that has passed since the Progressive era, few of the guiding principles and structures of schooling have changed. Reforms have come and gone, but the nature of teaching and learning has held steady (Tyack and Cuban 1995). While schools and education systems operate in much the same way as they did a century ago, US society has battled over educational access during this period of time. Different groups of people have waged fights for equal access to schools on parallel but distinct tracks. Indigenous Americans, African Americans, Asian Americans, Hispanic Americans, multilingual learners, women, and Americans with disabilities have all sought fair and equal access to schooling. Despite similar goals, these groups have faced distinct hurdles and made differential progress toward equal schooling. Much of the history of education in the United States—particularly that of the twentieth and twenty-first centuries—is defined by this struggle for access to an equal education. The following sections highlight how each of these groups' fights for educational equality define US education today.

Indigenous Americans' Access to Education

The history of Indigenous Americans' access to institutionalized education underscores the tension between using schooling to perpetuate the status quo and using schooling to bring about change. It is important to note that when those with power employ education to shift society in some manner, the change they seek often serves the desires of the governing class. There is no clearer case of the US government using education to serve its own purposes rather than the needs of those attending schools than with Indigenous American populations (Reyhner and Eder 2006).

From its inception, the US government sought to banish or perhaps eradicate Indigenous Americans. Even before the passage of the Bill of Rights, the US Congress signed the Naturalization Act of 1790, which excluded Indigenous American people—as well as any other person not deemed "white"—from obtaining citizenship. Throughout the nineteenth century, most of the US government's attention to Indigenous American populations focused on isolating them on undesirable land; however, the US government also used education to accomplish some of its goals. Most notably, Congress passed the Civilization Fund Act of 1819. This legislation provided Christian missionaries with funding to instruct Indigenous Americans in "the habits and arts of civilization" (Civilization Fund Act 1819). While the legislation stated that it was an effort to work "against the further decline and extinction of the Indian tribes," the fact that the US government initiated the Trail of Tears—displacing roughly 60,000 Indigenous Americans— a few years afterwards makes it impossible to believe this written intent (Ehle 2011). In reality, funds from the 1819 Civilization Fund Act supported efforts to eliminate Indigenous American cultures and indoctrinate Indigenous American people with Protestant ideals. Radical revisionist historians often highlight the ways in which Common School era school leaders mirrored this model of Indigenous American deculturalization in their efforts to "assimilate" immigrants (Spring 2004).

What began with Christian missionaries and the Civilization Fund Act later transformed into government-sponsored boarding schools under the purview of the US Commissioner of Indian Affairs. From the late 1800s through the early 1900s, the US government sponsored dozens of off-reservation boarding schools. One of the mottos of the Carlisle Indian School—a prominent off-reservation boarding school—was, "To civilize the Indian, get him into civilization. To keep him civilized, let him stay" (Pratt 2003: 283). Until the 1930s, the US government provided Indigenous Americans with few opportunities for schooling outside of these boarding schools even as educational access expanded across the country. In 1928, the US Secretary of the Interior commissioned a report by the Institute of Government Research at Johns Hopkins University that decried the off-reservation boarding schools and recommended community schools where Indigenous American children could remain connected to their culture (Meriam 1928). Following this report, the US government closed most of the off-reservation boarding schools and began funding individual states to build public education systems for Indigenous Americans.

Throughout much of the twentieth century, public education for Indigenous Americans was demonstrably inadequate. After releasing a report titled "Indian Education: A National Tragedy, a National Challenge," the US Senate passed the Indian Education Act of 1972 and the 1975 Indian Self Determination and Education Act, which provided Indigenous Americans with greater funding for culturally relevant public schooling. While Indigenous Americans have far more access to formal education than ever before and the school curriculum no longer explicitly strives to eradicate Indigenous cultures, achievement gaps persist and Indigenous communities struggle to nurture their cultures in schools (Reyhner and Eder 2006).

Black Americans' Access to Education

Before tracing the history of access to education for Black Americans, it is essential to lay bare the reality of contemporary systemic anti-Black racism. In almost all facets of American life, deeply embedded racism constrains and endangers Black Americans. We see this in acts of police brutality against Black bodies (Fryer 2019); in persistent racial segregation of neighborhoods, schools, and workplaces (Frankenberg et al. 2014; Reardon et al. 2009); and in the under-resourcing of Black communities (Darling-Hammond 1998;

Sadovnik et al. 2018). The fact that countless Black Americans have achieved immeasurable success across all fields of work is a testament to Black individuals and communities and not to equality of opportunity—equality of opportunity does not exist in the United States. Since the earliest days of this country, Black people have endeavored to make real the American promise of equality. As Nikole Hannah-Jones wrote in the *New York Times Magazine*'s *1619 Project*, "We were told once by virtue of our bondage, that we could never be American. But it was by virtue of our bondage that we became the most American of all" (Hannah-Jones 2019). The history of access to education for Black Americans underscores Hannah-Jones's observation that Black Americans have led this country on its unfinished journey to achieve its stated dream of equality.

Prior to the Civil War, state governments throughout the American South banned the education of enslaved Africans; yet some found a way to educate themselves in both informal ways across the country and more formalized ways in areas that had abolished slavery (Williams 2005). In the North, slavery persisted through the mid-1800s; yet more and more Black people claimed their freedom and created pathways to education. At the beginning of the nineteenth century, Black parents in Boston opened private schools for their children and advocated for public funding to provide their children with an education apart from the degrading biases of white children (Schultz 1973). It did not take long for Black families in Boston to realize that separate schooling meant the government maintained unequal schooling. As Siddle Walker chronicles in *The Lost Education of Horace Tate*, an immense network of Black teachers worked for generations to educate Black children, fund critical legal battles (including *Brown v. Board of Education*), and advance the entire United States toward equality (Walker 2018). Most importantly, this network of Black teachers promoted the central argument, as articulated by Rev. Dr. Martin Luther King Jr. (1967), that "Integration must lead us to a point where we share in the power that all of our society will produce."

To this day, schools remain deeply segregated by race despite an end to legal segregation, the ranks of Black educators are kept disproportionately low, the number of Black school and district leaders is even lower, Black children face dehumanizing bias in school discipline, and Black children rarely access the levels of educational opportunity experienced by their white peers (Johnson 2018). While progress has been made, largely through the efforts of persistent and passionate Black educators and leaders, the United States still fails to meet its obligations to provide educational equity to Black children.

Asian Americans' Access to Education

Throughout much of US history, the Asian American population was quite small. Still, Asian Americans struggled for basic rights as well as for access to education. In 1855, 1922, and 1923, the US Supreme Court repeatedly declared that Asians were not white and thus ineligible for citizenship under the 1790 Naturalization Act (Takaki 2012). Not until the 1952 McCarran-Walter Act overturned the racial restrictions of the 1790 Naturalization Act were all Asian people able to engage pathways to US citizenship available to others. Prior to the mid-1900s, state governments systematically worked to bar Asian Americans from receiving equal access to education (Low 1982). California's 1872 school code explicitly emphasized that the schools were open for the admission of white children, effectively excluding Asian American children. After years of battle with local school boards, an Asian American child won the right to receive a public education from a State Superior Court judge in 1885. Within weeks of this court decision, the California state legislature rewrote the school code to establish a system of segregated schooling. While some of the school segregation mandates for Asian Americans weakened in the early 1900s, many Asian Americans found that the US government directly limited their access to education until the middle of the century.

During the Civil Rights era of the 1960s, Asian American students found themselves in a previously unfathomable position—being upheld as the "model minority." After centuries of oppression, the internment of Japanese Americans during the Second World War, and efforts to segregate Asian Americans, white Americans constructed the model minority myth, placing Asian Americans in opposition to Black and Hispanic Americans. According to Museus and Kiang, "The model minority stereotype is the notion that Asian Americans achieve universal and unparalleled academic and occupational success" (2009: 6). The model minority myth, which persists to this day, has alternately opened doors and created barriers for Asian Americans. On the one hand, the model minority myth has helped Asian Americans overcome white Americans' biases and gain access to greater educational opportunities on par with those of white students. On the other hand, the model minority myth has created a stereotype and a set of behavioral expectations that can cause great harm to Asian American students (Lew 2006).

Hispanic Americans' Access to Education

Similar to Indigenous Americans, Black Americans, and Asian Americans, Hispanic Americans have tremendous within-group diversity that policymakers and the general population must not ignore.[3] Members of this large and growing group of Americans share some similar experiences when it comes to their history of access to schooling in the United States. Throughout much of US history, people of Mexican and Puerto Rican descent made up the majority of Hispanic Americans. At the conclusion of the Mexican-American War in 1848, the US Congress refused to grant US citizenship to Mexicans living on lands that Mexico ceded to the United States. As with other groups of people not of European descent, Mexican Americans struggled to gain full citizenship rights through the middle of the twentieth century (Montejano 1987). Puerto Ricans traveled a different pathway to gain US citizenship rights. Following the Spanish-American War in 1898, the US colonized Puerto Rico. Over the course of the twentieth century, Puerto Rican Americans slowly gained many of the rights of US citizenship. However, Puerto Rican Americans living in Puerto Rico are still unable to cast votes for the US President or send Senators and Representatives to the US Congress, despite being able to serve in the US military.

Just as Mexican Americans, Puerto Rican Americans, and other Hispanic Americans have had to fight for citizenship rights in a similar way as other marginalized groups, they have also had to fight for equitable access to education. State governments have oscillated between withholding educational access to Hispanic Americans and using education as a tool for control. After passing compulsory education laws at the turn of the twentieth century, many states opted not to enforce the laws for Hispanic Americans (Leon 2006). These actions kept many Hispanic American children out of school. However, as Hispanic Americans eventually began attending school in greater numbers, state governments employed familiar tools to create systems of segregated schooling. When Hispanic Americans were able to access a publicly funded education in the early 1900s, the government used schools to attempt to strip Hispanic Americans of their culture. Schools adopted English-only policies and used a curriculum that diminished the value of Hispanic Americans in contrast to Americans of European descent (Gonzalez 2013). In Puerto Rico, the US government worked even harder to use schools as a tool for Americanization and Puerto Rican deculturalization. Over the course of five decades, the US government imposed English instruction, the celebration of patriotic holidays, and a warped curriculum on children attending school in Puerto Rico (Spring 2004). Puerto Rican students and teachers fought against these policies throughout the first half of the twentieth century. When Puerto Rico gained commonwealth status in 1951, the people of Puerto Rico were able to take control of their education system, shift their curriculum, and return to using Spanish.

Today, the Hispanic population is growing across most of the United States. While the same Supreme Court ruling that outlawed the legal segregation of Black Americans applies to Hispanic Americans, many Hispanic children remain isolated in under-resourced schools where they rarely receive adequate language instruction or access to a culturally responsive curriculum (Schneider, Martinez, and Owens 2006).

Multilingual Learners' Access to Education

Schools have played a significant role in shaping how English is used in the United States and how people assimilate into American culture. Most Americans can trace their ancestral roots to people who spoke a language other than

English. The intimate connection between language and culture means that those Americans who no longer speak the same language as their ancestors have also lost an important tie to their families' cultures. Over the course of US history, some people have immigrated to the United States in search of opportunity, some have immigrated to the United States to escape various forms of oppression, some people simply lived on land taken by the US government, and some people were forcibly taken from their homes and brought to the United States as slaves. Many people, though not all, who chose to immigrate to the United States viewed learning English as a pathway to assimilation and economic stability. While new immigrants often worked to maintain their culture and language at home, they usually saw English instruction in school as a means to entry into the labor market and US society (Crawford 1989). Asian Americans who wanted to make the United States a permanent home often viewed learning English in this way; however, Asian people who hoped to return to their countries of origin, along with Asian Americans who wanted to maintain strong ties to their culture, sought opportunities to receive instruction in their native languages. A good number of more recent Hispanic immigrants share a similar view about maintaining their Spanish language (Cummins 2000). Groups of people whose sovereign land was taken by the US government have had a very different relationship with education and the forced assimilation into English-only schools. As noted earlier, the US government used schools to deculture Indigenous Americans, Mexican Americans, and Puerto Rican Americans. By providing English instruction and limiting or withholding instruction in native languages, schools worked to separate people from their culture and complete the process of colonialization or conquering. Black Americans who were subjected to the atrocities of slavery faced an even more violent separation from their native languages. Slavers actively worked to strip people of their native languages. As a result, most ancestors of enslaved people in the United States have little connection to a native language other than English. This legacy of stripping Black Americans of their language persists to this day. For example, many Black Americans have developed and nurtured African American Vernacular English only to have this dialect devalued by white society (McWhorter 2016). While there is debate about the source and cause of devaluing African American Vernacular English, it is clear that the workforce and other institutions have subordinated African American Vernacular English.

US policymakers, courts, and educational leaders have made some progress toward developing more inclusive approaches to instructing students whose primary language is something other than English (Wiley and Wright 2004). During the early years of public education, English-only instruction was the norm. However, as the US education system expanded in the early twentieth century, a series of court decisions affirmed the constitutional right of people to teach and learn in the language of their choice. These victories did not mean that the government provided sufficient resources for adequate language instruction. It was not until the 1968 Bilingual Education Act that the US federal government provided funding for districts to meet the needs of linguistically diverse students. Even then, bilingual education was not mandated until the 1974 *Lau v. Nichols* US Supreme Court decision required school boards to provide instruction in students' native languages. Today, multilingual learners encounter vastly different forms of education across the United States (Nieto 2017). Some education systems seek to quickly transition students away from speaking their native language, while others work to cultivate and celebrate fluency in multiple languages. Research and logic both demonstrate the value of multilingualism, and schools should view their multilingual learners as an asset to their learning communities and wider society (Calderon et al. 2019).

Women's Access to Education

The United States has maintained an oppressively patriarchal society throughout its history, and persistent misogyny continues to trammel women's access to equitable education to this day (Corbett, Hill, and St. Rose 2008). Women have been fighting for equality since the founding of the United States and have made tremendous progress in the face of unrelenting sexism. The history of women's access to education in the United States parallels the broader pathway toward women's equality. Well into the nineteenth century, few educational leaders saw a reason to provide comprehensive schooling to women. Girls who attended school generally terminated their education after learning basic literacy and numeracy skills. In 1848, the Seneca Falls Convention strengthened the budding Women's Rights movement and created a roadmap to equality with the attendees' Declaration of Sentiments. Part of this declaration noted that men had unjustly denied women "the facilities for obtaining a thorough education" (Stanton and Mott 1848). During the five decades that passed between the Seneca Falls Convention and the ratification of the 19th Amendment, which gave women the right to vote, women also made progress in gaining greater access to an education. The first women were admitted into a state university in 1856, and an increasing number of women's colleges opened their doors during this same period (Sadovnik et al. 2018).

Over the course of the twentieth century, women slowly gained access to all levels of education. Despite systematic efforts to hold women back from advancing academically, feminist movements succeeded in breaking down barriers. Initially, education systems funneled women into helping professions such as teaching, nursing, and clerical work. Through the persistent work of women who were committed to advancing gender equality, women made pathways for themselves into every field. In 1950, women only made up 32 percent of students attending postsecondary institutions in the United States (U.S. Department of Education 2020). By 1979 the number of women enrolled in postsecondary institutions surpassed the number of men; today, women comprise 57 percent of attendees at colleges and universities. Despite this progress, women continue to face rampant sexism in the US education system. During remarks made in 2005, then president of Harvard University, Lawrence Summers argued that biological differences help explain why men outperform women in math and science (Finder et al. 2006). Following this incident, Harvard's faculty approved a vote of no-confidence in Summers' leadership, and he eventually resigned from his post as Harvard's president. The overt sexism that Summers displayed persists across all levels of the US education system. While women are now able to access equal education, they continue to face deeply ingrained bias in schools as well as most aspects of life in the United States.

Access to Education for Other Marginalized Groups

Countless other groups of people have struggled to obtain equitable access to the US education system. Religion, disability status, sexuality, gender identity, and citizenship status have all shaped whether and to what degrees children could access school. In some instances, US education systems have created explicit barriers to entry, while in other cases, school personnel have made their institutions unwelcoming and unsafe for certain groups of children. Americans with disabilities have faced a particularly challenging pathway to gaining access to schooling in the United States. While some schools were formed in the nineteenth century to serve deaf children, most children with physical or mental disabilities were excluded from publicly funded schools (Hanes, Brown, and Hansen 2017). Not until the 1975 Education for All Handicapped Children Act (EHA), which was later reauthorized as the Individuals with Disabilities Education Act (IDEA), did the federal government mandate that states provide a free public education to children with disabilities. Despite laws such as the IDEA, children with disabilities encounter bias and discrimination in schools. Similarly, children who practice a religion other than Christianity, children who identify as LGBTQ+, and children who do not have US citizenship struggle for equity and full inclusion in US schools. Power and privilege have shaped access to education in the United States throughout history, and a child's identity continues to disproportionately influence the schooling they receive.

It is critical to note that an individual's identity is not defined by a single characteristic and that each of us has an intersectional set of identities that shape our experiences in society (Crenshaw 2015). Although the prior sections have looked at how individual components of identity shape people's education, an individual's path through the US education system is far more complicated because of our intersectional identities. For example, while the feminist movement advanced educational opportunities for women, white women benefited from these advances to a far greater degree than Black women. To better understand the complex ways in which people's intersectional identities often predetermine our educational pathways in the United States, I explore a range of institutional factors that have shaped educational access and equity.

INSTITUTIONAL FACTORS THAT SHAPE ACCESS AND EQUITY

Power structures and personal biases fuel educational inequality. Throughout the history of the United States, those in power have molded institutions to control access to education. However, reformers looking to expand educational access and equity have carefully studied the structures that govern schooling and strategically worked to reshape these institutions. Since the founding of the first public schools in seventeenth-century Massachusetts, the structures governing educational access in what became the United States have remained relatively constant. There has been ongoing realignment between different levels of government jockeying for oversight control of schools. Along with determining which levels of government have what degree of school oversight, policymakers and educational leaders have also been engaged in a continuous process of reconfiguring responsibility for funding schools. Policymakers and educational leaders with school oversight powers and control over school funding have used these tools to control educational access and equity. Similarly, those with the power to delineate school attendance areas and school admissions policies have also shaped equality of access to the US education system. These three institutional factors—school oversight, school funding, and school attendance areas—have alternately restricted and broadened educational access and equity to children in the United States.

In addition to these three factors, there are a number of structures within schools that have regulated who has access to what kind of education. School tracking systems, disciplinary structures, staffing plans, the curriculum, and pedagogy all play a role in shaping a child's equitable access to learning. In the following sections, I discuss how policymakers and educational leaders have employed this range of institutional factors to configure the educational experiences of children throughout US history.

School Oversight

The US education system involves countless individuals and institutions. As the US education system developed and grew, different states established their own education policies. Universal and compulsory schooling became the norm in the early twentieth century as states passed education legislation and adopted state constitutional provisions guaranteeing a free and public education. Because state law established the right to education, states have generally played the most significant role in overseeing public schooling. However, the federal government and local jurisdictions regularly exercise educational oversight powers as well.

A few key components of the US education system are centralized at the federal level, additional aspects of schooling are centralized at the state level, and many components of schooling are decentralized to individual districts. For most of US history, the federal government played little to no role in public schooling. Over time, the federal government has taken on new school oversight responsibilities. Often, the federal government's oversight of public schools is mediated through the judicial branch. Most famously, the Supreme Court attempted to end school segregation through its decision in *Brown v. Board of Education* (1954) (Patterson and Freehling 2001). While this particular Supreme Court decision increased the federal government's role in public schooling, the Supreme Court has regularly maintained that US citizens do not have a fundamental right to education. In *San Antonio Independent School District v. Rodriguez*, the Supreme Court declared that "Though education is one of the most important services performed by the State, it is not within the limited category of rights recognized by this Court as guaranteed by the Constitution" (1973: 2). Still, since passing the 1965 Elementary and Secondary Education Act, the federal government has played a significant role in funding and overseeing school programming. In 2001, the No Child Left Behind Act gave the federal government even more oversight power and established a nationwide standardized testing and accountability system that aimed to improve school quality and close the achievement gaps between students of different races, ethnicities, and socioeconomic backgrounds. The US government has since backed away from many of the oversight responsibilities it had established under No Child Left Behind due to their unpopularity and lack of effectiveness.

School Funding

School funding structures, which are intimately connected to the complex system of school oversight, have played a central role in determining educational access and equity. Gaps in education spending are not new to the United States. Throughout the decades of segregated schooling that followed emancipation, the doctrine of "separate but equal" generally led to separate and unequal education systems for Black and white children in many areas of the United States. During the Jim Crow era, white students in one South Carolina county received 347 percent of the funding that Black students received (Patterson and Freehling 2001). Such extreme gaps in education spending are less common today than during the Jim Crow era, but they still persist and lead to troubling forms of school inequality.

The federal government has steadily increased its education spending since founding the US Department of Education in 1979, but states and local governments still carry the most significant burden of funding public schools. New York currently has the highest per pupil spending on education at $24,040, and Utah has the lowest per pupil spending at $7,628. Such interstate gaps in education spending are shocking to some, but intrastate gaps can be even larger. In New York, per pupil spending ranges from a dramatic high of $152,539 to a low of $17,308 (Doran 2019). It is particularly troubling that education spending continues to correlate with the racial composition of US school districts, as it has throughout history (EdBuild 2019). Across the United States, districts serving a population of predominantly white students now receive an average of $2,226 more per student than other districts. In Arizona, districts that predominantly serve students of color spend 46 percent less per student than predominantly white districts. Education reformers seeking to make schools more equitable have made tremendous progress in restructuring school funding formulas since the Jim Crow era, but more work is needed (Baker 2018).

School Attendance Areas

When Massachusetts first established a system of public schooling in the seventeenth century, individual towns were responsible for educating their children. As public education systems expanded across the United States, policymakers used school attendance areas to delineate where children went to school. There is logic in tying school attendance to geography; however, given the complex system of school oversight and inequitable school funding structures discussed above, the process of delineating school attendance areas has been fraught with injustices throughout US history. More than other structural factors, school attendance areas have shaped educational access and equity since the middle of the twentieth century. Policymakers, educational leaders, and well-resourced citizens have used school attendance areas to control educational access by finding ways to exclude groups of people from living in certain school districts. Policymakers, banks, real estate agents, and community organizations implemented a wide range of discriminatory housing practices throughout the twentieth century to build and maintain a system of racial residential segregation that translated into school segregation (Rothstein 2017). Until Congress passed the 1968 Fair Housing Act, discriminatory housing ordinances and mortgage programs allowed white people to build segregated enclaves that either directly or indirectly excluded people of color. Today, de facto housing and school segregation persist in most communities across the United States as a result of the patterns that the government helped establish through discriminatory housing policies. Additionally, many people choose to move to segregated communities because of individual bias, and real estate agents continue the practice of steering clients toward residential areas based on race (Carrozzo 2019).

Education reformers seeking to advance equity have made some progress in altering school attendance areas to promote integration. Since the 1960s, the efforts of school integration advocates have led close to 200 school districts and charter schools to adopt student assignment policies that explicitly work toward integration (Potter and Burris 2020). Over 700 districts and charters are operating under a desegregation order or an explicit voluntary agreement aimed at integrating their schools.

In a separate example, student groups, community organizations, government panels, and scholars have been pressuring the New York City Department of Education to adopt new school assignment practices that ensure equitable access to the city's vast educational resources (Shapiro 2020). Since 1904, New York City has operated specialized high schools that have contributed to school segregation; and since the 1970s, New York City has overseen a gifted and talented program that has also persistently contributed to school segregation (Roda 2015). Spurred on by the disruptions resulting from the COVID-19 pandemic, New York City's mayor and school's chancellor responded to mounting pressure to change how children are assigned to the city's schools and announced a major restructuring of school admissions that will provide more equitable access to the city's most desired middle and high schools. Still, New York City's schools have a lot of work to do to ensure meaningful integration and equitable access to education.

Despite the numerous examples of education systems that are advancing equity by restructuring their use of school attendance areas, other districts are altering school attendance areas in ways that are intensifying segregation. There is a growing movement in school districts across the United States of wealthy enclaves seceding from their education systems and forming new school districts that are racially and socioeconomically isolated (Siegel-Hawley, Diem, and Frankenberg 2018). Because leaders of these secession movements frame their work around concepts of local control rather than racial exclusion, they often pass over legal hurdles that prohibit segregationist policies. These secession movements serve as a reminder and a warning that people will continue to use institutions to hoard opportunities and resources at the expense of other groups' access to equitable schooling as long as structures and the people who shape them allow.

School Structures and Processes

Policymakers and educational leaders use school oversight powers, school funding structures, and school zones to constrain or expand educational access at the macro-level; but there are countless other structures and processes within

US schools that also affect a child's access to an equitable education. Most notably, educators have long used tracking systems to separate children within schools (McCardle 2020). Although school leaders frame tracking around ability and meritocracy, tracking systems lead to intense levels of within-school segregation. Since the early 1900s, educators have often relied on IQ tests and other standardized tests to assign students to tracks; yet research demonstrates that these tests can be biased and that they fail to capture more than a limited scope of a child's academic abilities (Oakes 2005). Once children are assigned to a track, the track constrains the level and quality of coursework that they receive. As children progress through their schooling, these tracks intensify the gaps between children in upper and lower tracks. The use of tracking intensified following orders to desegregate schools in the 1960s and 1970s. In places where courts mandated school integration, educators used tracks to maintain and justify segregation within schools. While some diverse districts now place all children on a single track in an effort to advance equity, many maintain tracking systems with a range of course levels that overwhelmingly segregate Black, Hispanic, Indigenous, and low-income students into lower tracks and white, Asian, and high-income students into higher tracks (Burris and Garrity 2008).

Alongside tracking systems, US schools maintain disciplinary structures, pedagogical practices, staffing patterns, and a curriculum that privilege white, middle- and upper-class students. Far more work is needed to resolve the inequities within schools, but some districts have made notable progress and can act as models for policymakers and educational leaders hoping to expand access and equity for all students.

CONCLUSION

In the United States, it is not uncommon for larger political and cultural battles to play out within the education system. When civil rights activists sought an end to Jim Crow laws and segregation, they ushered the *Brown v. Board of Education* case through the Supreme Court and then used schools as the battleground for desegregation. Throughout history, groups of people have found similar ways to use school oversight powers, school funding systems, school assignment practices, and internal school structures to advance their goals. More often than not, racist, classist, sexist, and otherwise biased people in power have used these same institutional structures to privilege some and limit and control others. The history of schools and education systems in the United States demonstrates that people are continuously leveraging power to expand or constrain educational access and equity and to reshape society.

Education systems around the world have approached schooling in myriad ways over time, but people in power have consistently used education as a tool for advancing their goals. Although the US battle over educational access and equity is distinct, schools and education systems in other countries often follow similar patterns. For example, governments in all corners of the globe have adopted the same kinds of boarding schools for Indigenous children that the US government used to deculture and control Indigenous Americans. In some places, such as Canada and Australia, these boarding schools aimed to facilitate cultural genocide, and in other cases, such as Palestine and Saudi Arabia, they aimed to facilitate trade relationships between colonial powers and Indigenous communities (Smith 2009). Indigenous boarding schools are just one of countless analogues between the United States and other countries' experiences with education systems. This chapter's focus on the United States should not leave readers with the perspective that the experiences with schooling discussed here are unique to the United States; rather, readers should see the case of the United States as indicative of the ways in which humans often use education systems as part of a larger effort to shape and reshape society as a whole. Whether an elite ruling class has fashioned an education system to maintain control (Davies 2012) or a social welfare state has engaged education to advance the common good (Sahlberg 2014), those with power have used a range of institutional structures to shape educational access as they see fit.

There is an intimate and cyclical connection between education and power; history has shown that those who obtain an education are more likely to be able to exercise power. In the United States, as is true elsewhere, expansions in educational access have coincided with shifts in power dynamics. Many justice-minded people hope that access to quality education continues to expand and that this facilitates deeper transformations that allow for greater equity in our world. Past experiences indicate that such progress is possible, but that it is often slow and requires overcoming deep resistance.

NOTES

1. While countless similarities exist among the world's education systems, differences abound that embody the distinctions between societies. This chapter centers on the education system in the United States. While many of the features of the historical foundations of education of the United States explored in this chapter mirror what can be found elsewhere, not all lessons from this chapter are transferable outside of the United States.

2. It is important to note that reformers such as Mann and Dewey had visions of equality that were bound to their privilege as white men. Neither of them was a visionary of racial equality or gender equality. Instead, they primarily looked to schools as sources of social and economic equality for white men.

3. While I use the term "Hispanic" in discussing this group of people, many members of this group prefer to identify themselves as Latinos or Hispanic Americans (Torres 2018).

REFERENCES

Baker, Bruce D. (2018), *Educational Inequality and School Finance: Why Money Matters for America's Students*, Cambridge, MA: Harvard Education Press.

Bloom, Allan (1987), *The Closing of the American Mind: How Higher Education has Failed Democracy and Impoverished the Souls of Today's Students*, Cambridge, UK: Simon and Schuster.

Burris, Carol C. and Delia T. Garrity (2008), *Detracking for Excellence and Equity*, Alexandria, VA: ASCD.

Calderon, Margarita E., Maria G. Dove, Diane Staehr Fenner, Margo Gottlieb, Andrea Honigsfeld, Tonya Ward Singer, Shawn Slakk, Ivannia Soto, and Debbie Zacarian (2019), *Breaking Down the Wall: Essential Shifts for English Learners' Success*, Thousand Oaks, CA: Corwin Press.

Carrozzo, A. (2019), "Undercover Investigation Reveals Evidence of Unequal Treatment by Real Estate Agents," *Newsday*, last modified November 17, 2019. Available online: https://projects.newsday.com/long-island/real-estate-agents-investigation/ (accessed May 16, 2022).

Civilization Fund Act (1819), no. Pub. L. 15-85, 15th U.S. Congress.

Corbett, Christianne, Catherine Hill, and Andresse St. Rose (2008), "Where the Girls Are: The Facts about Gender Equity in Education," American Association of University Women Educational Foundation. Available online: http://eric.ed.gov/?id=ED501319 (accessed May 16, 2022).

Crawford, James (1989), *Bilingual Education: History, Politics, Theory, and Practice*, Los Angeles: Bilingual Educational Services.

Cremin, Lawrence (1970), *American Education; the Colonial Experience, 1607–1783*, 1st edn., New York: Harper & Row.

Cremin, Lawrence (1980), *American Education, the National Experience, 1783–1876*, New York: Harper and Row.

Cremin, Lawrence (1988), *American Education, the Metropolitan Experience, 1876–1980*, 1st edn., New York: Harper & Row.

Crenshaw, Kimberlé (2015), *On Intersectionality: The Essential Writings of Kimberlé Crenshaw*, New York: New Press.

Cummins, Jim (2000), *Language, Power and Pedagogy: Bilingual Children in the Crossfire*, Bristol: Channel View Publications.

Darling-Hammond, Linda (1998), "Unequal Opportunity: Race and Education," *Brookings*. Available online: https://www.brookings.edu/articles/unequal-opportunity-race-and-education/ (accessed May 16, 2022).

Darling-Hammond, Linda (2015), *The Flat World and Education: How America's Commitment to Equity Will Determine Our Future*, New York: Teachers College Press.

Davies, Brian (2012), *Social Control and Education (RLE Edu L)*, New York: Routledge.

Dewey, John (1900), *The School and Society*, Chicago: University of Chicago Press.

Dewey, John (1902), "The School as Social Center," *The Elementary School Teacher*, 3 (2): 73–86.

Doran, Elizabeth (2019), "See Schools that Spend the Most, the Least in NYS," *Syracuse.Com*, last modified August 9, 2019. Available online: https://www.syracuse.com/news/2019/05/which-school-districts-spend-the-most-the-least-in-new-york-state.html (accessed May 16, 2022).

EdBuild (2019), "$23 Billion," last modified 2019. Available online: http://edbuild. org/content/23-billion (accessed May 16, 2022).

Ehle, John (2011), *Trail of Tears: The Rise and Fall of the Cherokee Nation*, New York: Knopf Doubleday Publishing Group.

Finder, Alan, Patrick D. Healy, and Kate Zernike (2006), "President of Harvard Resigns, Ending Stormy 5-Year Tenure," *The New York Times*, February 22. Available online: https://www.nytimes.com/2006/02/22/education/22harvard.html (accessed May 16, 2022).

Finn, Chester (1991), *We Must Take Charge: Our Schools and Our Future*, New York: Free Press; Maxwell Macmillan Canada; Maxwell Macmillan International.

Frankenberg, Erica, Ee Jongyon, Jennifer B. Ayscue, and Gary Orfield (2019), *Harming our Common Future*. Available online: https://www.civilrightsproject. ucla.edu/research/k-12-education/integration-and-diversity/harming-our-common-future-americas-segregated-schools-65-years-after-brown/Brown-65-050919v4-final.pdf (accessed May 16, 2022).

Fryer, Roland G. (2019), "An Empirical Analysis of Racial Differences in Police Use of Force," *Journal of Political Economy*, 127 (3): 1210–61. https://doi. org/10.1086/701423.

Gonzalez, Gilbert G. (2013), *Chicano Education in the Era of Segregation*, Denton: University of North Texas Press.

Hanes, Roy, Ivan Brown, and Nancy E. Hansen (2017), *The Routledge History of Disability*, New York: Routledge.

Hannah-Jones, Nikole (2019), "America Wasn't a Democracy, Until Black Americans Made It One," *The New York Times*, August 14. Available online: https://www. nytimes.com/interactive/2019/08/14/magazine/black-history-american-democracy. html (accessed May 16, 2022).

Hirsch, E.D. (1988), *The Dictionary of Cultural Literacy*, Boston: Houghton Mifflin.

Hirsch, E.D. (2016), *Why Knowledge Matters: Rescuing our Children from Failed Educational Theories*, New York: Harvard Education Press.

Johnson, Rucker C. (2018), *Children of the Dream*, New York: Basic Books.

King, Martin L., Jr. (1967), *Revolution in the Classroom*, March 31.

Ladson-Billings, Gloria (1997), *The Dreamkeepers: Successful Teachers of African American Children*, San Francisco: Wiley.

Leon, Arnoldo D. (2006), *North to Aztlan: A History of Mexican Americans in the United States*, 2nd edn., Chichester, UK: Wiley-Blackwell.

Lew, Jamie (2006), *Asian Americans in Class: Charting the Achievement Gap Among Korean American Youth*, Washington, DC: Teachers College Press.

Low, Victor (1982), *The Unimpressible Race: A Century of Educational Struggle by the Chinese in San Francisco*, San Francisco: East/West Publishing Company.

Mann, H. (1848), *Twelfth Annual Report of the Board of Education, Together with the Twelfth Annual Report of the Secretary of the Board*, Commonwealth of Massachusetts, Board of Education. Available online: https://archives.lib.state. ma.us/handle/2452/204731 (accessed May 16, 2022).

McCardle, Todd (2020), "A Critical Historical Examination of Tracking as a Method for Maintaining Racial Segregation," *Educational Considerations*, 45 (2). Available online: https://newprairiepress.org/cgi/viewcontent.cgi?article=2186&context=edc onsiderations (accessed May 16, 2022).

McFarland, Joel, Jiashan Cui, Army Rathbun, and Juliet Holmes (2018), *Trends in High School Dropout and Completion Rates in the United States: 2018*. U.S. Department of Education and National Center for Education Statistics. Available online: https://nces.ed.gov/pubs2019/2019117.pdf (accessed May 16, 2022).

McWhorter, John (2016), *Talking Back, Talking Black: Truths About America's Lingua Franca*, New York: Bellevue Literary Press.

Meacham, Jon (2012), *Thomas Jefferson: The Art of Power*, New York: Random House.

Meriam, Lewis (1928), *The Problem of Indian Administration*, Institute for Government Research. Available online: https://eric.ed.gov/?id=ED087573 (accessed May 16, 2022).

Montejano, David (1987), *Anglos and Mexicans in the Making of Texas, 1836–1986*, Austin: University of Texas Press.

Museus, Samue and Peter P. Kiang (2009), "Deconstructing the Model Minority Myth and How it Contributes to the Invisible Minority Reality in Higher Education Research," *New Directions for Institutional Research*, 142 (5) (March): 5–15. https://doi.org/10.1002/ir.292.

Nieto, Sonia (2017), *Language, Culture, and Teaching: Critical Perspectives*, New York: Routledge.

Oakes, Jeannie (2005), *Keeping Track: How Schools Structure Inequality*, New Haven, CT: Yale University Press.

Orfield, Gary and Erica Frankenberg (2014), "Increasingly Segregated and Unequal Schools as Courts Reverse Policy," *Educational Administration Quarterly*, 50 (5) (October): 718–34. https://doi.org/10.1177/0013161X14548942.

Patterson, James T. and W.W. Freehling (2001), *Brown V. Board of Education: A Civil Rights Milestone and Its Troubled Legacy*, New York: Oxford University Press.

Potter, Halley and Michelle Burris (2020), "Here Is What School Integration in America Looks Like Today," The Century Foundation, last modified December 2, 2020. Available online: https://tcf.org/content/report/school-integration-america-looks-like-today/ (accessed May 16, 2022).

Pratt, Richard H. (2003), *Battlefield and Classroom: Four Decades with the American Indian, 1867–1904*, Norman: University of Oklahoma Press.

Reardon, Sean F., Chad R. Farrell, Stephen A. Matthews, David O'Sullivan, Kendra Bischoff, and Glenn Firebaugh (2009), "Race and Space in the 1990s: Changes in the Geographic Scale of Racial Residential Segregation, 1990–2000," *Social Science Research*, 38 (1): 55–70. https://doi.org/10.1016/j.ssresearch.2008.10.002.

Reyhner, John A. and Jeanne Eder (2006), *American Indian Education: A History*, Norman: University of Oklahoma Press.

Roda, Allison (2015), *Inequality in Gifted and Talented Programs: Parental Choices about Status, School Opportunity, and Second-Generation Segregation*, New York: Springer.

Rothstein, Richard (2017), *The Color of Law: A Forgotten History of How Our Government Segregated America*, New York: Liveright Publishing.

Sadovnik, Alan, Peter W. Cookson Jr., Susan F. Semel, and Ryan W. Coughlan (2018), *Exploring Education: An Introduction to the Foundations of Education*, 5th edn., New York: Routledge.

Sahlberg, Pasi (2014), *Finnish Lessons: What Can the World Learn from Educational Change in Finland*, New York: Teachers College Press.

San Antonio Independent School District v. Rodriguez (1973), Np. 71-1332, United States Supreme Court March 21, 1973.

Schneider, Barbara, Sylvia Martinez, and Ann Owens (2006), "Barriers to Educational Opportunities for Hispanics in the United States," in Marta Tienda and Faith Mitchell (eds.), *Hispanics and the Future of America*, 179–227, Washington, DC: National Academies Press (US).

Schultz, Stanley K. (1973), *The Culture Factory: Boston Public Schools, 1789–1860*, New York: Oxford University Press.

Shapiro, Eliza (2020), "New York City Will Change Many Selective Schools to Address Segregation," *The New York Times*, December 18.

Shores, Kenneth and Simon Ejdemyr (2017), "Pulling Back the Curtain: Intra-District School Spending Inequality and Its Correlates," *SSRN Electronic Journal*. https://doi.org/10.2139/ssrn.3009775.

Siegel-Hawley, Genvieve, Sarah Diem, and Erica Frankenberg (2018), "The Disintegration of Memphis-Shelby County, Tennessee: School District Secession and Local Control in the 21st Century," *American Educational Research Journal*, 55 (4): 651–92. https://doi.org/10.3102/0002831217748880.

Smith, Andrea (2009), *Indigenous Peoples and Boarding Schools: A Comparative Study*, United Nations Permanent Forum on Indigenous Issues. Available online: https://www.un.org/esa/socdev/unpfii/documents/E_C_19_2009_crp1.pdf (accessed May 16, 2022).

Spring, Joel (2002), *American Education*, New York: Routledge.

Spring, Joel (2004), *Deculturalization and the Struggle for Equality: A Brief History of the Education of Dominated Cultures in the United States*, 4th edn., New York: McGraw-Hill.

Spring, Joel (2018), *The American School: From the Puritans to the Trump Era*, New York: Routledge.

Stanton, Elizabeth Cady and Lucretia Mott (1848), *Declaration of Sentiments: Women's Grievances Against Men*, New York: Women's Rights Convention: Seneca Falls.

Takaki, Ronald (2012), *Strangers from a Different Shore: A History of Asian Americans (Updated and Revised)*, Boston: Little, Brown and Company.

Tyack, David B. and Larry Cuban (1995), *Tinkering Toward Utopia: A Century of Public School Reform*, Cambridge, MA: Harvard University Press.

U.S. Department of Education (2020), *Biennial Survey of Education in the United States*. Available online: https://nces.ed.gov/programs/digest/d19/tables/dt19_303.10.asp (accessed May 16, 2022).

Walker, Vanessa (2000), *Their Highest Potential: An African American School Community in the Segregated South*, Chapel Hill: Univeristy of North Carolina Press.

Walker, Vanessa (2018), *The Lost Education of Horace Tate: Uncovering the Hidden Heroes who Fought for Justice in Schools*, New York: New Press.

Wilkerson, Isabel (2020), *Caste: The Origins of Our Discontents*, New York: Random House.

Wiley, Terrence G. and Wayne E. Wright (2004), "Against the Undertow: Language-Minority Education Policy and Politics in the 'Age of Accountability,'" *Educational Policy*, 18 (1): 142–68. https://doi.org/10.1177/0895904803260030.

Williams, Heather A. (2005), *Self-taught: African American Education in Slavery and Freedom*, Chapel Hill: University of North Carolina Press.

CHAPTER FIVE

Learning and Human Development

Thinking Historically About Studying Childhood

SHAWN MICHAEL BULLOCK AND CÉCILE SABATIER BULLOCK

In this chapter we examine three historiographies of childhood and youth to highlight the ways in which competing conceptualizations of learning and human development have played out as significant conflicts between the adult ruling classes, children, youth, and adult advocates of young people. Our broad concern in this chapter is to outline historical challenges to learning and development using three case studies. First, we use the phenomenon of school strikes in the United Kingdom and North America to highlight the ways in which society reacts when children decide to leave schools in protest against injustice. The early twentieth-century school strikes against the use of corporal punishment, the more recent protests against wars in the Middle East, and protests in support of climate action provide our case studies. Second, we use the concept of the plurilingual child as a unit of analysis for thinking about the changing ways in which children who speak more than one language have been viewed by schools—mostly as being problematic, we argue. Finally, we situate some of the mythology of what it means to come of age in the new digital age within often uncited histories of the development of the internet. Our chapter concludes by using the nineteenth-century concept of the "ideal childhood" to frame the ongoing tension in connection with the structure of childhood and the agency of children themselves that characterizes the contested histories of how children learn.

CONSIDERING STRUCTURE AND AGENCY

In each of the sections that follow, we have tried to highlight the interplay between existing structures that attempt to direct the nature of certain kinds of youth experiences and various types of agencies that children and youth demonstrate in response to these structures. Simply put, we argue that historiographies of childhood and youth might be productively considered by trying to understand how the "rules of society" both enable and constrain young people. The choices made by children and youth, then, are both enabled and constrained by the rules and expectations society imposes.

To be sure, one of the standard contributions of childhood studies is to consider the ways in which adult populations restrict and direct the behavior of young people; one might argue that the concepts of childhood and youth are created by the structures that are imposed on them. Structures are dominant "rules and resources" (Giddens 1979: 64) that enable and constrain individual actions; they shape and are shaped by social practices. One simple example of structure is schooling; most countries around the world legislate that people of a certain age must attend school and follow a set curriculum, often defined at a national level. Going to school is part of childhood. As Bloch et al. put it, "Education, be it theory, practice, policy or childrearing has functioned as a means of constituting individuals, inscribing notions of normalcy, and socially administering freedom" (2006: 8). Structure might be thought of as an inherent stability of a system.

Agency, on the other hand, might be thought of as the ways in which social actors engage with structures. Emirbayer and Mische distinguish between an iterative, a projective, and a practical-evaluative dimension of agency in an attempt to "reconceptualise human agency as a temporally embedded process of social engagement" (1998: 963). The *iterative* element draws from Bourdieuian ideas such as *habitus* (i.e., agency informed by the past) and is focused on "past patterns of thought and action, as routinely incorporated in practical activity" (963). The *projective* element refers to the capacity of actors to imagine "future trajectories of action, in which received structures of thought and action may be creatively reconfigured in relation to actors' hopes, fears, and desires for the future" (963). Finally, the *practical-evaluative* element refers to the ways in which actors might make "practical and normative judgments among alternative possible trajectories of action, in response to the emerging demands, dilemmas, and ambiguities of presently evolving situations" (963).

We chose three sets of historical case studies to illustrate our point. The first two sections focus on the structure of school and the structure of the monolingual nation-state (imposed by school) as a way of highlighting how children and youth exhibit agency by responding to the dilemmas they encounter in mandatory societal structures by striking against school attendance and insisting on speaking their preferred home language. The third section explores the relationship between structure and agency within a very different rules-based system—that of social media, decided by large US corporations—that requires children and youth to enage in a practical-evaluative understanding of what personal privacy, and agency, mean in the digital age.

SCHOOL STRIKES

Historically, government authorities and members of adult populations have regarded school strikes—the action in which children and youth purposefully do not go to school as a form of organized process—with both concern and indignance. Most societies have decided that children need to spend a certain amount of time in formal schooling. Mandatory schooling, after all, is seen to be a crucial structure supporting the advancement of young people; it is, one might say, a job that most societies assign children for at least ten years of their lives. Children tend to have to comply with the significant structures of schooling with little input. Beyond their obligatory attendance, schooling is something that tends to be "done to" students with little input as to what they might learn, or how they might go about learning. In some cases, this is understandable—one would not want children to explore random sets of chemicals unsupervised in a misplaced interpretation of "discovery" approaches to science—but the fact remains that children spend most of their time in school being told what to do.

A failure to comply with the requirement to send one's children to school can bring serious consequences in many locations. In the UK, for example, parents or guardians can be prosecuted if their children (up to age sixteen) do not attend school. A local council might issue a "Parenting Order" that mandates that the parents attend classes, or a School Attendance Order that requires a student be sent to a specific school. Additionally, parents may be fined and, in some cases, sent to prison. Although home schooling is permitted, recent UK government policy for local authorities stipulates that "parents have a right to educate their children at home" before hastening to add "the past few years have seen a very significant increase in the number of children being educated at home, and there is considerable evidence that many of these children are not receiving a suitable education" (Department of Education 2019: 4). The specific evidence to support the statement is not listed and the document is issued by the state in support of state schooling. The same guidance states that it is the local (government) authority's responsibility to use "safeguarding powers" if it becomes clear that a child is not receiving a suitable education at home "to ensure that the child's development is protected from significant harm" (4). Clearly the UK considers school attendance to be a high priority, ostensibly because elected representatives and the general population believe that school attendance is an important part of learning and human development.

In this section we examine the ways in which schoolchildren have rebelled against schooling via strikes, the reasons behind striking, and the reactions of the adult public. Our case studies for analysis are the early nineteenth-century strikes against the use of corporal punishment, school strikes against the Iraq War, and school strikes in support of attention to the climate crisis (hereafter referred to as "climate strikes"). Our case studies in this section focus on strike actions in the United Kingdom.

From the waning decades of the nineteenth century to the Second World War, there were student-organized strikes in at least 100 schools in the UK, lasting anywhere from a few days to a few months (Humphries 1981). Those of 1889 and 1911 attracted the most national attention, as they were linked to larger labor unrest in the adult population. The two largest strikes were concurrent with practices used by the developing labor movement; in some cases, children wrote the word "picket" on a piece of paper and pinned it to their clothing. School strikes were often in protest against the use of corporal punishment and often occurred concurrently with labor strikes. Grigg (2003) highlighted that school strikes in Wales tended to be in the lower income area of industrialized towns; in the south the focal point of strikes was Llanelli—the tinplate capital of the world at the time. Historiography of this topic has focused on striking boys, mostly because they tended to be the victims of corporal punishment. Male students tend, in much of the literature, to be framed as active in organizing strikes at this time whereas female students tend to be framed as "going along" with strikes as observers, from time to time. These historiographies need to be interrogated, as there is evidence that female students were similarly active although their contributions may not have been reported. In part, the historiography may be shaped because of the ways in which violent behaviors of some striking boys were reported at the time (Cunningham and Lavalette 2016).

It is often difficult to find information on student-led school strikes because they were suppressed quickly and tended to have details stricken from official records. Many school officials refused to use the term "strike," perhaps for fear of acknowledging their link with the broader social movement of labor strikes (Humphries 1981). We thus rely on oral histories, photographs (often posted in pubs), and newspaper stories. There are linguistic elements at play as well; the strikes tended to be reported more often and in a more supportive fashion in Welsh-language newspapers compared with English-language newspapers in Wales and beyond.

Student-led school strikes in this time period can be viewed through the wider tensions between working and upper classes throughout the UK, particularly given the rhetoric used to describe the motivations of children and youth on strike. In many ways, commentaries on striking young people were proxies for critique of their working-class parents. As Humphries noted:

> School strikes were frequently viewed as an expression of anti-social, adolescent rebelliousness, aggravated by the pernicious influence of delinquent ringleaders [...] which in turn was often attributed to the increasing moral laxity of working-class parents, improved social conditions, and "progressive" teaching methods.
>
> (1981: 98)

Furthermore, Humphries's (1981) analysis of official and public explanations for school strikes instigated by children can be grouped into three general categories:

1. Working-class children and youth are rather gullible and likely to imitate the behavior of others, particularly working-class members of the labor movement.

2. Working-class children and youth tend to engage in violence and vandalism in general; the majority of "ringleaders" were in "street gangs" who used physical threats to coerce other children into joining them.

3. The behaviors of working-class children and youth, particularly with reference to school strikes, are symptomatic of a general moral decay in a more permissive and less proper society, particularly among the working classes.

Humphries's summation of English school strikes at this time fits well with Grigg's (2003) characterizations of school strikes in Wales. He cites the comments of the chairman of the Llanelli borough education committee as saying that the school strikes were in "the spirit of the times," a comment itself referencing the railway dispute meetings on Saturday afternoons held in local schools (Grigg 2003: 137). Rather than taking the concerns of students who were striking seriously—and these concerns were often linked to the use of corporal punishment, although occasionally rote teaching methods were targeted—government officials and newspaper opinion-makers tended to use striking schoolchildren at this time period as a barometer of a society in decline. Cunningham and Lavalette note that although some parents cooperated with school officials in trying to secure an end to student strikes, "many of the parents had in the previous months been on strike and subjected to the most extreme forms of state coercion and brutality" and thus "support [for school strikes] was commonplace" (2016: 82). Grigg indicated the journalists of the time "tended to mock the actions of striking pupils, dismissing the strikes as frivolous and undeserving of much serious investigation" (2003: 134). Learning and development, in other words, had been at least partially outsourced to schools and any disruption to learning, particularly disruption instigated by children of the working classes, was unwelcome and seen as contrary to the ethos of schooling.

Jumping forward to the school strikes in the early 2000s against the Iraq War, one tends to find a similar theme of establishment frustration with youth protest. Notably, children and youth participating in the 2003 school strikes against the Iraq War were agitating not for improvement of their conditions in schools, but out of concern for the actions of the Tony Blair government in the Iraq War. Cunningham and Lavalette (2004) noted that "The overwhelming response of the educational establishment was to castigate and punish those who took part in the strikes."

Cunningham and Lavalette (2016) trace the origins of the 2003 school strikes to the mass protests against the meeting of the World Trade Organization (WTO) in Seattle in 1999. The WTO, having just been formed in 1995, might be seen as a "broadening of the agenda of liberalisation beyond tariff reduction to encompass 'harmonisation' of (formerly 'domestic') rules and regulations governing business insofar as these appear, from the liberal perspective, as potential non-tariff barriers to trade" (Rupert 2003: 191). Several commenters (Rupert 2003; Cox and Nilsen 2007; Cunningham and Lavalette 2016) identify these protests—and indeed general dissatisfaction with the concept of the WTO—as the genesis of a new set of social movements concerned broadly with protesting against capitalism and neoliberalism and in favor of peace, environmental justice, social justice, and Indigenous rights. Cox and Nilsen (2007) placed the Seattle protests within a larger "movement of movements" protesting against the acceleration of neoliberal globalization. The Stop the War movement, developed in the UK shortly after the terrorist attacks on 9/11, was cited by Murray et al. as a possible reason for the "significant, perhaps unprecedented, degree of sympathetic media coverage" (2008: 10) of anti-war protests. The movement frequently protested against the war strategies of President Bush and Prime Minister Blair; a protest with over 500,000 people on September 28, 2002 is often cited as proof of the robustness of the protest movement (Cunningham and Lavalette 2016).

In many countries, including the UK, the end of February and early March of 2003 saw a number of school strikes. School strikes in the UK were the subject of a 2015 film enititled *Iraq War Day X: The Largest School Strikes in UK History* (2015). In the film, we see interviews with students who took part in the protests. Some commented that their teachers followed them outside asking them to take homework papers with them. Other parts of the film show journalists interviewing student protesters, using questions that suggest that students should be in school as their first priority. Student strikes followed on

Stop the War (and related movements) protests on February 15, 2003—it is estimated that between six million and ten million people protested in up to sixty countries over that weekend (BBC 2003). Similar to the school strikes from the early twentieth century, we see many commentors arguing that youth should not be engaging in the adult activity of protest—and that those young people who engaged in strikes were somehow being misled by nefarious adults.

One of the ironies of the government's reaction to student protest against the Iraq War in the early 2000s is that, in many ways, the protests indicated that the education system was working. In 1998, the government's own advisory group on citizenship and education released what has become known as "The Crick Report." The participation of students in democratic protests might be seen as being in line with the report, which states in part that students at the end of Key Stage 4 (approximately sixteen years old)

know about the different ways in which MPs can be elected and the Government held accountable through parliament to the electorate, including the importance of voting, public opinion, opinion polls, the role of the media, lobbying, pressure groups and *different forms of protest*; the different electoral systems and understand the reasons for the differences.

(UK Citizen Advice Group 1998; emphasis added)

A key democratic value is the right to peaceful protest when one disagrees with policy decisions taken by the government. The UK government felt it important to introduce a coordinated approach to citizenship education in schools, ostensibly to aid in the learning and development of young people, in the late 1990s. Five years later, however, government officials were quick to condemn young people taking their democratic responsibilities seriously by protesting against what they believed was an unjust war. There is an inherent tension between the government's stated aims and its actions when faced with peaceful protest.

Our final case study considers the recent school strikes in support of climate justice. The Swedish student Greta Thunberg began protesting outside her country's parliament in mid-August of 2018, explicitly presenting her actions as a school strike: "Facts don't matter anymore, politicians aren't listening to the scientists, so why should I learn?" (Crouch 2018). Emilsson, Johansson, and Wennerhag argue that what Thunberg began in Sweden "has served as an invigoration for the environmental moment as such and a broadening of its social base as new groups have joined the moment and participated in its demonstrations" (2020: 4). The authors cite the numbers of protesters who have manifested in cities around the world in support of climate justice since 2018, including but not limited to 60,000 in Stockholm, 300,000 in Montreal, 200,000 in Berlin, and 100,000 in London. Their analysis of the school strike for the climate justice movement demonstrates that Thunberg's protest movement is unlike other climate protest movements, which have tended to be concurrent with events such as Earth Day or international climate summits. In contrast, Thunberg's regular school strikes focus on a frustration with government inaction more generally and have resonated with millions of people around the world. Yet Emilsson, Johansson, and Wennerhag also point to several hierarchies and internecine tensions within and outside the most recent range of student strikes for climate protests.

Once again, we find that many in positions of responsibility within the UK government have taken great issue with school strikes for climate justice. Writing in *The Telegraph*, Madeline Grant (2019) asked, "Can we please stop garlanding children for being wrong?" and stated, "The Nobel Committee is unwittingly adopting a common trope in contemporary debate, attributing, in biblical fashion, special insights to children despite their limited knowledge of complex subjects." Member of Parliament William Wragg wrote, "It's far more fruitful to learn about climate change in school. The idea of a day of protest, I don't see what learning will come out of it" (Speck 2019). Finally, the Association of School and College Leaders issued the following statement:

> While we understand the strength of feeling over the very important issue of climate change, we would urge pupils against walking out of school on Friday. It is extremely disruptive for a school to have to deal with unauthorised absences and pupils will be missing out on important learning time.
>
> (Association of School and College Leaders 2019)

Similar to other school strike actions, the message sent by those in power to children and youth is quite clear. In many cases, youth are framed as being tempted into adult activism, being too immature to understand what they are doing, and being too young to have meaningful thoughts on complex subjects. Learning and development is linked to school attendance above all else, regardless of what might be experienced and learned outside school walls. Thus children and youth are expected to prioritize participation in societal structures, decided by adults, over whatever their personal views might be. Unfortunately, the historiography of school strikes also indicates that many adults do not consider children capable of having informed personal viewpoints. The agency of children and youth—particularly the aforementioned *projective* element in which actors imagine future trajectories—are deemed irrelevant or immature. Even when the moral imperative of a particular cause is recognized, it may be framed as a matter to be taken up within school under the watchful eyes of adults. Regardless of young people's reasons for engaging in protest by striking instead of going to school, it seems that the message in the UK has been and continues to be: the place of young people is in school.

THE PLURILINGUAL CHILD

In language education, the structure–agency dialectic has shaped profoundly the ways in which many modern societies conceptualize learning and human development. Tensions between structure and agency become immediately apparent when exploring the complexities of relationships to language(s) and identities and examining the dynamics by which various actors position themselves and are positioned by others through practices of language(s). When reflecting on the dynamics of the relationship between structure and agency in language education, we need to ponder the interrelationship of the macrolevel social structures and the microlevel individual practices and consider the ways in which (societal, discursive, curricular, etc.) structures influence individuals' agency in learning and human development. We also need to consider how individuals exercise agency to engage with structures and mobilize resources to create new contexts, new practices, and new enunciative spaces (Bullock in press).

Throughout history, humans have most often been multi- and plurilingual, even though we might not have thought of ourselves in those terms. Simply put, humans have traditionally had to find ways to communicate with each other that cross what we would now consider to be linguistic boundaries. The shift toward monolingualism in many parts of the world was partly as result of the emergence and consolidation of modern nation-states in the eighteenth and nineteenth centuries. These nation-states, in many cases, aimed for certain kinds of homogeneity (social, religious, regional, linguistic) in the name of "national unity." The process of constructing and contrasting the ideas of "monolingualism" and "bilingualism" was politically motivated in modern nation states. Framing the debate in this way resulted in individuals' linguistic and cultural practices being both rejected from the public sphere and often condemned—all in the name of the *unitarisme* of the new political power. The quest for a sort of *linguistic purism* led to the repression of home languages in society at large; in formal education, bilingual language acquisition was often only undertaken with suspicion. Those in charge of modern nation-states, particularly in the twentieth century, often saw languages as separate external entities; bilingual language development was regarded as a kind of aberrant development of a single language. As a result, one often finds significant, government-backed language reform initiatives linked to the emergence of a nation state in the early twentieth century (e.g., Hungarian, Japanese, Turkish).

The historical and political construction of the French nation-state, for example, banned the historical languages (called "patois") spoken by peoples in France from French education and society (Escudé 2016). These "patois" languages were systematically eradicated for the sake of the unification of the nation. In 1794, during the upheaval of the French Revolution, Abbé Grégoire declared that the unity of the new French Republic depended on linguistic unity. Today, we see the modern link between language and state in Article 2 of the Constitution of the Fifth Republic, which states "The language of the Republic is French" ("La langue de la République est le français," Article 2 of the *Constitution de la Cinquième République*).

The rejection of the historical languages of peoples of France led to the sociological construction of a modern state that, through bureaucratic and social structures, closely associates the role of one language in conditioning (by constraining or enabling) a sense of belonging through language practices and thus denies actors (and especially children) any power and any other identities than the collective national identity. Social structures thus subsumed over individuals' agency when monoglossic ideologies overlooked multilingualism and centuries-long plurilingual identities (Canagarajah and Liynage 2012) and when individual plurilingualism was instrumentalized to explain learning difficulties in children.

As early as 1840, Simon S. Laurie promoted the thesis that bilingualism was harmful for children. His ideas were taken up across much of Europe as they reflected the consensus view of academics across major universities. Laurie stated that bilingualism exerted a negative influence on children's learning abilities and development:

> If it were possible for a child to live in two languages at once equally well, so much the worse. His intellectual and spiritual growth would not thereby be doubled but halved. Unity of mind and character would have great difficulty in asserting itself in such circumstances.
>
> (1890: 15)

Laurie's ideas had a lasting impact on many works in which bilingual children were thought to be suffering from cognitive impairments as a result of having to learn and speak two (or more) languages throughout the nineteenth and twentieth centuries (Baker [1993] 2006; Tabouret-Keller 2016). Bilingualism was also seen to contribute harmful effects on morality and social behaviors, as social structures appeared to be called into question by maintaining diverse linguistic practices. This "deficit" perspective based on the misunderstanding of the phenomenon of multilingualism and on a very normative and structuralist approach to language(s) has long conditioned the vision that twentieth-century language policies and practices in education have developed about languages in contact. At the beginning of the twentieth century, many scholars (Saer 1923; Pichon 1936) emphasized the negative effects of bilingualism on children's intelligence and cognition and concluded that bilingual children were at a disadvantage in thinking compared with monolingual youngsters. The standard against which bilingualism was established was a monolingual conception of language acquisition and in the context of language learning and language development, "the tendency [was thus] to view individuals acquiring a second language as aspirant, and for the most part, failed native speakers" (Leung and Valdés 2019: 308).

In contrast with Laurie's ideas turning bilingual children into deficient subjects, in 1913, linguist Jules Ronjat nonetheless explored the enactments of children's agency through their language practices. Ronjat (1913) discussed the benefits of bilingualism in young children by describing his own son's bilingual language development. In one of the first monographs on bilingual language development in children, *Le Développement du langage observé chez un enfant bilingue*, Ronjat (1913) described his son's learning experiences in two languages as harmonious, in an autonomous way according to the principle "one person, one language." Even though his ideas went against the mainstream condemnation of bilingualism, Ronjat's case study falls within a linear additive and monolingual salient conception of language learning. In his view, bilingual language acquisition was based on the monolingual native speaker norm and a balanced mastery of languages in contact. Bilingualism was seen as transitional toward two monolingualisms inhabiting the same speaker.

The very definitions of bilingualism and bilingual speakers circulating during these decades also testify to the prevalence of this monolingual mindset of bilingual language acquisition. In 1933, Bloomfield defined bilingualism as "native-like control of two languages" (Bloomfield 1933: 56); in 1953, Haugen stated that a bilingual individual produces "complete and meaningful utterances in other languages" (1953: 6) and Weinreich considered bilingualism "the practice of alternately using two languages" (1953: 1). For decades, children speaking and/or acquiring an additional (second or third) language were consequently seen as having a "linguistic handicap" (Pinter and Keller 1922) or as being "deficient" (Bereiter and Engelmann 1966) or "semilinguals" (Skutnabb-Kangas and Toukomaa 1976), as the differences in cognitive development were only mediated by differences in language development. The concept of interference between the two languages of bilingual individuals, conceived as "deviations from the norms of either language" (Weinreich 1953: 1), made it then difficult to acknowledge the role of speakers' agency in learning and human development. "Many early studies, carried out from around 1920 to 1960, indicated that bilingualism exerted a negative influence on children's academic development" (Frost 2003: 130). The interplay in language learning between structure on the one hand, and agency on the other tilted in favor of structure over agency, as the former influenced education policy and practice by reproducing discourses of the dominant classes in power and shaped the daily experience of individuals by maintaining a sense of control and constraint in society.

The linguistic agency and identities of multilingual young people caused a critical turn in language education from 1968 onward and the subsequent social turn (Block 2003) that followed in the 2000s that called into question the structuralist approaches prevalent in many Western societies—particularly with respect to the systems of power and privilege. As new immigration patterns encouraged the development of new theories on how children and youth learn and use language(s) (Lüdi and Py [1986] 2003; Dabène and Billiez 1987; Billiez 1992; Deprez 1994; Milroy and Muysken 1995; Rampton 1995), the emergence of post-structuralism and post-modernity probed the binary opposition between structure and agency by reflecting on ways of communicating (Hymes 1966; Fishman 1967), constructing collective and individual identities (Goffman 1959; Pavlenko and Blackledge 2004), and framing discourse authority (Foucault 1971) from a dialogical perspective.

Such movements helped researchers to view young learners as having complex social identities, which in turn affect their approaches to language learning and their socialization (Bourdieu and Passeron 1964, 1970; Doise and Mugny 1981). A more critical stance on language learning contested the traditional view that language learning and child development was a linear process. Rather, it was argued young language learners were in constant negotiations between social structures and their individual agencies. Learning a language, then, was at least partially about the ways in which children were positioned within structural discourses and the roles they were assigned.

Schools that developed in the context of emerging modern nation-states had largely been built on monoglossic ideologies. As a result, the reemergence and recognition of linguistic plurality turned into a contentious sociocultural and political issue. The "monolingual habitus" (Gogolin 1997: 38) started to be rejected as a result of the critical and social turns, but structures tend to be rather resilient and conservative by nature. Cummins (2000) argued that bi- or multilingual individuals from migrant families were blamed for disrupting well-established social structures, including schools.

Picardo and Galante referred to the tension between existing homogenous school structures and the needs of the plurilingual child as a tension that demands a "new scenario" (2018: 147). In part, this scenario is a dialectic between structure and agency in educational settings that places more emphasis (1) on the role of social contexts in (language) learning (Lantolf 1994), and (2) on the (language) learner's agency and investment in their (language) learning (Norton Peirce 1995).

The shift in the rationale from languages as autonomous systems to bi-, multi-, plurilingual speakers and their linguistic repertoires has refocused attention on the individual that exists within the structures (Lahire 2001). However, agency should not be understood as a static property of individual children; agency emerges from the continuously co-constructed and renegotiated relationship with those around the individuals and with society (Yashima 2013). For most children and youth, these relationships are negotiated with family and friends and within and outside school contexts. As we shall see in the next section, such negotiations are increasingly mediated in online spaces. Therefore, according to García and Otheguy, bilingualism is strongly linked to social and political constructions and cannot therefore be analyzed without reference to the social order (2020: 71). In doing so, linguistic diversity is framed as a construct that shapes the daily lives and experiences of both individual children and worlds they inhabit.

Children's and youth's experiences with multiple languages make teaching and learning situations more complex, particularly if one wishes to consider the potential of plurilingual individuals within the classroom. After over a century debating whether or not schools should take linguistic diversity into account, many language educators are openly critical of the existing conceptualization of language as separate entities that independently inhabit a young person. Labeling someone as bi-, multi-, or plurilingual no longer refers to the native-speaker-like mastery of a particular language or the existing of multiple languages within a particular context (Grosjean 1984; Cummins 2007; García 2009). This shift requires reconceptualization of multilingual children and young language learners (May 2014). The constructed nature of language leads to a multiplicity of individuals' roles, affiliations, social position/ings, and practices. Collective and individual identities are developed through the multiple language experiences of individuals, in particular of children and youth (Sabatier 2006). A call for a multilingual turn (Conteh and Meier 2014; May 2014) in second language acquisition and in applied linguistics also gives voice to language learners and frees language teaching from exclusive reliance on monolingual instructional approaches (Cummins 2007; May 2014).

In schools, the disruption of the traditional understanding of multilingualism and the associated language education programs (traditional bilingual education programs such as immersion programs, for example) requires us to question the terms (such as mother tongue, first and second language, bi-, multi-, or plurilingualism, etc.) used to think about how young people learn and use their linguistic repertoires. Multiple scholars (Marshall and Moore 2018; Picardo 2018; Leung and Valdés 2019) have called for a focus on language plurality to transform the linguistic capacities of young people into assets for learning. The term *plurilingualism* has emerged to take better account of the construction of learners' concept of self through a wide range of discursive resources in linguistically complex communities (García and Otherguy 2019).

Plurilingualism brings to the forefront individual biographies and life experiences, focuses on voice rather than languages, and offers a counter discourse to the monolingual mindset on languages and bi- or multilingualism seen in a monoglossic perspective. Of particular importance for learning and development, the concept of plurlingualism opens up complex and dynamic enunciative spaces for a plurality of languages, cultures, and identities and focuses on the role of social contexts in (language) learning/teaching and on learners' agency. In consideration of how children and youth use and learn language, the turn to plurilingualism requires a shift toward a plurilingual educational practice developed as a conceptual and pedagogic framework in which the ability of learners and speakers to act independently and to make their own free choices is the foundation for linguistic tolerance. Plurilingual education advocates for the language rights of plurilingual speakers to overcome the century-long misguided assumption that the use or support of home, first, or primary language in schools is detrimental to the development of children and youth.

THE DIGITAL CHILD

This third and final section outlining historical challenges to learning and development concerns perhaps the most prevalent discussion on child development in recent years: that of the digital child and how they learn. Unfortunately, much of this discussion has been formed around a problematic, in our view non-academic, article written at the turn of the twenty-first century. It is difficult to overstate the impact of Prensky (2001), as his assertions are regularly referenced in both popular and academic discourse and often without attribution. His core claim was that the education systems needed to change in response to the ways children and youth learn in the digital age. Although seemingly innocuous at first glance, this claim was first asserted within ageist, techno libertarian ideas using arguably xenophobic metaphors (the title of the article was "Digital Natives, Digital Immigrants," for example). Prensky believes that those who grow up with access to particular technologies are digital natives and thus have an intuitive understanding of how to use technology to learn. Those who do not—older generations, especially—are framed as digital immigrants, who must learn to catch up with the ways in which young people learn and develop socially and cognitively in the digital age. It is not difficult to find examples of Prensky-inspired alarmist rhetoric about how education systems are falling behind their technology-enabled students.

It is important to first question the rhetorical device that Prensky uses to frame the debate: the word immigrant is used to denote a slower, out-of-date, other who is holding up the progress of the agile, up-to-date, native. Such rhetoric is divisive, xenophobic, and, as Helsper and Eynon (2010) convincingly showed in a review, not supported by peer-reviewed literature. Framing the discussion from the perspective of the sociology of technology and education, danah boyd wrote:

> The notion of the digital native, whether constructed positively or negatively, has serious unintended consequences. Not only is it fraught, but it obscures the uneven distribution of technological skills and media literacy across the youth population, presenting an inaccurate portrait of young people as uniformly prepared for the digital era and ignoring the assumed level of privilege required to be "native." Worse, by not doing the work necessary to help youth develop broad digital competency, educators and the public end up reproducing digital inequality because more privileged youth often have more opportunities to develop these skills outside the classroom. Rather than focusing on coarse generational categories, it makes more sense to focus on the skills and knowledge that are necessary to make sense of a mediated world. Both youth and adults have a lot to learn.
>
> (2014: 179)

From an historical perspective, boyd pointed out connections between children with intuitive technological knowledge and the techno-utopian/cyber-libertarian ideas espoused on the early days of the public World Wide Web in the 1990s. boyd cites comments from John Perry Barlow (former lyricist for the Grateful Dead, among other things) as foundational to Prensky's arguments: "You [adults] are terrified of your own children, since they are natives in a world where you will always be immigrants" (2014: 177). As boyd points out, Barlow's words tap into intergenerational fears, not least of which is the "idea that 'natives' have singular power and skills" (178).

It seems clear that, however frustratingly popular it may be, we should leave Prensky's framing of the digital child to the side in our consideration of learning and human development in the digital age. Instead, we believe it helpful to consider learning and development from sociohistorical perspectives, many of which challenge taken-for-granted assumptions about digital youth culture. For example, an analysis of children's use of technology across seven European Union countries revealed both that young children do not view digital technologies as a dominant part of their lives, and that digital activities are often undertaken to support "offline" life interests (Chaudron 2015). Moreover, young children were able to articulate clearly problems and limitations they faced using digital technologies for educational purposes, and many regarded the use of technology in schools for learning as infantilizing.

Livingston and Blum-Ross (2017) offer some helpful recommendations for how research on the learning and development of children might be undertaken with respect to questions raised by the current digital age. In particular, they touch on the importance of understanding the role that *mediation* plays in understanding the experiences of children and youth. Livingston and Blum-Ross also call attention to the ways in which children and youth write themselves "into being" in a digital context. One example of the consequences of finding space in the digital world is provided by Richardson (2017), who discussed the concept of "promposals." He demonstrates convincingly the ways in which spaces such as YouTube and Instagram create perceived requirements for young people, particularly in the United States in this case, to film elaborate proposals to potential dates to prom in high school. These promposals also tend to reinforce heteronormative, racial, and gender stereotypes, given that the vast majority of promposal videos feature young men asking young women to prom. Richardson concluded, in part, "the marriage of technology and high school romance has led to a reassertion of deeply conservative values and voices under the guise of connectedness" (Livingston and Blum-Ross 2017: 82).

A final important set of considerations for the learning and development of children and youth concerns the changing requirements around online social performances and negotiating private and public spaces. boyd (2014) helpfully offers the concept of *networked publics* to aid in our thinking about the new forms of digital learning required of children and youth. In part, boyd argues that social media has created a new public space: a space that is not only permanent and replicable, thanks to recording technologies, but also newly searchable. For example, it has been possible to audio record, and then to video record, events in a public space since the late nineteenth and early twentieth century. These recordings have provided a persistent record that is replicable— one can view, say, a public event without ever having attended and make copies of the recorded media. But social media has enabled "tagging"—the process of labeling content for purposes of cross-linking—and the tagging process is often done by those who did not create the original content. Although prevalent since the early days of social media, tagging has taking on a new urgency with the idea of "hashtagging" on platforms such as Instagram and Twitter. Events and, even more crucially, people can become part of the public discourse by having their name become a hashtag (started by anyone) that is replicated and amplified on social media. One can be "hashtagged" into a particular kind of public existence, without consent. Such is the nature of the networked public and one of the many things that children and youth learn to navigate if they engage with the internet and related digital tools.

As Livingston and Blum-Ross argue, researchers need to theorize about "the interplay between visibility and invisibility" and the reproduction of asymmetrical power relationships experienced by children and youth (2017: 66). Too often, particularly in the 1990s and early 2000s, the platforms that emerged to create new opportunities and affordances for public internet users were enveloped in a kind of cyber-libertarianism. New platforms, particularly those that facilitated easy access to publishing on the World Wide Web and that were often frequented by young people (Geocities, Livejournal, Blogger, etc.)

were heralded as a new path for democratic engagement of the global citizenry. After all, argued many platform enthusiasts, the ability to publish and connect online created unimaginable possibilities for young people to make their marks on the world, a world that would be inherently more socially just because it included more voices.

Except, of course, that not all youth had (or have) access to the online affordances in question (Hilbert 2016). Many could not connect online and those that did often used digital tools to replicate existing social structures. Part of boyd's (2008) work, for example, demonstrated that youth who believed that they would attend university would invest time and energy in the early versions of Facebook, whereas those who did not focused on MySpace. At least a part of this divide developed from the explicit "exclusivity" built into the earliest iterations of Facebook, which required a university email account to join, initially. Universities thus began targeting advertising and recruitment at Facebook, reinforcing social divides. Fast forwarding to the early 2020s, one might question the ways in which universities use social media giant Twitter: universities, faculties, departments, and programs of study (to say nothing of many academics and students themselves) routinely send out short messages and share links in an attempt to "engage" with young people. Such engagement assumes that all young people have access to the internet, the devices required to access the internet, and the time to "engage" back. In this way, universities reinforce their availability to certain well-off groups of young people. Lewin-Jones (2019) argues that university marketing pages tend to promote a narrow view of internationalization, for example, in an effort to appeal to students seeking particular conceptualization of success and employability. There have also been high-profile cases of potential students having their places in universities revoked due to prior problematic posts on social media. It seems that a new requirement for university enrollment, and indeed for those attend or work at these institutions, is the successful management of networked publics. As boyd commented, "The internet will not inherently make the world more equal, nor will it automatically usher today's youth into a tolerant world. Instead, it lays bare existing and entrenched social divisions" (2014: 175).

The use of social media platforms is a part of development for many children and youth all over the world. Adult debates about the ways in which young people use social media tend to focus on the age that youth should be allowed to use particular sites and the potential for children and young people to be harmed and/or exploited by nefarious actors. These debates often miss the fact that some decisions are made by a law called COPPA (the Children's Online Privacy Protection Act) because most popular social media platforms are headquartered in the United States. This de facto acceptance of US law, and its effects internationally on the experiences children and youth can and cannot have online, is problematic. The law itself dates back to 1998, before any of the current platforms became widely used. Many young people (often with consent of their parents) ignore or do not read the terms and conditions of use and enforcement of who engages with social media is relatively lax. Finally, although adult discussions of the use of social media amongst young people tends to focus on privacy, boyd (2014) remind us that youth often strongly disagree with the concept of "privacy" as constructed by older generations.

Social support is frequently listed as the biggest benefit to use of social networking for all age groups. The social support of one's peers is obviously important for the development of children and youth, and so it is important to consider the ways in which social media interacts with social support. Dunne, Lawlor, and Rowley (2010) found, in part, that social media and online affordances offered a space for young people to work out how to manage their identities and negotiate relationships without some of the pressures of face-to-face interactions. In a study by Radovic et al. (2016), adolescent participants who struggled with depression reported that finding positive content (images, quotations, etc.) online could be particularly helpful. Participants also highlighted the value of joining online social groups aimed at supporting others who had experienced challenges to their mental health (Radovic et al. 2016). Wang and Edwards (2016) built on the idea that online spaces offer a chance to practice identity and relationship development for young people, but went further to outline some of the ways in which social media is used to augment existing social capital between young people.

Often, though, the history of the development of the technologies underpinning social media go under-examined in consideration of the effects of social media on the development of children and youth. Most of the features of major social media platforms, such as the "Like" or "Favorite" buttons, and the ability to repost existing content with or without additional modifications, comes from internet message boards that were created in the late 1990s and early 2000s. These message boards, which included *amezou* (First Channel) and 2chan, 4chan, and their subsequent iterations, were founded on principles of anonymous posting and letting posts rise in popularity based on "up-voting." As Beran (2019) points out, the purpose of these boards was to share content and determine the merits of the content via anonymous members. Many of the memes shared via email originated in one of these spaces (LOLCats, for example). A significant amount of content, also voted on, featured horrific imagery, pornography, evidence of cyber-bullying, and so forth. Beran notes:

> As for-profit social media began to replace open-source message boards, social media companies were particularly interested in co-opting memes. Sites like Facebook transitioned from voyeuristic quasi-dating sites to content aggregators with ranked 4chan-style feeds ... [And now] Twitter users compete with one another to elaborate on new memes while generating

an endless flow of gibbering nonsense, as if it were 4chan in 2007. And users in Facebook and Instagram groups have replicated much of what 4chan once was *using their real names*.

(2019: 62; emphasis added)

One of the key differences in the for-profit social media platforms, then, is that users often (but not always) use their real names to produce the same kinds of content that was once anonymous and far less available. A small subset of youth culture was involved in the creation of an original technological platform for online discussions that has since been co-opted by large corporations that manage widely used products. This particular version of youth culture was both a part of and inspired by ideas of "tuning out" and living completely online. Beran (2019) argues that tuning out can lead to nihilism, which in extreme cases leads to a sense that the future has already been destroyed by the behavior of adult populations.

The social media platforms in wide use today, including but not limited to Facebook, Instagram, and Twitter, offer new spaces for performances of privacy for youth cultures in particular. Although adult populations tend to focus on the ideas of safety and protection for children and youth online, digital sociologists have argued that the concepts of the private and the public have fundamentally changed and that we should pay considerably more attention to these changes in research on the development of children and youth. In the study by Radovic et al. (2016) cited earlier, for example, participants were also quick to point out the challenges they faced in using social media: sharing risky behaviors, bullying, sharing negative updates with great frequency, making detrimental comparisons of themselves to others, and encountering triggering content. These challenges are all inextricably linked to the negotiations of new public and private spaces—what was once considered private and ephemeral can now easily be accessible to various publics, often without consideration for the consequences to self or to others.

Finally, greater attention also needs to be paid to the role of the history of technology in the creation of spaces for the "digital" child. Social media platforms, widely used by children and youth with access to technology, are grounded in technologies that encourage particular kinds of behaviors. Often these behaviors are performative and reinforce existing divides in societies. As Leurs noted: "Contemporary digital culture remains power-ridden, which urges us to reconsider the early notion of the digital divide; more attention is also needed for the empowerment users experience when negotiating digital inequalities and hierarchies" (2016: 61). Instead of the problematic rhetoric of the digital divide in the digital "natives" debate—a debate without research merit—we believe it is crucial to explore the power divides in digital culture and in access to digital devices, platforms, and infrastructures.

CONCLUSION: LEARNING, HUMAN DEVELOPMENT, AND THE "IDEAL" CHILD

The nineteenth century brought with it the notion of an "ideal child"—one who is innocent and unconcerned with the trials and tribulations of adulthood. Although this idea seems outdated and particularly Eurocentric nowadays, it is not hard to see how an idealized notion of childhood continues to pervade and shape societal expectations of learning, human development, the structure of childhood, and the agency of children themselves. In many ways, the structures—those rules and resources such as compulsory schools, the linguistic nation-state, and the technological infrastructures of childhood—reported in our three case studies were, at least tacitly, developed to support the belief in an idealized childhood. The fervent enthusiasm that adult society has for children remaining in school is clear when one looks at adult reactions to striking pupils—regardless of whether they were protesting the conditions of their learning or their concern for global events. Schools were structures that supported what children and youth were supposed to be doing and, as we saw from the second case study, most modern schools were also founded on a rhetoric of protecting children from the negative cognitive and behavioral effects of speaking more than one language. Finally, our discussion of the digital child reveals the ways in society is concerned with how online structures support existing social structures in the maintenance of an ideal childhood. The example of the "promposal" provides a significant illustration of the ways in which social grammars are often unproblematically translated to online spaces. In their retrospective critique of the sociological "turn" that created what is now thought of as "childhood studies," Tishdall and Punch concluded, in part, that "a focus on relationships can shed light on the complexities and interconnections of childhoods in a globalising world" (2012: 260). It is for this reason that we highlighted some of the details of the concept of agency at the beginning of the chapter, taking on board the idea that agential behaviors can be both historically laden and look to the future. For example, striking schoolchildren learned about collective action from adults and then took action of their own in an attempt to change their futures—what Emirbayer and Mische (1998) referred to as a practical-evaluative agency. Conceptualising children and youth as plurilingual rather than mono-, bi-, or multilingual challenges researchers and educators to attend to the personal histories and life experiences of young learners (Emirbayer and Mische 1998: 971). Once again, linguistic repertoires invite iterative agency, grounded in home language practices, but also encourage young people to imagine how they might form their identities (a projective agency) given the complexities of their experiences via different languages. The tensions between agency and relationships is certainly clear in a consideration of a digital child, in which the habitus of privacy and publics imposed by adult society seems to bear little resemblance to how children and youth wish to engage with imagined possibilities online.

Throughout this chapter, we have called attention to particular challenges to learning and human development faced by children and youth. Although our work has necessarily required both sociological and linguistic analyses, we have deliberately chosen history as the discipline that drove our considerations. While we concur with the recent calls to move beyond a structure–agency divide in understanding experiences of childhood, we also feel it is important to historicize the discussions and debates. Consider, for example, the continuous attempts to conceptualize children as less capable others—less capable of engaging in civic action, less capable of negotiating linguistic landscapes, and less capable of mediating their lives online. We believe that the historiographies contained in this chapter offer ample evidence that the history of ideas about children and youth are often overlooked in the mainstream educational discourse on learning and human development.

REFERENCES

Association of School and College Leaders (ASCL) (2019), "Climate Change Protest," February. Available online: https://www.ascl.org.uk/Help-and-Advice/Leadership-and-governance/Health,-safety-and-safeguarding/Climate-change-protest (accessed May 24, 2022).

Baker, Colin ([1993] 2006), *Foundations of Bilingualism and Bilingual Education*, 4th edn., Clevedon: Multilingual Matters.

Barton, Geoff (2019), "The Climate Strikes Threaten the Safety of our Pupils," *TES*, February 15. Available online: https://www.tes.com/news/climate-strikes-threaten-safety-our-pupils (accessed May 24, 2022).

Beran, Dale (2019), *It Came from Something Awful: How a Toxic Troll Army Accidentally Memed Donald Trump into Office*, New York: All Points Books.

Bereiter, Carl and Siegfried Engelmann (1966), *Teaching Disadvantaged Children in the Preschool*, Englewood Cliffs, NJ: Prentice-Hall.

Billiez, Jacqueline (1992), "Le 'parler véhiculaire interethnique' de groupes d'adolescents en milieu urbain, in Actes du colloque de Dakar," in Robert Chaudenson (ed.), *Des langues et des villes*, 117–26, Paris: Didier-Érudition.

Bloch, Marianne N., Devorah Kennedy, Theodora Lightfoot, and Dar Weyenberg (2006), "Introduction: Education and the Global/Local Construction of the Universal, Modern, and Globalized Child, School, and Nation," in Marianne N. Bloch, Devorah Kennedy, Theodora Lightfoot, and Dar Weyenberg (eds.), *The Child in the World/the World in the Child: Education and the Configuration of a Universal, Modern, and Globalized Childhood*, 3–17, New York: Macmillan.

Block, David (2003), *The Social Turn in Second Language Acquisition*, Edinburgh: Edinburgh University Press.

Bloomfield, Leonard (1933), *Language*, New York: Holt.

Bourdieu, Pierre and Jean-Claude Passeron (1964), *Les héritiers. Les étudiants et la culture*, Paris: Les Éditions de Minuit.

Bourdieu, Pierre and Jean-Claude Passeron (1970), *La Reproduction. Éléments d'une théorie du système d'enseignement*, Paris: Les Éditions de Minuit.

boyd, danah (2008), "Taken out of Context: American Teen Sociality in Networked Publics," Ph.D. diss., unpublished, University of California, Berkeley.

boyd, danah (2014), *It's Complicated: The Social Lives of Networked Teens*, New Haven, CT: Yale University Press.

British Broadcasting Corporation (BBC) (2003), "School Children March Against War," March 20. Available online: http://news.bbc.co.uk/1/hi/education/2867923. stm (accessed May 24, 2022).

Bullock, Cecile (in press), "Migrants' Identities in Multilingual Cities: Plurilingualism as Transformative Social Asset," in Linda Fisher and Wendy Ayres-Bennett (eds.), *Multilingualism and Identity: Interdisciplinary Perspectives*, Cambridge: Cambridge University Press.

Canagarajah, Suresh and Ubduja Liynage (2012), "Lessons from Pre-colonial Multilingualism," in Marilyn Martin-Jones, Adrian Blackledge, and Angela Creese (eds.), *The Routledge Handbook of Multilingualism*, 49–65, London: Routledge.

Chaudron, Stéphane (2015), *Young Children (0–8) and Digital Technology: A Qualitative Exploratory Study Across Seven Countries*, Report EUR 27052. Available online: https://op.europa.eu/en/publication-detail/-/publication/1f8b73cc-d900-406a-927c-0f8c0f202ed4/language-en (accessed May 24, 2022).

Conteh, Jean and Gabriela Meier, eds. (2014), *The Multilingual Turn in Education: Opportunities and Challenges*, Clevedon, UK: Multilingual Matters.

Cox, Laurence and Alf G. Nilsen (2007), "Social Movements Research and the 'Movement of Movements': Studying Resistance to Neoliberal Globalisation," *Sociology Compass*, 1 (2): 424–42.

Crouch, David (2018), "The Swedish 15-year-old Who's Cutting Class to Fight the Climate Crisis," *The Guardian*, September 1. Available online: https://www. theguardian.com/science/2018/sep/01/swedish-15-year-old-cutting-class-to-fight-the-climate-crisis (accessed May 24, 2022).

Cummins, Jim (2000), *Language, Power and Pedagogy: Bilingual Children in the Crossfire*, Clevedon, UK: Multilingual Matters.

Cummins, Jim (2007), "Rethinking Monolingual Instructional Language Strategies in Multilingual Classroom," *Canadian Journal of Applied Linguistics*, 10 (2): 221–40.

Cunningham, Steve and Michael Lavalette (2004), "'Active Citizens' or 'Irresponsible Truants'? School Student Strikes against the War," *Critical Social Policy*, 24 (2): 255–69.

Cunningham, Steve and Michael Lavalette (2016), *Schools Out! The Hidden History of Britain's School Student Strikes*, London: Bookmarks Publications.

Dabène, Louise and Jacqueline Billiez (1987), "Le parler des jeunes issus de l'immigration," in G. Vermès and J. Boutet (eds.), *France, pays multilingue*, vol. 2, 62–77, Paris: L'Harmattan.

Department for Education (2019), "Elective Home Education: Departmental Guidance for Local Authorities," last modified April 2019. Available online: https://www.gov. uk/government/publications/elective-home-education (accessed May 24, 2022).

Deprez, Christine (1994), *Les enfants bilingues: langues et familles*, Paris: Didier-Crédif.

Doise, Willem and Gabriel Mugny (1981), *Le développement social de l'intelligence*, Paris: InterÉditions.

Dunne, Áine, Margaret-Anne Lawlor, and Jennifer Rowley (2010), "Young People's Use of Online Social Networking Sites: A Uses and Gratifications Perspective," *Journal of Research in Interactive Marketing*, 4 (1): 46–58.

Emilsson, Kajsa, Hakan Johansson, and Magnus Wennerhag (2020), "Frame Disputes or Frame Consensus? 'Environment' or 'Welfare' First Amongst Climate Strike Protesters," *Sustainability*, 12 (3): 882.

Emirbayer, Mustafa and Ann Mische (1998), "What is Agency?" *American Journal of Sociology*, 103 (4): 962–1023.

Escudé, Pierre, ed. (2016), *Autour des travaux de Jules Ronjat, 1913–2013. Unité et diversité des langues Théorie et pratique de l'acquisition bilingue et de l'intercompréhension*, Paris: Edition des archives contemporaines.

Fishman, Joshua A. (1967), "Bilingualism With and Without Diglossia; Diglossia with and Without Bilingualism," *Journal of Social Issues*, 23 (2): 29–38.

Foucault, Michel (1971), *L'ordre du discours*, Paris: Gallimard.

Frost, E.D. (2003), "Bilingualism or Dyslexia- Language Difference or Language Disorder?" in Lindsay Peer and Gavin Reid (eds.), *Multilingualism, Literacy and Dyslexia: A Challenge for Educators*, 190–9, London: Routledge.

García, Ofelia (2009), *Bilingual Education in the 21st Century: A Global Perspective*, Malden, MA: Wiley/Blackwell.

García, Ofelia and Ricardo Otheguy (2020), "Plurilingualism and Translanguaging: Commonalities and divergences," *International Journal of Bilingual Education and Bilingualism*, 23 (1): 17–35.

Giddens, Anthony (1979), *Central Problems in Social Theory: Action, Structure, and Contradiction in Social Analysis*, Berkeley: University of California Press.

Goffman, Erving (1959), *The Presentation of Self in Everyday Life*, New York: Anchor Books.

Gogolin, Ingrid (1997), "The 'monolingual habitus' as the Common Feature in Teaching in the Language of the Majority in Different Countries," *Per Linguam*, 13 (2): 38–49. https://doi.org/10.5785/13-2-187.

Grant, Madeleine (2019), "Can We Please Stop Garlanding Children for Being Wrong?" *The Telegraph*, May 16. Available online: https://www.telegraph.co.uk/news/2019/03/16/can-please-stop-garlanding-children-wrong/ (accessed May 24, 2022).

Grigg, Russell (2003), "The Origins and Significance of the School Strikes in South Wales, 1911," *Local Historian*, 33 (3) (August): 133–47.

Grosjean, François (1984), *Life with two Languages – An Introduction to Bilingualism*, Cambridge, MA: Harvard University Press.

Haugen, Einer (1953), *The Norwegian Language in America: A Study of Bilingual Behavior*, Philadelphia: University of Pennsylvania Press.

Helsper, Ellen J. and Rebecca Eynon (2010), "Digital Natives: Where is the Evidence?" *British Educational Research Journal*, 36 (3): 503–20.

Hilbert, M. (2016), "The Bad News is that the Digital Access Divide is Here to Stay: Domestically Installed Bandwidths Among 172 Countries for 1986–2014," *Telecommunications Policy*, 40 (6): 561–81.

Humphries, Stephen (1981), "School Strikes: Parents and Pupils Protest," in *Hooligans or Rebels: An Oral History of Working-Class Childhood and Youth (1889–1939)*, 90–120, Oxford: Basil Blackwater.

Hymes, Dell H. (1966), "Two Types of Linguistic Relativity," in William Bright (ed.), *Sociolinguistics*, 114–58, The Hague: Mouton.

Iraq War Day X: The Largest School Strikes in UK History (2015), [Film] Dir. Katya Nasim, Independent. Available online: https://www.stopwar.org.uk/article/iraq-war-day-x-the-largest-school-strikes-in-uk-history/ (accessed May 24, 2022).

Lahire, Bernard (2001), *L'homme Pluriel*, Paris: Armand Colin.

Lantolf, James P. (1994), *Sociocultural Theory and Second Language Learning*, Oxford: Oxford University Press.

Laurie, S.S. (1890), *Lectures on Language and Linguistic Method in School*, Cambridge: Cambridge University Press.

Leung, Constant and Guadalupe Valdés (2019), "Translanguaging and the Transdisciplinary Framework for Language Teaching and Learning in a Multilingual World," *Modern Language Journal*, 103 (2): 348–70.

Leurs, Koen (2016), "Digital Divides in the Era of Widespread Internet Access: Migrant Youth Negotiating Hierarchies in Digital Culture," in Michel Walrave, Koen Ponnet, Ellen Vanderhoven, Jacques Haers, and Barbara Segaert (eds.), *Youth 2.0: Social Media and Adolescence*, 61–78, Dordrecht: Springer.

Lewin-Jones, Jenny (2019), "Discourses of 'Internationalisation': A Multimodal Critical Discourse Analysis of University Marketing Webpages," *Research in Post-Compulsory Education*, 24 (2): 208–30.

Livingstone, Sonia and Alicia Blum-Ross (2017), "Researching Children and Childhood in the Digital Age," in Pia Christensen and Allison James (eds.), *Research with Children: Perspective and Practices*, 3rd edn., 66–82, London: Routledge.

Lüdi, Georges and Bernard Py ([1986] 2003), *Être bilingue*, Bern: Peter Lang.

Marshall, Steven and Danièle Moore (2018), "Plurilingualism Amid the Panoply of Lingualisms: Addressing Critiques and Misconceptions in Education," *International Journal of Multilingualism*, 15 (1): 19–34.

May, Stephen, ed. (2014), *The Multilingual Turn: Implications for SLA, TESOL, and Bilingual Education*, London: Routledge.

Milroy, Lesley and Pieter Muysken, eds. (1995), *One Speaker, Two Languages: Cross-disciplinary Perspectives on Code-switching*, Cambridge: Cambridge University Press.

Murray, Craig, Katy Parry, Piers Robinson, and Peter Goddard (2008), "Reporting Dissent in Wartime: British Press, the Anti-War Movement and the 2003 Iraq War," *European Journal of Communication*, 23 (1): 7–27.

Norton Peirce, Bonny (1995), "Social Identity, Investment, and Language Learning," *TESOL Quarterly*, 29 (1): 9–31.

Pavlenko, Aneta and Adrian Blackledge, eds. (2004), *Negotiation of Identities in Multilingual Contexts: Bilingual Education and Bilingualism*, Clevedon, UK: Multilingual Matters.

Picardo, Enrica (2018), "Plurilingualism: Vision, Conceptualization, and Practices," in Peter Pericles Trifonas and Themistoklis Aravossitas (eds.), *Handbook of Research and Practice in Heritage Language Education*, 207–25, New York: Springer.

Picardo, Enrica and Angelica Galante (2018), "Plurilingualism and Agency in Language Education: The Role of Dramatic Action-Oriented Tasks," in Julie Choi and Sue Ollerhead (eds.), *Plurilingualism in Teaching and Learning: Complexities Across*, 147–64, London: Routledge.

Pichon, Edouard (1936), *Le développement psychique de l'enfant et de l'adolescent, évolution normale, pathologie, traitement. Manuel d'étude*, Paris: Masson.

Pinter, Rudolph and R. Keller (1922), "Intelligence Tests for Foreign Children," *Journal of Educational Psychology*, 13: 1–23.

Prensky, Mark (2001), "Digital Natives, Digital Immigrants Part 1," *On the Horizon*, 9 (5): 1–6.

Radovic, Ana, Theresa Gmelin, Bradley D. Stein, and Elizabeth Miller (2016), "Depressed Adolescents' Positive and Negative Use of Social Media," *Journal of Adolescence*, 55: 5–15.

Rampton, Ben (1995), *Crossing: Language and Ethnicity Among Adolescents*, London: Longman.

Richardson, John M. (2017), "The Promposal: Youth Expressions of Identity and 'Love' in the Digital Age," *Learning, Media and Technology*, 42 (1): 74–86.

Ronjat, Jules (1913), *Le Développement du langage observé chez un enfant bilingue*, Paris: Champion.

Rupert, Mark (2003), "Globalising Common Sense: A Marxian-Gramscian (Re-)Vision of the Politics of Governance/Resistance," *Review of International Studies*, 29: 181–98.

Sabatier, Cécile (2006), "Figures Identitaires des Elèves issus de la Migration Maghrébine à L'école Elémentaire en France," *Education et Francophonie*, 34 (1): 111–32.

Saer, David John (1923), "The Effects of Bilingualism on Intelligence," *British Journal of Psychology*, 14: 25–38.

Skutnabb-Kangas, Tove and Pertti Toukomaa (1976), *Teaching Migrant Children's Mothertongue and Learning the Language of the Host Country in the Context of the Sociocultural Situation of the Migrant Family*, Helsinki: The Finnish National Commission for UNESCO.

Speck, D. (2019), "Heads' Union Backs Pupils Strike Over Climate Change." *TES*, February 10. Available online: https://www.tes.com/news/heads-union-backs-pupils-strike-over-climate-change (accessed May 24, 2022).

Tabouret-Keller, A. (2016), "Le Bilinguisme en Procès du XIXe Siècle au Début du XXe Siècle: le Cas Rebelle de Jules Ronjat (1864–1925)," in Pierre Escudé (ed.), *Autour des travaux de Jules Ronjat, 1913–2013. Unité et Diversité des Langues Théorie et Pratique de L'acquisition Bilingue et de L'intercompréhension*, 29–42, Paris: Edition des archives contemporaines.

Tisdall, E. Kay M. and Samantha Punch (2012), "Not so 'New'? Looking Critically at Childhood Studies," *Children's Geographies*, 10 (3): 249–64.

UK Citizen Advisory Group (1998), *Education for Citizenship and the Teaching of Democracy in Schools* (The Crick Report), London: Qualifications and Curriculum Authority. Available online: https://www.teachingcitizenship.org.uk/sites/teachingcitizenship.org.uk/files/6123_crick_report_1998_0.pdf (accessed May 24, 2022).

Wang, Victoria and Simon Edwards (2016), "Strangers Are Friends I Haven't Met Yet: A Positive Approach to Young People's Use of Social Media," *Journal of Youth Studies*, 19 (9): 1204–19.

Weinreich, Uriel (1953), *Languages in Contact, Findings and Problems*, The Hague: Mouton.

Yashima, Tomoko (2013), "Agency in Second Language Acquisition," in Carol A. Chapelle (ed.), *The Encyclopedia of Applied Linguistics*, 1–7, Oxford: Blackwell Publishing.

CHAPTER SIX

Teaching and Teacher Education

The Interplay of Bureaucratic Rationalization and Occupational Professionalism

DOROTHEA ANAGNOSTOPOULOS AND JACK SCHNEIDER

At the beginning of the twenty-first century, concerns about teaching and teacher education moved to the center of global educational improvement efforts. Casting teachers as both villains and saviors of educational reform, policymakers in multiple nations sought to improve "teacher quality" by altering who enters the profession, how teachers are prepared, and how their work is evaluated (Goodwin 2021). Though apparently novel, efforts to improve public schools via reforms to the teaching profession have a long history.

This chapter examines such efforts within and across four eras in the United States: the late 1800s "system-building era," the early twentieth-century "Progressive era," the 1960s "postwar prosperity" years, and the early twenty-first-century "standards and accountability era." Rather than drawing specific attention to particular time periods, which are elastic at their margins, and which we define broadly, we are chiefly interested in identifying patterns and themes. Though we focus on the United States, the tensions identified across the historical periods pose fundamental questions relevant to all large-scale, publicly funded educational systems that serve students on an open-enrollment basis.

At the core of our analysis is an examination of the interplay between two key forces: bureaucratic rationalization and occupational professionalization. Policymakers, administrators, school boards, and public sector leaders have regularly attempted to improve schooling by defining, directing, and constraining teaching and teachers' work, often in the context of fiscal constraints. Teaching and teacher education, in other words, have occurred in the context of bureaucratic rationalization, or the coordination of teacher labor through hierarchical authority and control, designed to produce standardization and efficiency. Teacher licensure and evaluation systems are typical in this regard.

Teachers, however, have not been passive actors in this process. Pursuing their own personal, professional, and civic ambitions, they have shaped their work and its conditions. Decisions about whether to teach or how to organize instruction, for instance, generally have been made either exclusively or chiefly by individual teachers. Classroom teachers have also organized to advance the shared aim of occupational professionalization, or the collegial coordination of labor by skilled workers, who exchange specialized knowledge and competency for prestige and autonomy.

Rather than viewing bureaucratic rationalization and occupational professionalization as distinct and conflicting processes, we identify their concurrent influence, which manifests in several reoccurring themes. One such theme concerns how teachers' efforts to establish their professional status are often complicated by the professionalization efforts of other educators, especially educational administrators and university researchers, who have historically vied for authority over the knowledge and practice of teaching (Labaree 1992; Popkewitz 1994; Lagemann 1997). A second theme examines how government officials and policymakers have sought to limit teachers' autonomy and control over their work; whereas administrators and university researchers have limited teacher professionalism by asserting various jurisdictional claims, policy and political leaders have done so through the use of rules, guidelines, and procedures. Our third theme, alluded to earlier, highlights how teachers have actively navigated and challenged constraints on their professionalism to advance their own interests. Across all three themes, issues of gender and race shape the interplay of bureaucratic rationalization and occupational professionalization.

These themes, which emerge across all four time periods, complicate the story of teachers and teacher education in the United States. Rather than a slow evolution (Grant and Murray 2002), teachers' efforts to control their work and establish their professional status have taken a jagged path marked by collaboration and conflict with other educators, policymakers, reformers, and the public.

THE LATE NINETEENTH-CENTURY SYSTEM-BUILDING ERA

Who Taught

Though most teachers in the early years of white colonial settlement in North America were males, throughout the nineteenth century, women came to dominate the teaching force. Supported first by an early emphasis on "republican motherhood" and then by the mid-century "common school" movement's embrace of the ideology of domesticity, the feminization of teaching intensified throughout the latter half of the nineteenth century. During this time, leaders of the nation's nascent education system turned to women to fill the ranks of the expanding teaching force. These predominantly male administrative reformers viewed women as well suited for the subordinated role they imagined teachers playing in the school hierarchy (Tyack 1974). Hiring women additionally allowed administrators to contain costs while expanding schools—a significant concern in population-dense urban areas where immigration and industrialization fueled a growing demand for mass schooling (Strober and Lanford 1986). Between the 1870s and early 1900s, female teachers were paid 50 percent to 60 percent less than male teachers (Perlmann and Margo 2001). Ironically, the same administrative reformers who contributed so significantly to feminizing teaching would later bemoan the sparsity of male teachers as impeding the professionalization of teaching (Tyack 1974).

Administrative reformers also advanced a racial agenda. The teaching force in nineteenth-century urban public schools was more ethnically homogenous than the student body; school boards hired mostly native-born, English-speaking women (Leroux 2006). By the century's end, women from ethnic groups who could "pass" as white, particularly Jewish and Irish American women, began pursuing education through the public high schools, graduation from which often served as sufficient preparation for teaching. Still, racial segregation and prejudice prevented people of color from entering teaching in significant numbers (Strober and Lanford 1986: 216).

In segregated schools, the story was somewhat different. Though Northern white women and Southern white men and women taught in Black schools established after the Civil War, Black teachers constituted a disproportionately large number of these schools' teachers (Jones 1979; Buthart 2010). Though segregated schools were grounded in white racism, Blacks proudly embraced a predominantly Black teaching corps. The rise of Black teachers, particularly in the South, affirmed racial pride and freedom from white control (Fairclough 2004). During Reconstruction, schools became pillars of the Black community and Black teachers became important figures in the continued struggle for freedom (Siddle Walker 2005). Like the clergy, Black teachers were viewed by their communities as a critical source of racial uplift, as well as professionals who possessed knowledge of literacy and other subjects (Butchart 2010). Black teachers' professionalism, resting partly on increasing educational levels, both resembled and differed from the professionalism their white counterparts pursued.

How Teachers Were Trained

Prior to the late nineteenth century, there were no standards for entry into teaching. The chief gatekeepers for those seeking positions were local school boards, which tended to prioritize criteria such as the ability to maintain order (Sedlak 1989).

As historian Geraldine Clifford recounts, one aspiring teacher in Texas was asked three questions by the examination board: "What are your qualifications? What is your religious denomination? Do you play the piano?" (Clifford 2014: 177). Academic qualifications were minimal, often requiring only that teachers complete some schooling beyond the level they would teach (Labaree 2018).

This was, partly, a product of supply. In rural areas and the West, no formal training was available for most teachers. In the East, short-term teacher "institutes," rather than college- or university-based preparation, were the norm (Mattingly 1975). Minimal training was also a product of demand for teachers. As schools cropped up in new settlements, and as enrollments expanded, the need for new teachers often meant that anyone looking for work in the field could find it. As historian Donald Warren observed: "The opening of new schools and the frequent movement of teachers to new jobs or out of teaching altogether combined to create absolute shortages" (1985: 7). Pre-professional training, then, would have required not only an unnecessary expense but also an unnecessary delay of earned income.

As reformers worked to legitimize a nationwide system of common schools—in which teachers would be public employees paid with public funds—they sought to establish some minimal guarantee of quality and uniformity (Schneider 2018). As David Labaree writes: "When education shifted from an *ad hoc* and voluntaristic mode of delivery to a systematic and publicly sponsored form, teaching became a kind of public trust, which required systematic training and professional certification" (2018: 292). The bureaucratic response to teacher training was, partly, a means of legitimizing the use of public tax revenues to support universal schooling.

The first so-called normal school was established in Lexington, Massachusetts in 1839. By 1890, over 100 such institutions—academically equivalent, at the time, to high schools—had been established for the purpose of training teachers. Over the next two decades, the number of normal schools nearly doubled. But because the need for teachers continued to outstrip the number of trained teachers, it remained impossible to require training. Consequently, quality assurance was managed through the establishment of licensure exams. These tests varied widely in their nature and were often issued at both the state and local level.

To incentivize formal training, policy leaders in various states—twenty-eight by the turn of the century—began exempting normal school graduates from licensure tests (Cook 1921). This had little effect. According to David Tyack, in 1898, normal schools graduated no more than a quarter of new teachers (Tyack 1967). And, as Christine Ogren writes, "the academic curriculum was necessarily low-level, and the teacher-education curriculum was immature" (2005: 4). Still, it represented significant progress. Moreover, normal schools served women, unlike many other institutions, and also began to educate people of color (Butchart 2010).

How Teachers Were Evaluated

Prior to the late nineteenth century, though teachers exercised considerable autonomy within schoolhouse walls, community members visited classrooms to assess schoolhouse upkeep and alignment of content and instruction with community mores (Tracy 1995). In the absence of common or objective measures of teachers' effectiveness, educators were often assessed on personal characteristics such as morality and grooming. While visiting committees provided teachers suggestions intended to improve instruction, they more often simply fired a teacher who did not meet their expectations (Sedlak 1989).

School boards in rural districts would continue to appoint and dismiss teachers throughout the nineteenth century and into the twentieth. In city systems, however, superintendents began to manage the supervision of teachers. According to Jeffrey Glanz (1991), doing so was central to administrators' efforts to establish and assert their own professional status. City superintendents viewed supervision as a means of controlling a chaotic system of schooling and inculcating bureaucratic values. As they expanded their authority over a range of functions, including finances and the maintenance of new school buildings, superintendents positioned themselves as "teachers of teachers" who, unlike local school boards, possessed the expert knowledge necessary to improve the efficiency of poorly trained teachers (Tracy 1995). Superintendents visited individual teachers' classrooms to observe student recitations and evaluate teachers' content knowledge, ability to manage student behavior, and overall deportment (Glanz 1991: 14–15).

Though superintendents wrapped their supervisory practices in the language of science and expertise, they also viewed supervision as a means of imposing discipline, obedience, and order in schools (Fitzpatrick 1893; Glanz 1991). This was driven, partly, by the growing scale of urban districts. For example, in 1890, the city of Baltimore had two superintendents to oversee 1,200 teachers (Glanz 1991). Though superintendents asserted their authority over teacher supervision, they shifted much of their direct supervisory responsibilities to school principals and supervisors.

As teachers in city schools became increasingly subject to supervisors' personal prejudices and preferences, they complained that supervisors' criticism was "destructive and discouraging" and provided little basis for improvement (Brooks 1897). City teachers' federations organized against superintendents' expanding jurisdiction over teaching. Asserting their own professional status, the federations, often led by women teachers, demanded greater autonomy and respect, as well as better pay and pensions (Ogren 2005). Historian Wayne Urban describes how the New York City Teachers Association organized against superintendents usurping the community's role in hiring and supervising teachers in the mid-1890s (Urban 1976). Teachers asserted that they retained a degree of autonomy and closeness with their students and communities under the ward system that would be lost if superintendents, typically Anglo-Saxon and Protestant, gained the power to appoint and dismiss teachers (Urban 1976: 38). In the late 1890s, the Chicago Teachers Federation defeated a school reform bill promoted by William Rainey Harper, a prominent schoolman and president of the University of Chicago, that would have granted superintendents sole rights to hire and fire teachers (Goldstein 2014).

THE EARLY TWENTIETH-CENTURY PROGRESSIVE ERA

Who Taught

By 1920, fully 86 percent of teachers were women (Tyack 1974). Men continued to constitute a significant percentage of high school teachers and to be paid more than elementary school teachers. Teaching, however, had effectively become women's work.

Though organizationally subordinated within schools, female teachers began organizing to affect the growth of the school system, their role in it, and the educational reforms promulgated during this era (Urban 1976). Much of this happened within nascent teachers' unions. By the early twentieth century, female teachers comprised the majority of the National Education Association's (NEA) membership. They pushed NEA leaders to recognize their claims to better salaries, pensions, and tenure, and to redress the gendered authority structures of city school systems (Urban 2001; Goldstein 2014). The NEA created the Department of Classroom Teachers in 1912, fully constituting it in 1922, with the stated aim of securing "higher educational qualifications for teachers," greater teacher participation in school management, better pay, and greater employment security (Winn 1925: 563).

In the South, Black teachers continued to teach in segregated schools. In 1932, there were over 50,000 Black teachers in public elementary and high schools in seventeen Southern states and the District of Columbia; roughly 42,000 were women elementary teachers (Caliver 1935). During the early twentieth century, Black teachers, like their white counterparts, began organizing to promote their professional interests. Marginalized or excluded from white-dominated teacher associations such as the NEA and its Southern affiliates, Black teachers built their own associations. Black teachers in Southern states founded the National Colored Teachers Association in 1903, expanding it in 1907 to include white teachers teaching in Black schools and renaming it the National Association of Teachers in Colored Schools (NATCS) (Karpinski 2010). During the 1920s, the NATCS forged a relationship with the NEA to further Black teachers' professionalization. The NATCS and its later manifestation in the American

Teachers Association lobbied state legislatures to redress racial inequities in teachers' salaries and school facilities (Siddle Walker 2013).

Black teacher associations worked to preserve and promote education for Blacks in the South. As white Southerners reasserted their political power and disenfranchised Blacks, they seized control of the public school system that Black teachers had been instrumental in building (Anderson 1988), severely underfunding Black schools (Fultz 1995a) and often violently attacking Black schools and teachers. Siddle Walker documents how, as Black teachers used their associations to challenge educational inequalities, the associations helped form an organizational infrastructure for the civil rights movements of the 1950s and 1960s (Siddle Walker 2005, 2013).

How Teachers Were Trained

By the 1920s, nearly all teachers were required to earn a license. Unlike the previous period when only a small minority of educators were prepared on college and university campuses, many would-be teachers of this period sought entrance into the profession via a certified training program. Although alternatives such as licensure exams still existed in many states, they were rapidly being phased out (Frazier 1935). A new corps of administrators, oriented toward efficiency and determined to advance a "science" of education, worked tirelessly to build what they viewed as rational systems of training and licensure (Angus 2001: 15).

Bureaucracy, however, was not the only force driving teachers into college- and university-based programs. By the 1920s, most normal schools had been transformed into teachers' colleges and were undergoing a second transformation into state colleges (Orgen 2005). According to David Tyack, eighty-eight such conversions took place between 1911 and 1930, endowing these institutions with a newfound prestige (Tyack 1967). A university diploma was attractive to would-be teachers, particularly women and people of color for whom access to such credentials had long been limited. Perhaps more important was the pay they would earn in larger urban districts, which prized teachers with formal training.

The actual content of college- and university-based training remained fairly basic. No standards for accreditation existed, and only a handful of states required aspiring teachers to major or minor in particular content areas. Instead, the period was characterized by a broad faith in the power of higher education, which remained a fairly exclusive reserve. Through the early 1940s, only approximately 5 percent of Americans attended even a single year of college (Snyder 1993).

Efforts were made during this period to develop a coherent pre-professional curriculum. Classes in pedagogy were a norm by the 1920s, and some programs began to differentiate teacher training by school subjects. Many college- and university-based programs also had associated "practice schools" where novice teachers could train with actual students (Frazier 1935). Nevertheless, demand for teachers continued to outstrip supply; only roughly half of states could set high school graduation as a minimum prerequisite for licensure. And college- and university-based training remained far more common among high school teachers and teachers in urban districts than among elementary school teachers and teachers in rural districts (Warren 1985).

Thus, structural growth and more universal training remained more central to the work of reformers than anything about the science of pedagogy. This was particularly true among Black communities in the South, which maintained insufficient access to high schools and higher education. As historian Michael Fultz writes, "An insufficiently trained, low-paid Black teaching corps was both an integral component of, and a natural outcome of, the state-sanctioned racist suppression of African American education" (1995b: 206).

How Teachers Were Evaluated

As the administrative tasks of running expanding school systems multiplied, administrators increasingly rationalized their supervisory practices. Drawing on emerging research in educational psychology, as well as from popular business productivity methods, superintendents began to use standardized rating schemes as measures of teacher efficacy. The first rating scales appeared around 1915, and several hundred were available by 1930 (Good and Mulryan 1990). Additionally, as standardized tests became more popular and more available, administrators also began to turn to achievement scores as ostensibly objective measures of teacher skill (Sears 1921). Though classroom visits by administrators remained popular, supervisors also wrote descriptive reports, employed checklists, or graded teachers on lists of qualities associated with instruction, discipline, professional interest, and personal characteristics such as character, appearance, and manner (Boyce 1922).

Beginning in the 1920s and 1930s, supervisors, convinced of the value of the science of education through their professional training, advocated for more cooperative approaches that invited input from teachers (Clifford and Guthrie 1988; Tanner and Tanner 1987). Calls for "cooperative" and "democratic" supervision further reflected prevailing concerns about the preservation of democracy, which emerged during and in the wake of the First World War (Marzano, Frontier, and Livingston 2011). They also represented efforts by supervisors, eager to establish their own professional standing, to align themselves with teachers while asserting their jurisdiction over teaching (Glanz 1991).

For their part, teachers organized against rating and evaluation schemes, viewing them as administrators' efforts to encroach on their work. They criticized supervisors as lacking training, providing harsh criticism, and being undemocratic (Hill 1919). Additionally, teachers viewed administrators' use of ratings to determine pay as especially threatening to teachers' professional claims of specialized training, jurisdictional authority over teaching, and individual autonomy. In a 1915 presentation to NEA's Department of Classroom Teachers, Ava L. Parrott, a New York City school teacher, detailed efforts by the city's Professional Teachers' Association to abolish a teacher rating scheme promoted by district superintendents (Parrott 1915). Parrott argued that the rating of teachers by the superintendents undermined teachers' efforts to establish themselves as professionals. Asking, "would anyone for a moment suggest that 'standardization' would be possible with physicians, lawyers, ministers?" she concluded: "The absurdity is made apparent there at once" (1915: 1170). Along with credentials, educational degrees, and entrance examinations, Parrott proposed compulsory parent observations of teachers and teachers' collective responsibility for helping weak teachers and identifying inefficient teachers for dismissal.

THE 1960S AND THE POSTWAR PROSPERITY ERA

Who Taught

During the 1960s, women continued to comprise the majority of teachers, though their overall representation did decline moderately—to roughly 70 percent of the workforce (Sedlak and Schlossman 1986). Unlike previous eras, many female teachers were married women. A postwar baby boom, supported by a pronatalist climate and increased anxiety about shifting gender roles led to a dramatic increase in the number of married female teachers; in 1960, they comprised just over two-thirds of female teachers (Donahue 2002).

The percentage of male teachers increased to roughly 30 percent, propelled by federal educational assistance through the GI Bill, as well as by rising teacher salaries that attracted working-class males (Sedlak and Schlossman 1986). Though the women's rights movement and teachers' growing frustration with city schools' increased bureaucratization fueled a growing assertiveness among all teachers, male teachers in the 1960s and early 1970s were influential in the movement to secure collective bargaining rights (Murphy 1990; Urban 2001).

The 1960s and 1970s represented the peak of teachers' collective power, especially in large cities. Though strikes remained illegal in many states, tens of thousands of teachers participated in work stoppages during the period. Across this period, there were over 100 teacher strikes nationwide; at least 1,000 school districts experienced a strike or threatened strike (Murphy 1990). During this period, teachers won salary and benefit increases and secured uniform salary schedules that ended gender and racial pay inequities. The NEA, historically reluctant to align itself with the AFT's more aggressive tactics, eventually partnered with the AFT to defend teachers' collective bargaining rights and fight anti-union efforts (Murphy 1990).

Though teachers, overall, made gains in salary and working conditions throughout the 1960s and 1970s, Black teachers in the South experienced massive job losses (Ladson-Billings 2004). The Supreme Court's landmark *Brown v. Board of Education* (1954) decision mandated the racial desegregation of students in the nation's segregated schools; it did not address the integration of teachers. Prior to 1954, approximately 82,000 Black teachers taught two million Black children in US public schools (Madkins 2011). In the wake of *Brown*, white school officials closed Black schools, bussed Black students to white schools, and dismissed roughly 40,000 Black teachers across seventeen Southern states (Ethridge 1979). Throughout the 1970s, despite continued court-ordered desegregation, Southern school districts also reduced the pool of Black educators by abolishing tenure laws, dismissing teachers without cause, and reassigning Black teachers to white schools where they faced racial hostilities (Tillman 2004).

How Teachers Were Trained

Until the mid-twentieth century, education professors at colleges and universities, bureaucrats inside state education departments, big city superintendents, and teachers were unified in their push for training-based professionalism. By 1960, they had pressed states to adopt the bachelor's degree as a minimum qualification for elementary school teachers, eliminated the certification exam, and created a national accrediting body—the National Council for the Accreditation of Teacher Education (NCATE)—to control standards. As a result, teachers followed professionals from other fields— particularly law, medicine, and the clergy—in shifting occupational preparation out of apprenticeships and into college and university classrooms. For their part, the public was reassured by the fact that teachers remained the best educated members of their communities.

Over the period of less than a century, bureaucratic licensure mandates, coupled with university-based training, had led to massive increases in the education of future teachers. The overwhelming majority of new teachers by the second half of the twentieth century were college graduates who had received at least a year of professionally focused training. In the eyes of critics, however, this came at a steep cost. As with college- and university-based training in other fields, teacher preparation often emphasized theory over practice. An even riper target for critique of the credential system, however, was the presumed emphasis on form over function—the completion of a certified program, rather than an assessment of teaching skill (Koerner 1963). And licensure requirements kept many capable people out of the profession, specifically those who had not taken the requisite coursework.

Meanwhile, teachers themselves began to abandon the consensus-driven approach that had for so long made college- and university-based training a policy priority. From the late nineteenth century through the 1960s, teachers worked in concert with members of the education establishment to advance the aim of professionalism. In the 1960s, the NEA and the AFT shifted away from earlier drives for professionalism, instead emphasizing collective bargaining for higher wages and better working conditions. As a result, teacher attention was drawn away from pre-professional training and, as historian David Angus writes, "made it difficult for other elements of the profession, such as education school faculty and state department staffers, to maintain a united front with [teachers]" (2001: 32).

After the dissolution of the long-standing teacher education consensus, and in response to the ostensible shortcomings of bureaucratically managed professionalization efforts, many policy leaders began to support alternatives. Notably, the long-standing aim of professionalizing teaching through college- and university-based preparation was still a work in progress. Schools of education, for instance, had only just begun to wrestle with sociocultural questions and the science of cognition, and were in the process of reimagining relationships with teacher placement sites and departments across the university—work that would extend across the next several decades.

At the same time, so much had been achieved on the bureaucratic front, chiefly through licensure standards, that it would have been easy to view the teacher education establishment as a fully realized system. Taking aim at what seemed a bloated and lumbering bureaucracy, reformers sought to restore some of the flexibility of earlier periods. They pushed for alternatives to licensure, such as the Masters of Arts in Teaching program, which functioned as a curricular "add-on" to traditional liberal arts training, the National Teacher Corps, a "service" approach modeled on the Peace Corps and funded by the federal government, and a variety of competency-based teacher education projects (Schneider 2011). Such programs set the stage for the so-called alternative certification movement of the 1980s and 1990s, which posed a major threat to college- and university-based teacher training.

How Teachers Were Evaluated

The 1960s witnessed the rise of "clinical supervision." Facing growing public criticism fueled by expanding school enrollments and budgets, superintendents increasingly turned to social science research on organizational and administrative processes to guide and justify their decisions. Clinical supervision, in intent, emphasized collaboration; the teacher and supervisor identified effective instructional practices through jointly analyzing holistic observations of teaching. In practice, however, administrators used the observations and conferences of clinical supervision for evaluating teachers (Marzano, Frontier, and Livingston 2011). District evaluation forms in use during the 1960s largely resembled prior rating schemes. Many assessed teachers' "instructional skill," "personal qualities," and "executive ability," based on evaluators' observations of the classroom environment. Many also assessed teachers on grooming, personality, and record-keeping (Stemnock 1969).

While evaluation practices in this period echoed Progressive era practices, the balance of power between teachers and administrators had shifted. Teachers' newly won collective bargaining rights provided protections from arbitrary dismissals by local school boards and administrators, significantly strengthening tenure protections. Teacher contracts delineated grievance procedures, with some stipulating teachers' access to their personnel files and notice of evaluation results (Stuart and Goldschmidt 1986). And contracts governing rating and observation procedures both rationalized teacher evaluation and constrained administrative discretion (McDonnell and Pascal 1979).

Though collective bargaining enabled teachers to assert more influence over teacher evaluation in their districts, state accountability pressures were mounting. Growth in teacher salaries spurred public concerns about value returned for public funds (Good and Mulryan 1990). In 1971, for instance, California passed the Stull Act, requiring the use of student achievement in evaluating teachers. Teacher evaluation would continue to revolve around classroom observations into the 1980s (Tracy 1995). Legislation such as the Stull Act, however, foreshadowed the accountability-driven teacher evaluation systems of the early twenty-first century.

THE EARLY TWENTY-FIRST-CENTURY STANDARDS AND ACCOUNTABILITY ERA

Who Teaches

In the first decades of the twenty-first century, the teacher workforce has remained both remarkably stable and increasingly uncertain. In 2017, women comprised roughly 76 percent of US teachers, including 89 percent of elementary school teachers (National Center for Education Statistics 2020). As in prior eras, most teachers (roughly 80 percent) are white. While the percentage of Latinx teachers grew to 9 percent of the teaching force by 2017, the percentage of Black teachers declined from 12 percent in 1970 to 7 percent (King 1993; National Center for Education Statistics 2020). The teaching force also remains segregated. Teachers of color remain more likely than white teachers to teach in under-resourced schools enrolling high percentages of students of color—schools where teacher turnover rates outpace the national average (Frankenberg 2008; Ingersoll, May, and Collins 2017).

While the teaching force has remained overwhelmingly white, students attending the nation's public schools have become increasingly diverse. Between 2000 and 2017, the percentage of white students decreased from 61 percent to 48 percent. While the percentage of Black students has remained largely unchanged, Latinx students have increased from 16 percent to 27 percent (National Center for Education Statistics 2020). Given these demographics, and growing evidence of the positive effects teachers of color have on the achievement of students of color, policymakers and educators of the period have targeted efforts on recruiting and retaining teachers of color (Villegas and Irvine 2010; Carver-Thomas and Darling-Hammond 2017; Gershenson et al. 2018).

Despite these long-running gender and racial trends, the number of teachers has increased dramatically. While student enrollment grew by 24 percent from 1987 to 2015, the number of teachers increased by 65 percent over the same time period (Ingersoll, Merrill, and Stuckey 2018). At the same time, the teacher attrition rate rose from 5 percent to 8 percent, creating a need for roughly 90,000 additional teachers each year (Carver-Thomas and Darling-Hammond 2017; Ingersoll and Collins 2017). Meanwhile, the number of people pursuing education degrees or completing teacher preparation programs dropped significantly (Garcia and Weiss 2019). By the early twenty-first century, the nation faced not only a growing racial divide among its teachers and students, but also a looming teacher shortage.

How Teachers Are Trained

After the 1960s, the coalition supporting the advancement of teacher professionalism through college- and university-based training began to unravel. Whereas bureaucratic rationalization had for several generations been framed as a solution to the perceived shortcomings in teachers and teaching, a new consensus began to emerge among US policy elites: that bureaucratic rationalization was the *problem* (Baker and Dickerson 2006). Seeing deregulation as a solution, leaders in and outside of government began to push for alternate certification programs that extended and further decentralized efforts of the 1960s.

The proliferation of alternate routes lowered barriers to entry and wound back the clock to an earlier era. And for some policy elites, de-professionalization was a conscious aim (Milner 2013). Envisioning teaching as short-term work, rather than a profession, they imagined a system guided not by bureaucracy and professionalism, but by entrepreneurialism and innovation. In the growing charter school sector, for instance, models arose that presumed a shorter commitment to teaching and adjusted training expectations accordingly.

If future teachers would only remain in classrooms for a short period of time, many charter networks reasoned that traditional teacher preparation was an unnecessary barrier to entry. In response, several of them banded together to create the Relay Graduate School of Education, which trains unlicensed teachers to employ a discrete set of classroom practices designed to improve student standardized test scores.

This is not to say that teacher education stopped evolving in the late twentieth and early twenty-first centuries. College- and university-based programs improved clinical experiences, developed reflection models and mentoring structures, strengthened content preparation, and worked to create programmatic coherence (Schneider 2018). Yet, growing efforts to treat teaching as a trade instead of a profession, worked to shift training away from college and university campuses and back to something closer to apprenticeship.

How Teachers Are Evaluated

The policy elites pushing for deregulation of the teaching profession simultaneously advanced efforts during this period to introduce new bureaucratic processes for teacher evaluation. Calls for accountability that emerged and intensified throughout the 1970s and 1980s led states in the 1990s to require schools to meet performance indicators, most prominently student achievement scores on state assessments. The passage of the federal No Child Left Behind Act (NCLB) in 2002 made test-based accountability universal across all fifty states. NCLB assumed that attaching high-stakes incentives to standardized performance indicators would compel recalcitrant local actors, including teachers, to alter and improve their practices (Mintrop and Sunderman 2013).

In 2009, the federal government launched the $4.35 billion Race to the Top (RTT) initiative. RTT used evaluation to intensify accountability pressures on teachers. RTT awarded states, reeling financially from the 2008 Great Recession, competitive grants to raise teacher performance standards, create large-scale information systems linking student achievement to individual teachers, and implement teacher evaluation systems that incorporated student achievement scores into teachers' ratings, compensation, and dismissal. Though only a few states received RTT funds, by 2015, nearly all states had enacted these changes.

Most contentiously, new evaluation systems incorporated value-added measures (VAMs) of individual teachers' contributions to student learning. VAMs were built on sophisticated statistical models and relied on large-scale, digital informational systems created by an array of actors outside of public schools, including education researchers, technical consultants and philanthropic institutions (Anagnostopoulos, Routledge, and Jacobsen 2013). As VAMs were integrated into teacher evaluation systems, these actors shaped which aspects of teaching and teachers' work counted.

These new evaluation systems represent a high-water mark for bureaucratic management. Though some districts have developed systems collaboratively with local teachers' unions (Donaldson and Papay 2017), evaluation in others are under state jurisdiction and not subject to collective bargaining (Pogodzinski, Umpstead, and Witt 2015). Some evaluation systems also include provisions requiring teachers to cede tenure protections (Hazi 2017). The evaluation systems thus rationalized teaching by subordinating teachers and their associations to multiple administrative measures and casting them as opposing public accountability.

Teachers waged several lawsuits contesting the use of VAMs and denouncing the violation of their collective bargaining rights (Sawchuk 2015: 15). In places such as New York City, teachers joined with parent and community anti-testing groups to protest the use of standardized test scores in evaluation systems. Individual teachers also used news and social media to publicly critique evaluation systems (Dunn 2018; Anagnostopoulos, Wilson, and Charles-Harris 2020). In 2015, the federal Every Student Succeeds Act, responding to increased public dissatisfaction with the standards and accountability movement, granted states waivers from testing mandates. Whether and how this will reshape teacher evaluation—and teaching—remains to be seen.

CONCLUSION

Teaching and teacher education have been shaped, over time, by both professionalization and bureaucratic rationalization. Looking across roughly a century of history, and using the case of the United States, reveals the extent to which each of these forces ebbs and flows within and across particular sociohistorical contexts. Sometimes they have worked in tandem. In the early twentieth century, for instance, bureaucratic approaches to teacher licensure helped advance teacher pay, elevate teacher status, and enhance teacher prestige. Most recently, the erection of so-called value-added evaluation systems and the construction of alternate pathways into teaching have undermined teachers' professional stature, bypassing university-based teacher preparation and eroding teachers' autonomy.

As public sector employees, teachers are subject to government oversight and their pay is constrained by the available tax base. Moreover, because an ostensibly equal public education is guaranteed to all young people in the United States, teaching is a mass occupation that must, by definition, include a large segment of the adult population. Unlike those in other fields, then, teachers' professionalization efforts fundamentally rely on cooperation and support from public officials.

Meanwhile, other educators, including administrators and educational researchers, have claimed jurisdiction over who teaches, how they are prepared, and how they are evaluated to establish their own professional status. While such efforts have often diminished teachers' autonomy and impeded their control of their work, in some cases, teachers' professionalization projects have been advanced. University-based, faculty-controlled preservice training, for instance, has typically enhanced the status of both teacher educators and future teachers.

Gender and race have shaped these advances in complex and varied ways. Women teachers have been organizationally subordinated and poorly paid. Yet, teaching also provided women in certain eras with a path to independence through increased access to formal education, work opportunities, and professional recognition. The same was true for marginalized racial groups who used such access to advance the causes of racial uplift and community liberation.

Teachers in the twenty-first century are unquestionably better trained, generally more experienced, and better paid than their nineteenth-century counterparts. Yet, they are not held in higher esteem. As more Americans began attending college in the second half of the twentieth century, teachers became less exceptional in this regard. Their limited pay, though substantially better than in earlier periods, constrained the amount of pre-professional training that could be required. And women were increasingly drawn away from teaching by economic opportunities in other fields, even as the profession remained feminized.

In sum, the matters of who teaches, how teachers are trained, and how teachers are evaluated never exist in a vacuum. They are shaped by the twin forces of professionalism and bureaucratic rationalization, which in turn are shaped by broader social and political contexts. Teaching and teacher education have evolved in a complex system that has produced contradictory phenomena of progress and regress. Teaching advances; but it also retreats and repeats. Its future is both assured and unpredictable.

REFERENCES

Anagnostopoulos, Dorothea, Stacey A. Routledge, and Rebecca Jacobsen (2013), "Mapping the Information Infrastructure of Accountability," in Dorothea Anagnostopoulos, Stacey A. Routledge, and Rebecca Jacobsen (eds.), *The Infrastructure of Accountability: Data Use and the Transformation of American Education*, 1–20, Cambridge, MA: Harvard Education Press.

Anagnostopoulos, Dorothea, Suzanne Wilson, and Sian Charles-Harris (2020), "Contesting Quality Teaching: Teachers' Pragmatic Agency and the Debate about Teacher Evaluation," *Teaching and Teacher Education*, 98. https://doi.org/10.1016/j.tate.2020.103246.

Anderson, James D. (1988), *Black Education in the South, 1860–1935*, Chapel Hill: University of North Carolina Press.

Angus, David L. (2001), *Professionalism and the Public Good: A Brief History of Teacher Certification*, Washington, DC: Thomas B. Fordham Foundation.

Baker, Bruce D. and Jill L. Dickerson (2006), "Charter Schools, Teacher Labor Market Deregulation, and Teacher Quality: Evidence from the Schools and Staffing Survey," *Educational Policy*, 20 (3): 752–78.

Boyce, A.C. (1922), *The Fourteenth Yearbook of the National Society for the Study of Education, Part II: Methods for Measuring Teachers' Efficiency*, Bloomington, IL: Public School Publishing Company.

Brooks, Sarah L. (1897), "Supervision as Viewed by the Supervised," *National Educational Association Journal of Proceedings and Addresses*: 225–32. https://hdl.handle.net/2027/mdp.39076007018406.

Butchart, Ronald E. (2010), *Schooling the Freed People: Teaching, Learning, and the Struggle for Black Freedom, 1861–1876*, Chapel Hill: University of North Carolina Press.

Caliver, Ambrose (1935), "Some Problems in the Education and Placement of Negro Teachers," *Journal of Negro Education*, 4 (1): 99–112.

Carver-Thomas, Desiree and Linda Darling-Hammond (2017), *Teacher Turnover: Why It Matters and What We Can Do About It*, Palo Alto, CA: Learning Policy Institute.

Clifford, Geraldine J. (2014), *Those Good Gertrudes: A Social History of Women Teachers in America*, Baltimore: Johns Hopkins University Press.

Clifford, Geraldine J. and James W. Guthrie (1988), *Ed School: A Brief for Professional Education*, Chicago: University of Chicago Press.

Cook, Katherine M. (1921), *State Laws and Regulations Governing Teachers' Certificates*, U.S. Bureau of Education, *Bulletin No. 22*.

Donahue, David M. (2002), "Rhode Island's Last Holdout: Tenure and Married Women Teachers at the Brink of the Women's Movement," *History of Education Quarterly*, 42 (1): 50–74.

Donaldson, Morgaen L. and John P. Papay (2017), "An Idea Whose Time Had Come: Negotiating Teacher Evaluation Reform in New Haven, Connecticut," *American Journal of Education*, 122 (1): 39–70.

Dunn, Alyssa H. (2018), "Leaving a Profession after It Has Left You: Teachers' Public Resignation Letters as Resistance Amidst Neoliberalism," *Teachers College Record*, 120 (9): 1–34.

Ethridge, Samuel B. (1979), "Impact of the 1954 Brown v. Board of Education of Topeka Decision on Black Educators," *Negro Educational Review*, 30 (4): 217–32.

Fairclough, Adam (2004), "The Costs of Brown: Black Teachers and School Integration," *Journal of American History*, 91 (1): 43–55.

Fitzpatrick, F.A. (1893), "How to Improve the Work of Inefficient Teachers," *Proceedings of the International Congress of Education*, New York: National Educational Association. https://hdl.handle.net/2027/miua.0677752.1893.001.

Frankenberg, Erica (2008), "The Segregation of American Teachers." *Education Policy Analysis Archives*, 17 (1). Available online: http://epaa.asu.edu/epaa/v17n1/ (accessed August 20, 2020).

Frazier, B.W. (1935), "History of the Professional Education of Teachers in the United States," *National Survey of the Education of Teachers*, 5: 1–86.

Fultz, Michael (1995a), "African American Teachers in the South, 1890–1940: Powerlessness and the Ironies of Expectations and Protest," *History of Education Quarterly*, 35 (4): 401–22.

Fultz, Michael (1995b), "Teacher Training and African American Education in the South, 1900–1940," *Journal of Negro Education*, 64 (2): 196–210.

Garcia, Emma and Elaine Weiss (2019), *U.S. Schools Struggle to Hire and Retain Teachers: The Second Report in 'The Perfect Story in the Teacher Labor Market' Series*, Economic Policy Institute. Available online: https://www.epi.org/publication/u-s-schools-struggle-to-hire-and-retain-teachers-the-second-report-in-the-perfect-storm-in-the-teacher-labor-market-series/ (accessed August 21, 2020).

Gershenson, Seth, Cassandra Hart, Joshua Hyman, Constance Lindsay, and Nicholas W. Papageorge (2018), "The Long-Run Impacts of Same-Race Teachers," Working Paper #25254, National Bureau of Economic Research. Available online: https://www.nber.org/papers/w25254 (accessed August 20, 2020).

Glanz, Jeffrey (1991), *Bureaucracy and Professionalism: The Evaluation of Public School Supervision*, Rutherford, NJ: Fairleigh Dickinson University Press.

Goldstein, Dana (2014), *The Teacher Wars: A History of America's Most Embattled Profession*, New York: Anchor Books.

Good, T.L. and C. Mulryan (1990), "Teacher Ratings: A Call for Teacher Control and Self-Evaluation," in Jason Millman and Linda Darling-Hammond (eds.), *The New Handbook of Teacher Evaluation: Assessing Elementary and Secondary School Teachers*, 191–215, Newbury Park, CA: Sage.

Goodwin, A. Lin (2021), "Teaching Standards, Globalization, and Conceptions of Teacher Professionalism," *European Journal of Teacher Education*, 44 (1): 5–19.

Grant, Gerald and Christine E. Murray (2002), *Teaching in America: A Slow Revolution*, Cambridge, MA: Harvard University Press.

Hazi, Helen M. (2017), "VAM Under Scrutiny: Teacher Evaluation Litigation in the States," *The Clearing House*, 90 (5–6): 184–90.

Hill, Sallie (1919), "Defects of Supervision and Constructive Suggestions Thereon," *Journal of Education*, 89 (12): 321–6.

Ingersoll, Richard M. and Gregory J. Collins (2017), "Accountability and Control in American Schools," *Journal of Curriculum Studies*, 49 (1): 75–95.

Ingersoll, Richard M., Henry May, and Gregory Collins (2017), "Minority Teacher Recruitment, Employment, and Retention: 1987 to 2013," Learning Policy Institute. Available online: https://learningpolicyinstitute.org/product/minority-teacher-recruitment-report (accessed August 15, 2020).

Ingersoll, Richard M., Lisa Merrill, and Daniel Stuckey (2018), *The Changing Face of Teaching*, Philadelphia: University of Pennsylvania Graduate School of Education.

Jones, Jacqueline (1979), "Women Who Were More than Men: Sex and Status in Freedmen's Teaching," *History of Education Quarterly*, 19 (1): 47–59.

Karpinski, Carol F. (2010), "'We have a long way to go': H. Councill Trenholm, Educational Associations, and Equity," *Pedagogica Historica*, 46 (1–2): 51–67.

King, Sabrina H. (1993), "The Limited Presence of African American Teachers," *Review of Educational Research*, 63 (2): 115–49.

Koerner, James D. (1963), *The Miseducation of American Teachers*, Boston: Houghton Mifflin.

Labaree, David (1992), "Power, Knowledge, and the Rationalization of Teaching: A Geneaology of the Movement to Professionalize Teaching," *Harvard Educational Review*, 62 (2): 123–54.

Labaree, David (2018), "An Uneasy Relationship: The History of Teacher Education in the University," in Julie Gorlewski and Eve Tuck (eds.), *Who Decides Who Becomes a Teacher? Schools of Education at Sites of Resistance*, 290–306, New York: Taylor & Francis.

Ladson-Billings, Gloria (2004), "Landing on the Wrong Note: The Price we Paid for Brown," *Educational Researcher*, 33 (7): 3–13.

Lagemann, Ellen C. (1997), "Contested Terrain: A History of Educational Research in the United States, 1890–1990," *Educational Researcher*, 26 (9): 5–17.

Leroux, Karen (2006), "Lady Teachers' and the Genteel Roots of Teacher Organization in Gilded Age Cities," *History of Education Quarterly*, 46 (2): 164–91.

Madkins, Tia C. (2011), "The Black Teacher Shortage: A Literature Review of Historical and Current Trends," *Journal of Negro Education*, 80 (3): 417–27.

Marzano, Robert J., Tony Frontier, and David Livingston (2011), *Effective Supervision: Supporting the Art and Science of Teaching*, Alexandria, VA: ASCD.

Mattingly, Paul (1975), *The Classless Profession: American Schoolmen in the Nineteenth Century*, New York: New York University Press.

McDonnell, Lorraine and Anthony H. Pascal (1979), *Organized Teachers in American Schools*, Santa Monica, CA: RAND.

Milner, H. Richard, IV (2013), *Policy Reforms and De-Professionalization of Teaching*, National Education Policy Center. Available online: https://nepc.colorado.edu/publication/policy-reforms-deprofessionalization (accessed August 23, 2020).

Mintrop, H. and G.L. Sunderman (2013), "The Paradoxes of Data-Driven School Reform: Learning from Two Generations of Centralized Accountability," in Dorothea Anagnostopoulos, Stacey A. Routledge, and Rebecca Jacobsen (eds.), *The Infrastructure of Accountability: Data Use and the Transformation of American Education*, 23–40, Cambridge, MA: Harvard Education Press.

Murphy, Marjorie (1990), *Blackboard Unions: The AFT and the NEA, 1900–1980*, Ithaca, NY: Cornell University Press.

National Center for Education Statistics (2020), *The Condition of Education 2020*. US Department of Education.

Ogren, Christine (2005), *The American State Normal School: "An Instrument of Great Good,"* New York: Palgrave Macmillan.

Parrott, Ava L. (1915), "Abolishing the Rating of Teachers," *National Education Association Addresses and Proceedings*. Available online: https://archive.org/details/addressesproce1915natiuoft/page/1168/mode/2up (accessed June 14, 2020).

Perlmann, Joel and Robert A. Margo (2001), *Women's Work? American Schoolteachers, 1650–1920*, Chicago: University of Chicago Press.

Pogodzinski, Ben, Regina Umpstead, and Jenifer Witt (2015), "Teacher Evaluation Reform Implementation and Labor Relations," *Journal of Educational Policy*, 30 (4): 540–61.

Popkewitz, Thomas S. (1994), "Professionalization in Teaching and Teacher Education: Some Notes on its History, Ideology, and Potential," *Teaching and Teacher Education*, 10 (1): 1–14.

Sawchuk, Stephen (2015), "Teacher Evaluation Heads to the Courts," *Education Week*, 35 (7): 15. Available online: https://www.edweek.org/ew/section/multimedia/teacher-evaluation-heads-to-the-courts.html (accessed May 26, 2020).

Schneider, Jack (2011), *Excellence for All: How a New Breed of Reformers is Transforming America's Public Schools*, Nashville, TN: Vanderbilt University Press.

Schneider, Jack (2018), "Marching Forward, Marching in Circles: A History of Problems and Dilemmas in Teacher Education," *Journal of Teacher Education*, 69 (4): 330–40.

Sears, J.B. (1921), "Measurement of Teaching Efficiency," *Journal of Educational Research*, 4 (2): 81–94.

Sedlak, Michael W. (1989), "Let Us Go and Buy a Schoolmaster," in Donald Warren (ed.), *American Teachers: Histories of a Profession at Work*, 257–90, New York: Macmillan.

Sedlak, Micael W. and Steven L. Schlossman (1986), *Who Will Teach? Historical Perspectives on the Changing Appeal of Teaching as a Profession*, Santa Monica, CA: RAND Corporation.

Siddle Walker, Vanessa (2005), "Organized Resistance and Black Educators' Quest for School Equality, 1878–1938," *Teachers College Record*, 107 (3): 355–88.

Siddle Walker, Vanessa (2013), "Tolerated Tokenism, or the Injustice of Justice: Black Teacher Associations and their Forgotten Struggle for Educational Justice, 1921–1954," *Equity & Excellence in Education*, 46 (1): 64–80.

Stemnock, Suzanne K. (1969), *Evaluating Teaching Performance: Educational Research Circular Number Three*, Washington, DC: American Association of School Administrators.

Snyder, Thomas D. (1993), *120 Wears of American Education: A Statistical Portrait*, Washington, DC: National Center for Education Statistics.

Strober, Myra H. and Audri G. Lanford (1986), "The Feminization of Public School Teaching: Cross-Sectional Analysis, 1850–1880," *Signs*, 11 (2): 212–35.

Stuart, Leland E. and Steven M. Goldschmidt (1986), *Collective Bargaining in American Public Education: The First 25 Years*, Washington, DC: Center for Educational Policy and Management.

Tanner, Daniel and Laurel Tanner (1987), *Supervision in Education*, New York: Macmillian.

Temin, Peter (2002), "Teacher Quality and the Future of America," *Eastern Economics Journal*, 28: 285–300.

Tillman, Linda C. (2004), "(Un)Intended Consequences? The Impact of the Brown V. Board of Education Decision on the Employment Status of Black Education," *Education and Urban Society*, 36 (3): 280–303.

Tracy, Saundra J. (1995), "How Historical Concepts of Supervision Relate to Supervisory Practices Today," *The Clearing House: A Journal of Educational Strategies, Issues and Ideas*, 68 (5): 320–5.

Tyack, David B. (1967), *Turning Points in American Educational History*, Waltham, MA: Blaisdell.

Tyack, David B. (1974), *The One Best System: A History of American Urban Education*, Cambridge, MA: Harvard University Press.

Urban, W.J. (1976), "Organized Teachers and Educational Reform During the Progressive Era: 1980–1920," *History of Education Quarterly*, 16 (1): 35–52.

Urban, W.J. (2001), "Courting the Woman Teacher: The National Education Association, 1917–1970," *History of Education Quarterly*, 41 (2): 139–66.

Villegas, Ana M. and Jacqueline J. Irvine (2010), "Diversifying the Teaching Force: An Examination of the Major Arguments," *Urban Review*, 42: 175–92.

Warren, Donald (1985), "Learning from Experience: History and Teacher Education," *Educational Researcher*, 14 (10): 5–12.

Winn, Agnes (1925), "NEA Department of Classroom Teachers," *Journal of Education*, 102 (21): 563–4.

CHAPTER SEVEN

Assessment and Evaluation

Assessment is Posited within Evaluation

CORRIE REBECCA KLINGER AND DON A. KLINGER

In 1968, Benjamin S. Bloom offered a lengthy discussion about what assessment is and how it is used. He described assessment as "the attempts to assess the characteristics of individuals in relation to a particular environment, task, or criterion situation" (1968: 10). In response to Bloom, Michael Scriven argued that assessment is not distinct from evaluation and that evaluation is a twofold task, "determining appropriate criteria and applying them" (1967: 9). Years later, Scriven asserted:

> Assessment is often used as a synonym for evaluation, but sometimes the subject of valiant efforts to differentiate it, presumably to avoid some of the opprobrium associated with the term "evaluation" in the minds of people for whom the term is more important than the process.
>
> (1991: 60)

With these differing takes on assessment from two prominent scholars in the field, it is unsurprising that assessment and evaluation continue to be mired in unresolved controversy. It is within this ongoing, contentious environment that we explore the history of assessment and evaluation.

Evaluation has been defined as the process of making judgments based on some criteria (Bloom et al. 1956). Ralph W. Tyler (1942), often referred to as the father of evaluation and assessment, used the term "testing" within and as a part of evaluation when he outlined the purposes of evaluation for educational institutions. More recently, Scriven defined evaluation as "the process of determining merit, worth, or significance" (2016: 36). Michael Quinn Patton added to that definition, "credibility, and utility of whatever is being evaluated, for example, a program, a policy, a product, or the performance of a person or team" (2018: 185). And further expanding on the definition, Scriven (n.d.) advocated for "The Three Revolutions" in evaluation that transforms evaluation to the "alpha discipline," thus positioning assessment within evaluation. About the alpha discipline:

> Evaluation has that power because all disciplines are completely dependent for their legitimacy on the quality of their intradisciplinary evaluation, i.e., their ability to identify good vs. bad theories, data, hypotheses, explanations, etc., the tools of every discipline's expertise.
>
> (Scriven n.d.: para. 4)

Patton added to this revolution by articulating an "Evaluation Science," which asks, "*What are the factors that contribute to, methods for determining, and criteria for judging interventions' successes and failures?*" (2018: 187).

Sound assessment methods are essential for the evaluative process. And, the assessment of learning is situated within evaluation. We are not undervaluing the assessment process when we posit it within evaluation. According to Scriven, assessment is one of the "Duties of the Teacher":

> The terms "assessment" and "testing" are here construed in the widest sense, to involve any systematic and objective process that leads to either evaluative classification (e.g., identification of learning disability) or determination of the merit of student work. Assessment may involve the use of structured and recorded observation, conversation, project or portfolio analysis, as well as paper and pencil, computerized, or verbal testing or questioning.
>
> (2015: 20–1)

Even though we currently use the terms assessment and large-scale assessment as standalone endeavors, historically, evaluation was the term more often used by scholars, not assessment. As we know it today, assessment is grounded in evaluation. In 1958, evaluation was used in the name of the first large-scale standardized international studies of the International Association for the Evaluation of Educational Achievement (IEA). With the IEA studies, worldwide large-scale standardized assessments developed within and as a part of evaluation. The connotation of assessment as unaccompanied with evaluation seems to have occurred after the National Assessment of Educational Progress used the term assessment in its name in 1969. Measurement driven instruction policies of the 1980s solidified the controversial nature of assessment being detached from evaluation with largely unquestioned and unexamined uses of large-scale assessments, leading to often problematic interpretations and misuse of assessment information to support educational policies and practices. We argue that assessment as a standalone endeavor emerged from an intersection of evaluation and advances in psychometrics that provided conditions for measurement driven instruction of the 1980s to the controversial utilization of large-scale standardized tests for accountability purposes. In this chapter, we provide a brief historical account of how large-scale assessments resulted after a coalescence of evaluation and psychometrics, which provided the conditions that gave rise to measurement driven instruction, thus leading to the presumption that assessment is separate from and not posited within evaluation.

A PROBLEM WITH ASSESSMENT TODAY

A problem exists because the competent use of assessment has been compromised by the contentious nature of the educational policies within many countries that use test scores for sorting purposes rather than the development of human beings. These uses of tests equate higher scores with success, either in relation to other students, established standards, or some combination of the two. School access is based on test scores in European and Asian countries, with most pressure on the student to meet specified standards (Manns 2018). Other countries such as Finland and New Zealand use "multiple measures of performance … (e.g., teacher observations and diverse evidence of student achievement)" (Nichols and Harris 2016: 41). Some countries, including the United States of America, judge schools, administrators, and teachers based mainly on one test score (Kifer 2001; Nichols and Harris 2016: 41). As a further example, countries increasingly use international test results to rank order themselves in relation to other countries and set broad educational policies. Some scholars argue that international tests have made "the globe a commensurate space of measurement and governance" (Lingard and Lewis 2016). Through the years, policymakers have been called on to stop misusing standardized test scores with these types of stakes (Hood 1998; Berliner and Biddle 1999; Kifer 2001; American Evaluation Association [AEA] 2006; Nichols, Berliner, and Harvard University, Graduate School of Education 2007; Berliner and Glass 2014; Gordon 2016; Nichols and Harris 2016; Arbuthnot 2017; Wood, Thrupp, and Barker 2021).

Even though good tests tend to straightforwardly and clearly state appropriate uses of their results, controversial and invalid judgments about students, teachers, schools, and education at large, continue. Erroneously, human beings swiftly "adopt simplistic causal explanations (e.g., scores are low, so bad teaching is to blame), even when such conclusions are not warranted" (Nichols and Harris 2016: 41). These errors seem to happen because the current educational policy arena focuses on test scores that are ends outcomes, while means inputs are absent. "By merely focusing on the test results, we sidestep the more crucial question of the proper role of testing" (Madaus and Russell 2016: 28). A proper role of testing is to use the results to evaluate differences in achievement while making sense of the interconnectedness of inputs and outcomes (Kifer 2001: 4; AEA 2006; American Educational Research Association [AERA], American Psychological Association [APA], and National Council on Measurement in Education [NCME] 2014). For example, IEA studies include large-scale assessments within their investigations of means and ends (Kifer 2001: 4). Respectable large-scale tests tend to provide appropriate score interpretations and uses for each test or set of tests (AERA, APA, and NCME 2014; Ferrara and Lai 2016; Ferrara et al. 2016; Zieky 2016; Mislevy 2018) in relation to the curriculum or behaviours that have been assessed. But, today, the curriculum is an input that seems to have been forgotten by the use of large-scale assessments as standalone outcomes (Kifer 1997: 627). Individuals who are not trained in psychometric principles rarely make sense of the proper conclusions that ought to be drawn from large-scale assessments (627) because they need to make sense of the tests within the test's established curricular or behavioral parameters. The use of assessments as outcomes would be better served positioned within a process to evaluate means and ends together instead of perpetuating assessments as standalone endeavors. Tests such as the Programme for International Student Assessment (PISA) do not seem to examine inputs such as curriculum therefore they may unknowingly be adding to the controversial judgments about students, teachers, schools, and education. Even though scholars within the assessment and evaluation communities of psychometrics and measurement may agree with Edward Kifer that it is appropriate to use test scores "to make inferences about the efficacy of a curriculum" (627), time and again, they are caught between their "controversial history on the one hand and its important achievements on the other" (Wijsen and Borsboom 2021: 332).

MOVING THROUGH HISTORY

The evaluation and assessment of learning have a long historical record. Ancient China used the keju system to identify future civil servants and military officers. Evaluative judgments to develop student knowledge and reasoning skills were developed with the Socratic method. And centuries later, the use of examinations to select and rank students was found throughout Europe in the eighteenth and nineteenth centuries.

Ancient China

The Chinese keju system, in place for an extensive amount of time, 605–1905, played a critical role in "identify[ing] and recruit[ing] the most capable and virtuous individuals into government instead of relying on members of the hereditary noble class" (Zhao 2014: 32). These high-stakes examinations had critical consequences, "doing well could offer a way out of poverty and into positions of nobility and power" (Nichols and Harris 2016: 40). Limited numbers of those writing the examinations were successful. In an attempt to make fair and accurate decisions, the examinations were administered at specific locations, numbers rather than names identified students, and scribes would reproduce the completed examinations to prevent those marking the examinations from identifying the examinees or to use the quality of writing to interfere with the evaluation of performance. Even though fair and accurate decision-making were some of the reasons for this system, the purpose was to sort and select citizens into jobs. The keju system influenced assessment practices in other nearby Asian countries. Indeed, there continue to be parallels to these ancient examinations to large-scale tests used today, especially considering university entrance examinations or certification examinations for entry into professions (e.g., architecture, law, medicine).

The Socratic Method

In contrast to the explicit career orientation of the keju system, the Socratic method, which Plato promoted, is a dialectical evaluation structured to build knowledge and reasoning. We discuss the Socratic method as a historical example of the use of evaluative judgments for developmental purposes. The Socratic method was designed as a verbal argumentative dialogue based on asking and answering questions. The evaluative purpose was to identify assumptions while analyzing a problem to enhance logic and reasoning.

The Socratic method involves a type of evaluative judgment that is authentically tied to and embedded within the learning activities, which is different from the keju system and the current use of large-scale tests. Large-scale standardized tests tend to be written and given externally from the learning activities. Even though the Socratic method is a series of questions and answers, its verbal nature is not the type of data collection method that lends itself to replicating multiple forms of questions given to large numbers of students found on most standardized large-scale tests used under accountability policies. Currently, the Socratic method is used in classrooms worldwide and tends to be used at universities within schools and faculties of law.

Europe of the Eighteenth and Nineteenth Centuries

The keju system may have influenced examinations that selected and ranked students throughout Europe in the eighteenth and nineteenth centuries. These European practices subsequently expanded to the New World, including Canada, the United States of America, and countries across Central and South America (Wilbrink 1997; Klinger, DeLuca, and Miller 2008; Klinger and DeLuca 2009). As Ben Wilbrink notes, "where earlier one's family, wealth and relations were decisive to get attractive government positions, now merit was becoming the prime criterion" (1997: 40). There is evidence that educators were held accountable for student achievement in England during the 1800s (Scriven 1991). While educators were responsible for the education of their students; student achievement was measured for ranking and selection purposes.

THE RISE OF PSYCHOMETRICS AND STANDARDIZATION

From the late 1800s through the early 1900s, making sense of human learning and intelligence emerged within philosophy and psychology. Advances in statistics and psychometrics came out of this work. Psychometrics is a field that studies and theorizes about measurement techniques. Most often, psychometricians work in psychological or educational testing, measurement, assessment, evaluation, and other related areas. The field tends to be concerned with technical processes to develop valid and reliable measures of personality, achievement, and skills, to name a few.

Also, during the late nineteenth century and into the twentieth century, there was worldwide momentum for standardization. Standards for the design and specifications of screws, nuts, and bolts were set for common sizes and threads. Before standards were set, there were no common sized screws, nuts, or bolts. Engineers were developing standards for composites in building materials so that there was agreement about the standards for safety and economic reasons. They wanted to make sense of the composition of materials purchased anywhere in the world.

With good reason, the standardization movement made its way into areas of social development. From 1886 through 1902, Charles Booth designed a study that made sense of the living and labor conditions in London, Great Britain. During this study, Charles Booth served as President of the Royal Statistical Society. According to Booth, he used a "double method of inquiry" to collect data and triangulate findings with the 1891 census records. School board members went to every house on every street collecting data about family size, birthplaces, head of household occupation, hours of work for anyone working, and their wages, while noting religious affiliations. Each school board member used the same approach to collect data. Data were charted onto maps to depict social conditions throughout London (Booth 1892, 1893, 1902). As data were charted onto the maps, the same approach was used to depict the data on the map. Following the same scripted processes for data collection and analysis created a standardized approach. This seminal work was replicated across the globe, which led to the worldwide implementation of standardized data collection methods (Lagemann 2009).

Globally, schooling and education as a discipline of study emerged simultaneously with measurement, statistics, evaluation, psychometrics, and standardization. By 1920, there seemed to be a sentiment in the United States of America that standardized methods were indispensable from the evaluation of educational programs (Lagemann 2009: 87). Standardized meant that one or multiple researchers used the same common script for data collection and analysis. Edward L. Thorndike had a profound influence on the use of standardized procedures in education (Lagemann 2009: 87; Plucker 2016; Wijsen and Borsboom 2021). Additionally, Charles Spearman, Louis Leon Thurstone, and Lee Cronbach made critical psychometric and statistical contributions that have shaped our evaluation and assessment practices (Lagemann 2009: 87; Plucker 2016; Wijsen and Borsboom 2021).

The contributions of these scholars are crucial to discuss because their advances in statistics and psychometrics from the early 1900s into the 1950s led to the development of standardized tests. Standardized tests were the backbone for the policies of measurement driven instruction of the 1980s, which provided the conditions for the change away from the use of evaluation to the use of the term assessment, which gave rise to the sentiment that assessment is a standalone endeavor.

Edward L. Thorndike, 1874–1949

Edward L. Thorndike mobilized standardized methods in both educational research and educational psychology. He believed that by using the same standard data collection methods and analysis, researchers could design objective, impartial, unbiased, and fair measures. Thorndike and others believe that objectivity is attainable and that these types of measures are not influenced by any factors such as attitudes, feelings, perceptions, circumstances, or individual interpretation. Objective measures can be described as measuring a person's performance on a task in a controlled environment. Thorndike tended to use stimulus and response tasks in his quest to measure intellectual level objectively (Plucker 2016). He "formulated ideas that were more suited to translation into formulas for educational practice" (Lagemann 2009: 57). By 1917, Thorndike "had developed methods for measuring a wide variety of abilities and achievements" (Plucker 2016). Thorndike's determination to implement standardized data collection and analysis methods coincided with the worldwide development of standardization in education thanks to Charles Booth's seminal works (Lagemann 2009).

According to Ellen Condliffe Lagemann (2009), Thorndike's approach was not without controversy. John Dewey, Thorndike's peer, had a different approach that may better relate to the approach of the Socratic method than Thorndike's quest for standardized methods. For Dewey, "freedom combined with intellectual cooperation provided a better way to ensure effective teaching" (Lagemann 2009: 51). Dewey believed that evaluating learning was more complex than Thorndike's stimulus and response approach. Dewey argued that an individual's interpretation of the situation influences the response to a stimulus. His ideas challenge Thorndike's notion of objective measures. Dewey's work suggests that subjectivity influences each measurement; thus, calling into question the notion of objectivity.

Even with the controversy between Thorndike and Dewey, we see that Thorndike's quest for the use of standardized methods seems to have been realized with the global use of standardized tests.

Charles Spearman, 1863–1945

As an experimental psychologist, Charles Spearman was one of the first to measure functions of the human mind using mathematics (Plucker 2016). He "combined psychological problems he was struggling with, with the development of statistical tools that he needed to tackle those problems," which led to technical advances in statistics (Wijsen and Borsboom 2021: 331). Spearman became known for creating the method of factor analysis. He hypothesized that human intelligence was produced by one single *general factor* (often referred to as *g*), and he designed a rank-order correlation coefficient that is used to describe the strength and direction of a relationship between two variables (Spearman 1904; Plucker 2016; Wijsen and Borsboom 2021).

Spearman's contributions cannot be discussed without also addressing eugenics. In the late 1800s and into the 1900s, Spearman supported the eugenics movement based on the idea that intelligence was genetically inherited. Therefore, selective breeding could improve the human population to enhance genetic makeup (Gould 1981; Plucker 2016; Wijsen and Borsboom 2021). His work reveals underlying controversies and disagreements within and without psychometricians' contributions. As Lisa D. Wijsen and Denny Borsboom (2021) note, the history of psychometrics is loaded with a dichotomy of controversy and accomplishments (Wijsen and Borsboom 2021).

Inherent within the eugenics movement are issues of race, class, and gender. Issues of race, class, and gender are inseparable from quality evaluation and assessment but are beyond the scope of the thesis of this chapter. For in-depth works of race, class, and gender, look within the published literature about culturally responsive assessment and evaluation. For example, Edmund W. Gordon (2016) has been a leading scholar addressing "Human Diversity and Equitable Assessment." See Keena Arbuthnot's work, such as *Global Perspectives on Educational Testing: Examining Fairness, High-Stakes and Policy Reform* (2017).

Louis Leon Thurstone, 1887–1955

Louis Leon Thurstone "wanted to explain the human mind. He both had an interest in measurement and an interest in understanding how the mind functions" (Wijsen and Borsboom 2021: 331). Thurstone developed "new statistical techniques" and added to statistical procedures developed by others (Plucker 2016). "'Thurstone made the discipline ... and created quantitative psychology'" (Wijsen and Borsboom 2021: 331). In testing, technical processes to develop valid and reliable measures come from Thurstone's contributions of measuring perceptions of an object. Thurstone used factor analysis to challenge Spearman's *general factor* of intelligence. He found that intelligence takes the form of seven independent factors, primary abilities: word fluency, verbal comprehension, spatial visualisation, number facility, associative memory, reasoning, and perceptual speed (Thurstone 1938). In subsequent work, Thurstone found the presence of both a common *general factor* and the seven primary abilities (Plucker 2016). Along with Edward Thorndike and Joy Paul Guilford, Thurstone founded the Psychometric Society and *Psychometrika*.

Lee J. Cronbach, 1916–2001

Moving into the 1950s, as an educational psychologist, Lee Cronbach made historically significant contributions to psychological testing and measurement through program evaluation, measurement theory, and instruction. Robert "Mislevy praises Cronbach for thinking critically about psychological measurement and the inferences or conclusions you can draw based on certain data, referring here to generalizability theory (Cronbach et al. 1972): 'he laid down some real mileposts, about how psychometrics is not just about measurement, it is about the quality and the nature of inferences that you're making'" (Wijsen and Borsboom 2021: 331).

Lee Cronbach also strongly influenced the concepts of reliability and validity. His name is often recognized because of Cronbach's alpha (Cronbach 1951). Cronbach's alpha is a measure of internal consistency for a test or scale, a reliability estimate. Reliability relates to the consistency and dependability of results from a measurement or calculation. A measure is said to have high reliability when that measure produces similar results under similar conditions. "According to Willem Heiser, Cronbach's paper on the reliability coefficient is one of his most significant contributions, due to its applicability to practical problems in research, not only in psychology but also in medical science or other fields where measurement plays a central role" (Wijsen and Borsboom 2021: 331). Subsequently, Cronbach, Nageswari Rajaratnam, and Goldine C. Gleser (1963) introduced Generalizability theory (G theory) as a statistical approach to evaluate reliability and reduce sources of error to increase reliability and dependability. In terms of validity, Cronbach and Paul Meehl (1955) introduced the notion of construct validity, measuring what is intended to be measured.

Addressing controversy, Cronbach (1967) asked researchers to value applied research in the same esteem as lab and experimental research. With this plea, he discussed the interconnectedness of lab and experimental research with applied research (Cronbach 1967). Hence it is not surprising that much of Cronbach's work has impacted practice across multiple environments and fields of study.

Relevant to the classroom setting, a purpose for Cronbach's work was to enhance students' responses to instruction during the learning process. He seemed to understand that how a student engages in the classroom makes a difference in the learning process. For Cronbach, assessment is not an isolated standalone activity. A purpose for assessment in schools is to create better learning contexts for better instruction to develop better student responses during the learning process.

Of importance, Thorndike's, Spearman's, Thurstone's, and Cronbach's contributions made sense of the human mind and the learning process. Their contributions illustrate statistical and psychometrics advancements that occurred throughout the early to mid-twentieth century that provided the conditions for the unresolved disagreements about assessment and evaluation. Even though assessment was not a standalone endeavor during that time, standardized methods for data collection began to take form from the 1900s and into the 1960s. Crucially, these historically significant contributions to psychometrics gave rise to the statistical processes used to develop standardized large-scale assessments.

EVALUATION TAKES FORM

Evaluation was the term most often used by scholars concerning student learning from the 1930s (Tyler 1934) through the 1960s.

Basic Principles of Curriculum and Instruction, 1949

In his 1949 book, *Basic Principles of Curriculum and Instruction*, Ralph W. Tyler set forth a path to formatively evaluate learning. For Tyler, it was all about evaluation. As far back as 1934, "Tyler proposed that educational testing be concerned with the changes in students produced by educational means.

He used the term _evaluation_ to refer to a set of procedures for appraising changes in students" (Bloom 1968: 5).

According to Tyler (1949), one step in the evaluation process is using instruments to collect evidence of learning. Tyler considered it critical that the evaluative purpose of an instrument be aligned to clearly stated concise learning objectives. As Scriven (2015) noted, systematically collecting evidence of learning is part of the assessment process. But, assessment was not an isolated standalone endeavor for Tyler. The assessment instrument is essential but is not the focus; the focus is on using the data collection instrument within the classroom while learning is taking place to collect evidence of affective and cognitive learning. Significantly, Tyler (1949) suggested that learning be evaluated based on gaps, emphasis, and needs, creating the concept of achievement gaps that is still used today.

Taxonomy of Educational Objectives Handbook I: The Cognitive Domain, 1956

The _Taxonomy of Educational Objectives Handbook I: The Cognitive Domain_ is a historically significant contribution like no other that is still widely used today. Benjamin S. Bloom, Max D. Engelhart, Edward J. Furst, Walter H. Hill, and David R. Krathwohl were the first to pull from biology's use of taxonomies to construct a taxonomy of educational goals or objectives. In biology, the use of taxonomies ensures accurate communication of and a system for "organization and interrelation of the various parts of the animal and plant world" (Bloom et al. 1956: 1). According to Bloom et al. this taxonomy

> is intended to provide for the classification of the goals of our educational system. It is expected to be of general help to all teachers, administrators, professional specialists, and research workers who deal with curricular and evaluation problems. It is especially intended to help them discuss these problems with greater precision.
>
> (1956: 1)

Interestingly, this quote also demonstrates the predominance of evaluation over assessment at that time. Assessment was not a standalone endeavor for Bloom et al. in 1956.

The taxonomy is ordered by theoretical complexity from simple to cognitively complex tasks: knowledge, comprehension, application, analyses, synthesis, and evaluation. Knowledge consists primarily of cognitive functions such as recalling or recognizing terminology, facts, processes, procedures, rules, and principles. Comprehension is changing something from one form into another form, such as paraphrasing to state the meaning of a sentence or text into a different composition. Application is to use information in a unique or novel way. Analysis is examining something complex and breaking it into its parts. Synthesis is to put information together in a unique or novel way, generally to solve a problem. Evaluation is making a judgment based on some criteria. This taxonomy has been replicated in many publications by different authors, demonstrating its ubiquitous use to describe and measure learning (Bloom, Hastings, and Madaus 1971; Guskey 1997, 2005; Gronlund and Brookhart 2009).

The cognitive domain is distinct from the affective and psychomotor domains. Taxonomies for educational objectives were developed for these two domains. The affective domain relates to attitudes, interests, work habits, and methods of adjustment (Krathwohl, Bloom, and Masia 1964). The psychomotor domain relates to motor skills and kinesthetics (Simpson 1966).

In practice, learning objectives, verbs, and content are placed within the Taxonomy as a tool for educators to use as they design the curriculum, instruction, and assessments to evaluate student learning (Bloom, Hastings, and Madaus 1971; Guskey 1997, 2005). Although many educators have a connotation of this Taxonomy, it is questionable if most accurately denote it as the authors of the work did. Table 7.1 summarizes the Taxonomy along with a brief description and a few verbs to illustrate the types of learning to be measured within each cognitive level (Bloom et al. 1956; Bloom, Hastings, and Madaus 1971; Guskey 1997, 2005; Gronlund and Brookhart 2009).

In 1971, Benjamin S. Bloom, J. Thomas Hastings, and George F. Madaus demonstrated the use of this taxonomy as a framework to create tables of specifications to organize the content and skills taught within units of study for different subject areas such as history, biology, and language arts in the book, *The Handbook on Formative and Summative Evaluation of Student Learning*. Currently, tables of specifications are used for designing large-scale assessments, typically using some form of the taxonomy to ensure assessment items cover a desired range of the cognitive domain. Tables of specifications map out the knowledge and skills measured with an assessment and are used to provide an estimate of the content or tasks to be measured. Another valuable aspect of these tables of specifications is that they indicate relationships between the content placed into the categories. Even today, most sound standardized large-scale tests share a version of the table of specifications used to construct the test. For example, the National Assessment of Educational Progress (NAEP) calls these "Assessment Frameworks" and provides them on the World Wide Web for each assessment (National Center for Education Statistics [NCES] 2021).

TABLE 7.1 Summary of the *Taxonomy of Educational Objectives Handbook I: The Cognitive Domain* (1956) by Benjamin S. Bloom, Max Englehart, Edward J. Furst, Walker Hill, and David Krathwohl.

Cognitive Level	Summary	Examples of Verbs at this Level
Knowledge	Recall or recognize	Name Repeat List
Comprehension	Change from one form to another	Describe Paraphrase Compute
Application	Apply or use information in a new situation	Interpret Use Solve
Analysis	Examine something complex and break it down into its parts	Contrast Infer Differentiate
Synthesis	Put information together in a unique or novel way	Integrate Construct Formulate
Evaluation	Make a judgment based on some criteria	Argue Justify Defend

The combination of advances in statistics and psychometrics with Ralph W. Tyler's approach to evaluation and the *Taxonomy of Educational Objectives Handbook I: The Cognitive Domain* created an intersection that provided favorable conditions for developing standardized tests with tables of specifications that organize and classify the curriculum to be evaluated. This intersection was crucial to develop the techniques necessary to examine psychometric test properties such as validity and reliability, which led to the design and implementation of large-scale standardized assessments.

LARGE-SCALE STANDARDIZED ASSESSMENTS

As described, the availability of large amounts of data collected through standardized methods ushered in an age of advances in statistics and psychometrics. These advances were furthered by those interested in using mathematics to make sense of the human mind and learning. Using frameworks such as the *Taxonomy of Educational Objectives Handbook I: The Cognitive Domain*, test items and data collected with the tests could be organized and analyzed in new ways to make sense of learning and functions of the mind. Large-scale standardized tests that measured what students knew and were able to do began taking shape with the formation of the International Association for the Evaluation of Educational Achievement (IEA) in 1958 and the NAEP after 1963. Implementing sound psychometric principles, these large-scale standardized assessments provided critical and useful information about student learning, the curriculum, and achievement. Subsequently, as more standardized large-scale assessments were designed and implemented, they impacted policy, practice, and perceptions of education over time.

International Association for the Evaluation of Educational Achievement (IEA)

In 1958, a group of scholars including psychometricians, sociologists, and educational psychologists at the United Nations Educational, Scientific and Cultural Organization's (UNESCO) Institute for Education in Hamburg, Germany, met to discuss issues related to evaluating school effectiveness and student learning. IEA grew out of these discussions and became a legal entity in 1967. For the first time, large-scale standardized testing began taking shape with IEA. It is historically relevant that this entity's name included the term evaluation. Once again, we note the absence of the concept of assessment when IEA was formed. Undoubtedly, the work of this organization gave rise to the large-scale international tests that we have today.

   Because the current educational policies across the globe controversially focus on outcomes, it is important to note that, according to IEA, both inputs and outputs (or outcomes) are essential to make sense of school effectiveness and student learning. Kifer suggests,

> Because IEA's search is for variables that explain achievement differences, it focuses on outcomes (ends) and inputs (means). The studies are based on what I think is a proper notion: Ends and means are inextricably entwined. One cannot change schools without dealing with both.
>
> (2001: 4)

IEA has carried out international comparative studies focusing on educational policies and practices. Each IEA study has a specified purpose and tends to be made up of several different methods of collecting data. IEA studies "support Berliner's (1987) notions of classroom instruction, which included OTL [opportunity to learn], students' engagement in learning, students' experiences of success, pacing, structuring, and monitoring" (Kifer 2001: 4). IEA studies cover topics including mathematics and science education (Third International Mathematics and Science Study, TIMMS), reading and literacy (Progress in International Reading Literacy Study, PIRLS), or citizenship (International

Civic and Citizenship Education Study, ICCS). These studies generally extend over a period of time, providing longitudinal data. For example, the TIMMS study has administered its assessment and survey every four years since 1995. IEA offers sound methods for using large-scale assessments, unlike the policies that came out of measurement driven instruction in the 1980s.

National Assessment of Educational Progress (NAEP)

In 1963, Ralph Tyler took a memorandum to John Tukey and Fred Mosteller that suggested it would be interesting to have a national test in the United States of America to find out what students and adults knew and what they were able to do (Hazlett 1973; Kifer 2001). Thus began a significant phase in standardized large-scale assessments, as this memo became the basis for the NAEP. The vision of NAEP was subsequently realized in 1969 (Education Testing Service [ETS] n.d.). Of importance for our work, the formation of NAEP, and the use of the term assessment in its name, provides a historically significant shift away from the use of the term evaluation and the beginning of the use of the term assessment.

NAEP continues to be widely used by educators, policymakers, and test designers as it "produces both current results and trends over time, some of which extend to the late 1960s" (Kifer 2001: 9). In the early stages of NAEP, reading, writing, mathematics, science, art, health, and citizenship were assessed, making it one of the broadest large-scale assessments in use. Advancing the discipline, NAEP was an early leader in sampling and measurement techniques to evaluate various school children in various age groups. "Arguably, NAEP's most important function is monitoring achievement patterns over time" (17). There are no stakes associated with NAEP. The quality of NAEP set the bar for worldwide large-scale assessments that we see today.

Both IEA and NAEP pioneered the effort to make sense of learning externally because they are given outside the classroom teaching and learning cycle. IEA and NAEP were early examples of using large-scale assessments to measure and monitor achievement patterns rather than individual achievement.

THE CONFLUENCE OF PSYCHOMETRICS AND LARGE-SCALE ASSESSMENTS

By the 1960s, we see the conditions that set the stage for the use of large-scale assessments to make sense of learning across the world. Advances in statistics and psychometrics from contributions made by Spearman, Thurstone, Cronbach, and Thorndike were being implemented in experimental psychology and educational research. Statistical methods were further refined and implemented. Thorndike's work convinced researchers to use standardized methods. Spearman began the technique of using mathematics to analyze the human mind. Thurstone's work taught us how to measure what we are interested in through perceptions and relationships. Cronbach's contributions led to the use of reliability and validity coefficients and Generalizability theory. Connecting these pieces on the path toward large-scale standardized assessments was Tyler's proposition that:

> educational testing be concerned with the changes in students produced by educational means .... His stress on appraisal of change meant that, theoretically at least, testing had to be done at two or more points in time on each individual to determine the extent of change.
>
> (Bloom 1968: 5)

Combining, one, the advances in statistics and psychometrics, and two, Tyler's emphasis on appraisal and multiple testing points to show change in students with, three, the use of the Taxonomy of 1956 to organize and classify curriculum and learning, the conditions were ripe for organizations such as IEA and NAEP to map content onto a table of specifications to guide the development of standardized assessment items. The same test items could be completed by large numbers of students in a standardized way across geographic regions. The data collected could be analyzed statistically to make sense of the repeatability, reliability of the inferences being made from the data, and the extent to which the content that was being measured was the content intended to be measured, validity. Now, IEA and NAEP could map data analysis onto a table of specifications to make sense of various levels of the learning. IEA and NAEP move Tyler's theoretical proposition of assessment at multiple moments in time into a large-scale reality.

Assessment and Evaluation

As noted above, we see a shift in terminology using the term assessment in NAEP's name. Chronologically, the term evaluation was used until the 1960s, not assessment. IEA used the term evaluation in its name at its inception in 1958. During the time NAEP was taking shape (1963–9), the disagreement between Bloom and Scriven about assessment and evaluation that we referenced at the beginning of this chapter was emerging. Bloom published a paper in which he described assessment as "the attempts to assess the characteristics of individuals in relation to a particular environment, task, or criterion situation" (1968: 10). Central to Scriven's response, he argued that the very essence of all scientific inquiry is evaluation because it is about making "good and better explanations, principles, and classifications ..., and the use of the valuational terms 'good' and 'better' in that claim is essential" (5). Fascinatingly, in 1969, NAEP used the term "assessment" in its name. In 1971, Bloom published the text titled, *The Handbook on Formative and Summative Evaluation of Student Learning* with Hastings and Madaus. Did Scriven convince Bloom of the soundness of his position?

Measurement Driven Instruction

IEA and NAEP had been operating for about two decades by the 1980s. During this time, advances in computers led to much more efficient and quicker statistical and psychometric calculations. Thus, advances in computers provided quick analyses of large amounts of data collected anywhere in the world. Consequently, the use of large-scale standardized assessments was on the rise. Controversial uses of the data collected grew with the increased use of standardized large-scale evaluations across the globe.

In the 1980s, minimal competency tests grew in importance under measurement driven instruction (FairTest n.d.). The purpose of measurement driven instruction was to "make teaching to the test an explicit policy" without providing the actual test for instructional purposes (FairTest n.d.). The historical significance of measurement driven instruction was that it brought about the current age of accountability and stakes associated with assessment scores. In turn, this focus on assessment scores led to a widespread supposition that assessment is a standalone endeavor.

There is much controversy and disagreement about the educational policies that arose from measurement driven instruction that attaches stakes to standardized assessment scores. Even today, politicians and governing persons continue to support measurement driven instruction despite a lack of evidence to suggest it is improving learning (FairTest n.d.). Scholars continue to ask educational policymakers to top the use of policies that came about as a result of measurement driven instruction (Scriven 1994; Hood 1998; Berliner and Biddle 1999; Kifer 2001; AEA 2006; Nichols, Berliner, and Harvard University, Graduate School of Education 2007; Waugh and Gronlund 2013; Berliner and Glass 2014; Gordon 2016; Nichols and Harris 2016; Arbuthnot 2017; Wood, Thrupp, and Barker 2021).

The Kentucky Instructional Results and Information System (KIRIS) used from 1992 to 1998 is one example of the implementation of Measurement Driven Instruction. KIRIS attempted to "serve too many purposes with one assessment scheme" (Kifer 2001: 28). Hence, KIRIS is a prime example of how measurement driven instruction has too many purposes (Nichols, Berliner, and Harvard University, Graduate School of Education 2007; Madaus and Russell 2009). Purpose is something one intends to do, an intention or aim (Yarbrough et al. 2010). According to the Classroom Assessment Standards, Foundations standard number one, "Assessment Purpose: Classroom assessment practices should have a clear purpose that supports teaching and learning" (Klinger et al. 2015: 189). Formative and summative evaluative judgments are two distinctly different purposes for how assessments are used. These two types of evaluative judgments, formative and summative, were first described by Scriven in 1967 (Scriven 1967). Both are intended to make judgments about what has or has not been learned. As the name implies, formative functions use evidence about the learning for making changes to the curriculum or instruction so that the learner engages in new experiences to learn what still needs to be learned. Summative functions are those that also relay whether there is evidence that the learning has or has not taken place, but no changes in curriculum or instruction are made, and the learner does not engage in new learning experiences (Bloom, Hastings, and Madaus 1971; Guskey 1997). As Kifer (2001) notes, the ways KIRIS was attempting to do formative and summative functions simultaneously with the same assessment was too much. KIRIS intended to measure "expectations for achievement, attainment of cognitive goals, attendance rates, dropout and retention rates, reductions of barriers to learning and successful transitions" while summatively holding schools accountable with sanctions or rewards and trying to get them to formatively improve (Kifer 2001: 25). As further examples, many state assessments in the United States of America implementing measurement driven instruction attempt to measure: content, non-cognitive factors, schools, classrooms, the teacher, and the student, often with consequences associated with the scores. Relatedly, the pressures felt by educators and students due to the ways scores are used has led to perverse actions such as cheating, inappropriate test preparation, and suicide ideation (Amrein-Beardsley, Berliner, and Rideau 2010; Wang 2016).

From KIRIS and other examples, we learn that measurement driven instruction does not work. Even though Kentucky's legislation enacted the essence of measurement driven instruction by seeking to create a test worth teaching to, within six years, the legislators eliminated the performance-based nature of the assessment system, thus losing the original intent of education reform legislation.

If we believe that children attend school to continually learn things that they do not yet know, then development is a purpose of education (Bloom, Hastings, and Madaus 1971). Learning is messy. For example, the first time a human being learns to use a pencil to write his name, it looks quite messy, contrasted to a human being who has mastered the writing of her name with pencils and has recently progressed to using ballpoint pens. In this example, the teacher has continually assessed these students' progress and provided evaluative formative feedback that they are using to get better at writing their names. If we believe developing new skills and learning new things is a continuous process that uses assessments for evaluative purposes, then measurement driven instruction goes against the developmental purpose of schools and the continuous nature of learning. Measurement driven instructional policies take scores out of context and lead to wrongheaded casual conclusions "(e.g., scores are low, so bad teaching is to blame), even when such conclusions are not warranted" (Nichols and Harris 2016: 41). Assessments as standalone entities lose the evaluative context that promotes continuous development of teaching practices and student learning. It seems that the stakes for accountability and the selection of schools for rewards or sanctions have become more important than the engaging, messy, continuous process of learning. "I would argue that the main reason for the dramatic changes over a decade in the original [Kentucky] assessment came about because persons focused on accountability ignored the continuous assessment piece of the legislation" (Kifer 2001: 28). The legislation initially set forth a plan to improve schools but lost the improvement when accountability with standalone assessments became the focus.

CURRENT ACCOUNTABILITY PRACTICES FROM MEASUREMENT DRIVEN INSTRUCTION

Perhaps unintentionally, advances in statistics, psychometrics, and measurement driven instruction policies gave rise to the use of standardized large-scale assessments for accountability purposes. Simultaneously, as measurement driven instruction developed, professional organizations created standards and frameworks that led to the refinement of the curriculum, instruction, and the classroom and large-scale assessments. These standards and frameworks have become the basis for accountability indices. We believe the evidence suggests that standardized large-scale evaluations provide reliable information both at a single time point and over time which helps us make sense of education such as learning, achievement, the curriculum, instruction, and educational policies. The stakes associated with the assessment perverts the reasonable inferences that can be made.

Across the globe, current international policies equate success with standardized assessment scores (Kifer 2001; Miller, Linn, and Gronlund 2013; Waugh and Gronlund 2013; Block 2015: 12; Manns 2018). School access is based on assessment scores in European and Asian countries, with most pressure to meet specified scores on the student (Manns 2018). In the United States of America, most of the pressure seems to be on the school, including administrators and teachers. More countries sort students into schools based on large-scale assessment scores. Some countries, including the United States of America, judge schools, administrators, and teachers based on large-scale assessment scores. Nevertheless, there are counterexamples to such practices. In response to the realization that accountability policies were creating "winner" and "loser" schools, New Zealand had moved away from using these types of accountability policies by 1999 (Wood, Thrupp, and Barker 2021: 274). Canadian provinces continue to adapt their large-scale provincial assessment practices to reduce the impact on individual students while also providing more useful information to enhance teaching and learning.

However, unintended consequences of accountability continue to arise. For example, items on standardized assessments tend to be multiple-choice, with some constructed-response items. Measurement driven instruction may be about creating a test worth teaching to, but one of the consequences has been the appearance of immediate cost savings, which has led to the use of large-scale assessments made up of multiple-choice items (Kifer 2001; Nichols, Berliner, and Harvard University, Graduate School of Education 2007; Miller, Linn, and Gronlund 2013; Waugh and Gronlund 2013). The number of multiple-choice items has been increasing as the number of performance-type items and other types of items are decreasing or vacant (Kifer 2001; Madaus and Russell 2009; Miller, Linn, and Gronlund 2013; Block 2015). Measurement and psychometric scholars continue to share concerns that relying on multiple-choice items on large-scale assessments has led to a lack of application, analysis, synthesis, and evaluation types of assessment items (Kifer 2001; Madaus and Russell 2009; Miller, Linn, and Gronlund 2013; Block 2015). C. Keith Waugh and Norman E. Gronlund have contended:

> Many parents and teachers feel that there is too much emphasis on testing and that teachers are being forced to spend instructional time on rote memorization of content and repetition to prepare students for the test. They argue that this time should be spent on teaching students how to think critically and solve problems. While these concerns are prevalent, most will agree that assessment is necessary and accountability is needed.
>
> (Waugh and Gronlund 2013: 12)

CONCLUSION

Most scholars who have made historically significant contributions to evaluation and assessment articulate assessment within evaluation, not as a standalone endeavor. Assessment is one step in the teaching and learning process as it is crucial for systematically collecting data to make evaluative judgments about learning, instruction, and the curriculum (Tyler 1949; Scriven 1994, 2015; Kifer 2001). Assessing student learning is a critical endeavor, and assessment provides the criteria for expected outcomes that show learning took place. We agree with Kifer (1997) about why he likes test scores because they tell us these things about curriculum, what has or has not been taught or what has or has not been learned. Nevertheless, assessment cannot be the focus because outcomes are only part of the work. Outcomes and inputs are inseparably interwoven. Both are necessary to change education (Kifer 2001; Salkind 2008). Evaluation is how we examine inputs and outcomes. Further, assessment as the focus neglects its purposes and functions. The purposes and functions of assessment are situated within evaluation.

Despite the continual contentions surrounding the use of assessments for accountability purposes, large-scale assessments emerged out of sound evaluation methods and advances in statistics and psychometrics. Large-scale standardized assessments began to take shape during the 1960s and 1970s with IEA and NAEP. The use of the term assessment in NAEP was a historically significant change from the use of the term evaluation, which had been used most often before NAEP. Whether intentional or not, significant contributions over time provided the tools and conditions that gave rise to the controversial accountability policies of measurement driven instruction that set into motion the practice of teaching to a test. The association of rewards or sanctions with standardized test scores implied that assessment is a standalone activity.

Assessment and evaluation are all positioned within ongoing disagreements between controversies and achievements (Wijsen and Borsboom 2021). Thorndike represents the ongoing disagreements and controversy within and without the scholarly community of assessment, evaluation, measurement, and psychometrics. Since Thorndike's quest for the use of standardized assessment has been realized, there is hope that culturally responsive assessment practices may also be achieved following Thorndike's belief that culture is influential. New consideration needs to be given to Thorndike's suggestions that culture influences some measures (Plucker 2016). Maybe Thorndike's influence can be expanded for the common good.

Critical aspects of what assessment is and how it is used come from the historical role of eugenics and issues related to race, class, and gender. While the eugenics movement is no longer a driver in assessment, race, class, and gender continue to be important factors, albeit from a far different perspective. Edmund W. Gordon (2016) is a leading scholar addressing "Human Diversity and Equitable Assessment." According to Gordon, the challenge to educational assessment is to develop measures and procedures that are capable of:

(1)   engaging students from diverse backgrounds and experiences in assessment situations that are capable of eliciting performances and products appropriate to standards that are both universal and pluralistic;

(2)   providing assessment opportunities that are embedded in and complementary to teaching and learning experiences;

(3)   supporting the diverse learning and performance contexts necessary to the optimal expression of variously developed and expressed abilities;

(4)   managing and presenting information in ways that are meaningful and useful to a variety of audiences, but especially to teachers and students, in the improvement of teaching and learning; and

(5)   enabling reliable and valid judgements concerning the quality and adequacy of students' diverse developed abilities, documented performances, and collected products. (2016: 370)

Underlying these is the call for the use of culturally responsive assessments such as curriculum-embedded assessments and portfolio systems, in contrast to the simultaneous rise of measurement driven instruction that led to the increase of multiple-choice items in place of performance-based and portfolio type assessment items for accountability purposes. Performance-based items have been decreasing in large-scale assessments but are used within examinations for medical and health sciences education and licensure. Yet policymakers, who often do not have sufficient expertise in psychometrics or measurement, do not seem interested to use the body of evidence from those with such psychometrics or measurement expertise. Importantly related, the Socratic method discussed earlier embeds evaluation into the learning much like Gordon seeks.

In terms of standardized large-scale assessments, to be culturally responsive, it is incumbent upon educators and those who make and use large-scale assessments to take the time to learn about the cultures of the students being assessed so that the tools for measuring achievement are developed to measure what is intended to be measured without cultural barriers. Thus, leading to accurate and consistent analyses of achievement, the curriculum, and instruction instead of being unaware of the factors that potentially interfere with the attempt to measure specific characteristics, latent traits, or learning. As test items are being developed, attention needs to be given to demographic attributes such as socioeconomics, visual impairments and students whose first language is not the language of the assessment so that these are accounted for and do not "limit test takers access to the construct being measured" (Arbuthnot 2017: 9). Similarly, from the Classroom Assessment Standards, Quality standard one, "Cultural and Linguistic Diversity," states, "Classroom assessment practices should be responsive to and respectful of the cultural and linguistic diversity of students and their communities" (Klinger et al. 2015). Improving standardized large-scale assessments and classroom assessments is an interconnected process that necessitates attention be given to the ways culture and demographic attributes influence measurements of what is intended to be measured.

It is time to be wise about evaluation and assessment (Klinger and Klinger 2021). According to Scriven, assessment is not separate from evaluation; evaluation is a twofold task, "determining appropriate criteria and applying them" (1968: 9). It is time to stop negative connotations associated with the term evaluation (Scriven 1991) and put an end to the misinformed and consequential interpretations of assessment scores (Nichols and Harris 2016). It is time to realize evaluation as the "alpha discipline" (Scriven n.d. 2016) and make sense of large-scale assessments and classroom assessments as ends and means together seamlessly interconnected.

REFERENCES

American Educational Research Association (AERA), American Psychological Association (APA), and National Council on Measurement in Education (NCME) (2014), *Standards for Educational and Psychological Testing*, American Educational Research Association.

American Evaluation Association (AEA) (2006), "Public Statement: Educational Accountability," November 1. Available online: https://www.eval.org/Policy-Advocacy/Policy-Statements/Educational-Accountability-Statement (accessed May 24, 2022).

Amrein-Beardsley, Audrey, David C. Berliner, and Sharon Rideau (2010), "Cheating in the First, Second, and Third-Degree: Educators' Responses to High-Stakes Testing," *Education Policy Analysis Archives*, 18 (June): 14.

Arbuthnot, Keena (2017), *Global Perspectives on Educational Testing: Examining Fairness, High-Stakes and Policy Reform*, Bingley, UK: Emerald Publishing.

Berliner, David and Bruce J. Biddle (1999), *The Manufactured Crisis: Myths, Fraud, and the Attack on America's Public Schools*, New York: Basic Books.

Berliner, David and Gene V. Glass (2014), *50 Myths & Lies that Threaten America's Public Schools: The Real Crisis in Education*, New York: Teachers College Press.

Block, Corrie R. (2015), "Examining a Public Montessori School's Response to the Pressures of High-Stakes Accountability," *Journal of Montessori Research*, 1 (1): 12.

Bloom, Benjamin S. (1968), *Toward a Theory of Testing Which Includes Measurement-Evaluation-Assessment*, Center for the Study of Evaluation of Instructional Programs Occasional Report No. 9.

Bloom, Benjamin S., Thomas Hastings, George Madaus (1971), *Handbook on Formative and Summative Evaluation of Student Learning*, New York: McGraw Hill.

Bloom, Benjamin S., Max Englehart, Edward J. Furst, Walker Hill, and David Krathwohl (1956), *Taxonomy of Educational Objectives: The Classification of Educational Goals. Handbook I: Cognitive Domain*, London: Longmans, Green.

Booth, Charles (1892), "The Inaugural Address of Charles Booth, Esq., President of the Royal Statistical Society. Session 1892–93. Delivered 15th November, 1892," *Journal of the Royal Statistical Society*, 55 (4): 521–57. https://doi.org/10.2307/2979580.

Booth, Charles (1893), "Life and Labour of the People in London: First Results of an Inquiry Based on the 1891 Census. Opening Address of Charles Booth, Esq., President of the Royal Statistical Society. Session 1893–94," *Journal of the Royal Statistical Society*, 56 (4): 557–93. https://doi.org/10.2307/2979431.

Booth, Charles (1902), *Life and Labour of the People in London: First Series*, London: Macmillan.

Cronbach, Lee J. (1951), "Coefficient Alpha and the Internal Structure of Tests," *Psychometrika*, 16: 297–334.

Cronbach, Lee J. (1967), "The Two Disciplines of Scientific Psychology," in Douglas
    N. Jackson and Samuel Messick (eds.), *Problems in Human Assessment*, 22–39,
    New York: McGraw-Hill.
Cronbach, Lee J. and Paul E. Meehl (1955), "Construct Validity in Psychological
    Tests," *Psychological Bulletin*, 52: 281–302.
Cronbach, Lee J., Nageswari Rajaratnam, and Goldine C. Gleser (1963), "Theory
    of Generalizability: A Liberalization of Reliability Theory," *British Journal of
    Statistical Psychology*, 16 (2): 137–63.
Education Testing Service (ETS) (n.d.), "National Assessment of Educational
    Progress." Available online: https://www.ets.org/k12/assessments/federal/naep/?WT.
    ac=k12_36148_overwrite_naep_170105 (accessed November 16, 2021).
FairTest (n.d.), "Measurement Driven Instruction." Available online: https://www.
    fairtest.org/measurement-driven-instruction (accessed September 7, 2020).
Ferrara, Steve and Emily Lai (2016), "Documentation to Support Test Score
    Interpretation and Use," in Suzanne Lane, Mark R. Raymond, and Thomas
    M. Haladyna (eds.), *Handbook of Test Development*, 2nd edn., 603–23, New York:
    Routledge.
Ferrara, Steve, Emily Lai, Amy Reilly, and Paul D. Nichols (2016), "Principled
    Approaches to Assessment Design, Development, and Implementation," in
    Andre A. Rupp and Jacqueline P. Leighton (eds.), *The Handbook of Cognition and
    Assessment: Frameworks, Methodologies, and Applications*, 41–74, Chichester, UK:
    Wiley-Blackwell.
Gordon, E.T. (2016), "Human Diversity and Equitable Assessment," in Samuel
    J. Messick (ed.), *Assessment in Higher Education: Issues of Access, Quality, Student
    Development and Public Policy*, 203–11, London: Routledge.
Gould, Stephen J. (1981), *Mismeasure of Man*, Harmondsworth, UK: W.W. Norton &
    Company.
Gronlund, Norman and Susan M. Brookhart (2009), *Gronlund's Writing Instructional
    Objectives*, 8th edn., Upper Saddle River, NJ: Pearson/Merrill Prentice Hall.
Guskey, Thomas R. (1997), *Implementing Mastery Learning*, 2nd edn., Belmont, CA:
    Wadsworth Publishing.
Guskey, Thomas R. (2005), "Mapping the Road to Proficiency," *Educational
    Leadership*, 63 (3): 32–8.
Hazlett, James A. (1973), "A History of the National Assessment of Educational
    Progess, 1963–1973," Ph.D. diss., University of Kansas.
Hood, Stafford (1998), "Introduction and Overview: Assessment in the Context of
    Culture and Pedagogy: A Collaborative Effort, a Meaningful Goal," *Journal of
    Negro Education*, 67 (3) (July): 184–6.
International Association for the Evaluation of Educational Achievement (IEA)
    (n.d.-a), "History." Available online: https://www.iea.nl/about/org/history
    (accessed September 19, 2020).
International Association for the Evaluation of Educational Achievement (IEA)
    (n.d.-b), "TIMSS Trends in International Mathematics and Science Study."
    Available online: https://www.iea.nl/studies/iea/timss (accessed July 28, 2021).
Kifer, Edward (1997), "Why I Like Test Scores and What They Tell Me About
    Curriculum," *Journal of Curriculum Studies*, 29 (6): 627–35.
Kifer, Edward (2001), *Large-Scale Assessment: Dimensions, Dilemmas, and Policy*,
    Thousand Oaks: Corwin Press.

Klinger, Corrie and Don Klinger (2021), "Regarding Evaluation," *2020 Consortium for Research on Educational Assessment and Teacher Effectiveness Annual Conference Proceedings*, 1: 28–30.

Klinger, Don. A. and Christopher DeLuca (2009), *The History of Large Scale Achievement Testing in Ontario's Education System*, Toronto: Elementary Teachers' Federation of Ontario.

Klinger, Don A., Christopher DeLuca, and Tess Miller (2008), "The Evolving Culture of Large-Scale Assessments in Canadian Education," *Canadian Journal of Educational Administration and Policy*, (76): 1–34.

Klinger, Don A., Patricia J. McDivitt, Barbara B. Howard, Marco A. Munoz, W. Todd Roger, and E. Caroline Wylie (2015), *Classroom Assessment Standards for preK-12 Teachers: Joint Committee on Standards for Educational Evaluation*, [Kindle Edition].

Krathwohl, David R. (2009), "Historical Research," in David R. Krathwohl (ed.), *Methods of Educational and Social Science Research: The Logic of Methods*, 605–14, Long Grove, IL: Waveland Press.

Krathwohl, David R., Banjamin S. Bloom, and Bertram B. Masia (1964), *Taxonomy of Educational Objectives Handbook II: The Affective Domain*, London: Longmans.

Lagemann, Ellen C. (2009), *An Elusive Science: The Troubling History of Education Research*, Chicago: University of Chicago Press.

Lingard, Bob and Steven Lewis (2016), "Globalization of the Anglo-American Approach to Top-Down, Test-Based Educational Accountability," in Gavin Brown and Lois Harris (eds.), *Handbook of Human and Social Conditions in Assessment*, 1st edn., 387–403, New York: Routledge. https://doi.org/10.4324/9781315749136.

Madaus, George and Michael Russell (2009), "Paradoxes of High-Stakes Testing," *Journal of Education*, 190 (1/2): 21–30.

Manns, Mark (2018), *The Culture of Testing: Sociocultural Impacts on Learning in Asia and the Pacific*, Paris: UNESCO. Available online: https://unesdoc.unesco.org/ark:/48223/pf0000261955 (accessed May 24, 2022).

Miller, David M., Robert L. Linn, and Norman E. Gronlund (2013), *Measurement and Assessment in Teaching*, 11th edn., Boston: Pearson.

Mislevy, Robert J. (2018), *Sociocognitive Foundations of Educational Measurement*, New York: Taylor and Francis. https://doi.org/10.4324/9781315871691.

National Center for Education Statistics (NCES) (2021), "Assessment Frameworks: National Assessment of Educational Progress, " December 13. Available online: https://nces.ed.gov/nationsreportcard/assessments/frameworks.aspx (accessed March 1, 2022).

Nichols, Sharon L. and Lois R. Harris (2016), "Accountability Assessment's Effects on Teachers and Schools," in Gavin Brown and Lois Harris (eds.), *Handbook of Human and Social Conditions in Assessment*, 1st edn., 40–56, New York: Routledge. https://doi.org/10.4324/9781315749136.

Nichols, Sharon L., David C. Berliner, and Harvard University, Graduate School of Education (2007), *Collateral Damage: How High-Stakes Testing Corrupts America's Schools*, Cambridge, MA: Harvard Education Press.

Oliveri, María Elena, René Lawless, and Robert J. Mislevy (2019), "Using Evidence-Centered Design to Support the Development of Culturally and Linguistically Sensitive Collaborative Problem-Solving Assessments," *International Journal of Testing*, 19 (3): 270–300.

Patton, Michael Q. (2018), "Evaluation Science," *American Journal of Evaluation*, 39 (2): 183–200. https://doi.org/10.1177/1098214018763121.

Plucker, Jonathan (2016), "History of Influences in the Development of Intelligence Theory," last modified April 29, 2018. Available online: https://www.intelltheory.com/map.shtml (accessed May 24, 2022).

Salkind, Neil J. (2008), "Evaluation," in Neil J. Salkind (ed.), *Encyclopedia of Educational Psychology*, vol. 1, 363–73, Thousand Oaks, CA: Sage Publications.

Scriven, Michael (n.d.), "The Three Revolutions." Available online: http://michaelscriven.info/papersandpublications.html (accessed November 17, 2021).

Scriven, Michael (1967), "The Methodology of Evaluation," in Ralph W. Tyler, Robert M. Gagné, and Michael Scriven (eds.), *Perspectives of Curriculum Evaluation*, Vol. 1, 39–83, Chicago: Rand McNally & Company.

Scriven, Michael (1968), *Evaluation as a Main Aim of Science: Comments on Professor Bloom's Paper Entitled Toward a Theory of Testing Which Includes Measurement-Evaluation-Assessment*, CSE Report 10, Los Angeles: University of California; Los Angeles: Center for the Study of Evaluation.

Scriven, Michael (1991), *Evaluation Thesaurus*, 4th edn., Newbury Park, CA: Sage.

Scriven, Michael (1994), "Duties of the Teacher," *Journal of Personnel Evaluation in Education*, 8 (2): 33.

Scriven, Michael (2015), "Duties of the Teacher." Available online: http://michaelscriven.info/images/DUTIES_OF_THE_TEACHER.2.12.15-2.pdf (accessed November 17, 2021).

Scriven, Michael (2016), "Roadblocks to Recognition and Revolution," *American Journal of Evaluation*, 37: 27–44.

Simpson, Elizabeth J. (1966), "The Classification of Educational Objectives: Psychomotor Domain," Research Project No. OE-5-85–104, University of Illinois, Urbana.

Spearman, Charles (1904), "'General Intelligence,' Objectively Determined and Measured," *American Journal of Psychology*, 15 (2): 201–92.

Thurstone, Louis L. (1938), *Primary Mental Abilities*, Chicago: University of Chicago Press.

Tyler, Ralph W. (1934), *Constructing Achievement Tests*, Columbus: Ohio State Univeristy Press.

Tyler, Ralph W. (1942), "General Statement on Evaluation," *Journal of Educational Research*, 35 (7): 492–501.

Tyler, Ralph W. (1949), *Basic Principles of Curriculum and Instruction*, Chicago: University of Chicago Press.

Wang, Liang Choon (2016), "The Effect of High-Stakes Testing on Suicidal Ideation of Teenagers with Reference-Dependent Preferences," *Journal of Population Economics*, 29 (2): 345–64.

Waugh, C. Keith and Norman E. Gronlund (2013), *Assessment of Student Achievement*, 10th edn., New York: Pearson.

Wijsen, Lisa D. and Denny Borsboom (2021), "Perspectives on Psychometrics Interviews with 20 Past Psychometric Society Presidents," *Psychometrika*, 86 (1): 327–43. http://dx.doi.org.proxy.queensu.ca/10.1007/s11336-021-09752-7.

Wilbrink, Ben (1997), "Assessment in Historical Perspective," *Studies in Educational Evaluation*, 23 (1): 31–48.

Wood, Bronwyn, Martin Thrupp, and Michael Barker (2021), "Education Policy: Changes and Continuities Since 1999," in Graham Hassall and Girol Karacaoglu (eds.), *Social Policy Practice and Processes in Aotearoa New Zealand*, 272–85, Auckland: Massey University.

Yarbrough, Donald B., Lynn M. Shulha, Rodney K. Hopson, and Flora A. Caruthers (2010), *The Program Evaluation Standards: A Guide for Evaluators and Evaluation Users*, 3rd edn., Los Angeles: Sage. Available online: https://evaluationstandards. org/program/ (accessed May 24, 2022).

Zhao, Yong (2014), *Who's Afraid of the Big Bad Dragon? Why China has the Best (and Worst) Education System in the World*, San Francisco: Jossey-Bass.

Zieky, Michael (2016), "Developing Fair Tests," in Suzanne Lane, Mark R. Raymond, and Thomas M. Haladyna (eds.), *Handbook of Test Development*, 2nd edn., 81–99, New York: Routledge.

CONTRIBUTORS

Dorothea Anagnostopoulos is Professor and Associate Dean for Academic Affairs in the Neag School of Education at the University of Connecticut, USA. Her research examines teaching and teacher education policy and practice. She recently collaborated with colleagues across three universities on a large-scale, mixed-methods longitudinal study of beginning teachers' development of ambitious instruction.

Shawn Michael Bullock is Professor of Education at the University of Cambridge, UK. His research uses the lenses offered by the history and philosophy of science and technology to examine issues in education. Currently, he is particularly interested in the history of technology use in schools and the history of multilingual education. He also conducts research on teacher education and professional development, with a particular focus on self-study methodology.

Theodore Michael Christou is Professor of Education and the Associate Dean of Graduate Studies in the Faculty of Education at Queen's University, Canada. His research concentrates on curriculum history and social studies education. Theodore is currently developing mapping applications to digitize and support access to archival materials for public use.

Ryan W. Coughlan is Associate Professor at the Marxe School of Public and International Affairs, Baruch, College, City University of New York, USA. His research focuses on educational equity across PK-16 education systems. Ryan is currently conducting a geostatistical analysis of access to racially diverse and integrated spaces in neighborhoods, elementary schools, secondary schools, postsecondary schools, and workplaces across the United States.

Mark T.S. Currie recently completed his Ph.D. in Education at the University of Ottawa, Canada and is currently a part-time Professor of Education, also at University of Ottawa, Canada. His research examines connections between landscapes of colonialism and racist exclusions, and theorizes the potential for (re)creating anti-racist sociohistorical geographies. Mark is developing a study to investigate the ways that social studies and history education can help students become active participants in the (re)creation of anti-racist sociohistorical community spaces.

Rebecca S. Evans is a graduate student of Education at Queen's University, Canada. Her research focuses on civic learning in educational spaces beyond public schools. Rebecca is currently working on a research project that integrates historical thinking concepts with education for climate action.

Peter Hlebowitsh is Professor of Education and the Dean of the College of Education at the University of Alabama, USA. His work has focused on the development of the school curriculum and on the historic impact of the progressive movement on the action of the public schools in North America.

Corrie Rebecca Klinger, Ph.D., is Senior Research Fellow at the University of Waikato, New Zealand. She is the President of the Consortium for Research on Educational Assessment and Teacher Effectiveness and a Senior Fellow at the Pegasus Institute. Evaluation is her predominant area of research.

Don A. Klinger, Ph.D., is ProVice-Chancellor Te Wānanga Toi Tangata Division of Education, at the University of Waikato, New Zealand. His research focuses on the measurement and assessment of student outcomes and their associated consequences.

Christopher McCuaig is a graduate student in the Faculty of Education at Queen's University, Canada. His research interests include curriculum studies and history education. Having thirteen years of experience as a high school teacher, Christopher is currently investigating recent changes to the high school history curriculum in the province of Ontario.

Nicholas Ng-A-Fook is Full Professor of Curriculum Theory and Vice-Dean of Graduate Studies at the University of Ottawa, Canada. His teaching and research are situated within the wider international field of curriculum studies, history education, and life writing research. Dr. Ng-A-Fook has co-published several award-winning books including *Oral History and Education: Theories, Dilemmas, and Practices* (2017); and *Provoking Curriculum Studies: Strong Poetry and Arts of the Possible in Education* (2016).

Patrick Phillips is currently a Ph.D. candidate in the Faculty of Education at the University of Ottawa, Canada. His research foci include developing and applying under-theorized arts-based practices, including visualization and critique, toward research-creation that fosters better interconnectedness in teaching and learning without erasing difficult questions, or encounters between differing or alienated knowledge systems. His current research includes supporting the *Thinking Historically for Canada's Future* national project.

Jackson Pind is Postdoctoral Fellow in Indigenous Education in the Faculty of Education at Queen's University, Canada. He recently completed his dissertation on the history of Indian Day Schools in partnership with Curve Lake First Nation. His current research projects include incorporating ancient Anishinaabe history into the curriculum and understanding how history education can be used to face the climate crisis.

Jack Schneider is Associate Professor in the School of Education at University of Massachusetts Lowell, USA. His research examines how stakeholder perceptions shape decision-making and policy in K-12 public education. He is most recently the co-author (with Ethan Hutt) of a book about the quantification of student learning, past, present, and future.

Cécile Sabatier Bullock is Associate Professor of French Education in the Faculty of Education at Simon Fraser University (SFU), Canada. Her research documents and interprets plurilingual practices and attitudes to multilingualism in families, schools, and communities, as well as addressing issues relevant to teacher training and professional development. It emphasizes how languages mediate social inclusion and express a sense of belonging when speakers mobilize their plurilingual repertoires. Her current work focuses on problematizing the "multilingual turn" in language(s) education and the translingual perspective that has been emerging in its wake to bring back some historicity in the field of Language(s) Education.

INDEX

2chan/4chan 128–129

Aboriginal peoples 49
academic history 25–26
academic qualifications and teaching
 139–140
access to education 89–104
 Asian Americans 94–95
 Black people 93–94, 99–100
 and equity 100–104
 Hispanic Americans 95–96
 Indigenous Americans 92–93
 institutional factors 100–104
 LGBTQ+ 99
 multilingual learners 96–98
accountability era of teaching 137,
 148–151
accountability practices, measurement
 driven instruction 175–176
African American Vernacular English 97
"Age of Enlightenment" 40–41, 56
"age of improvement" (Tomkins) 45
*Age of Technoeconomic Labor and
 Progress* 46
agency of childhood development
 112–113, 118–124
Airton, L. 56
Aladejebi, F. 55, 57–58
alpha (Cronbach) 165–166
American Educational Research Association
 (AERA) 160

American Federation of Teachers
 (AFT) 145–146, 147
American Historical Association 29
American Psychological Association
 (APA) 160
American Revolution 90
amezou 128
analysis and cognitive assessment
 167–168, 169
Ancient China 160–161
Ancient China and the keju system
 160–161
Anderson, B. 24–25
anti-racism 40, 42, 48–60, 93–94
Apple 40
application and cognitive function
 167–168, 169
aqueduct bridges 27–28
Asian Americans 94–95, 97
Asian countries 159, 160–161,
 175–176
Assessment of Educational Progress
 (NAEP) 168, 171, 172, 173
assessment and evaluation 157–183
 current accountability practices
 175–176
 large-scale standardized
 assessment 169–171
 present-day problems 159–160
 psychometrics with large-scale
 assessments 171–175

psychometrics and
        standardization 162–166
    taking form of evaluation 166–169
    through history 160–162
Association Teachers in Colored Schools
        (NATCS) 142–143
Axelrod, P. 43–44

Bailyn, B. 4–5
bans on education 42, 94
Barlow, J.P. 125
Barman, J. 44
Battiste, M. 55
Benne, K. 19–20
Beran, D. 128–129
"best practices" movements 81
Bestor, A.E. 51
bias 102–103, 104
    anti-racism/racism 40–42, 48–57
    see also otherness
BigTech 39–40
bildung 82
Bilingual Education Act 89, 97–98
bilingualism 119, 120–121, 122–123
Bill of Rights 92
Black communities 40–41
    access to education 93–94, 99–100
    African American Vernacular
        English 97
    #BlackedOutHistory initiative 55
    "linear progressive narrative" of
        freedom 41–42
    Ontario Black History Society 55–56
    progressive era of teaching 142–143,
        144
    racial concepts 52–53
    racialization of Blackness 54
    school funding 101
    segregation 41, 93–94, 102–103, 139,
        142–143
    student demographics 148–149
    under-resourcing 93–94
    unemployment 146
    see also race
#BlackedOutHistory initiative 55
Blair, T. 114, 116–117
Bloch, M.N. 112
Bloom, A. 88
Bloom, B.S. 157, 168, 171–173

Bloomfield, L. 121
Blount, J.M. 56
Blum-Ross, A. 125–127
Bobbitt, J.F. 75–76, 79
Bode, B. 76
Booth, C. 162–163
Bourdieu, P. 112
Boyd, D. 126, 127–128
Brant-Birioukov, K. 51–52, 55, 57–58,
        59–60
British settler colonies 43–48
Brown v. Board of Education 89, 94, 101,
        146
"Browning" of curricula 53–54
bullying 128–129
bureaucratic rationalization 137–156
Burke, S.Z. 39
Bush Jr., G.W. 114, 116–117
Butts, F. 19–20

California Stull Act 148
Calls to Action (unsettling) 57
Canada 2, 11, 39, 42
    challenges of unsettling 57–60
    historical mindedness 29–30
    "historical thinking" 25–27
    "imagined community" concepts 24–25
    Ontario Black History Society 55–56
    public education and settler
        colonizers 43–48
    and racism 54
    and settler colonizers 40, 43–60
    social foundations 22–23
    statue defacements and toppling 11
    teacher education and liberal arts
        20–21
    Truth and Reconciliation
        Commission 44, 57
    unsettling of settler colonial
        education 48–50
Carlisle Indian School 93
Catholicism 44–45
causality 25–26
cause and consequence 26
Center for Education Statistics
        (NCES) 168
Challenging Mystification (Greene) 17–18
change over time concepts 25–26
Chicago Teachers Federation 141–142

child-centered position 70–71
Children's Online Privacy Protection Act (COPPA) 127–128
China and the keju system 160–161
Chomsky, N. 6
Christian Eurocentric doctrine 44–45
Christianity 92–93
citizenship 95–96
Civil Rights movement 95, 98, 99–100
Civilization Fund Act of 1819 92
Clark, P. 22
class
    eugenics movement 164–165
    school strikes 114–115
Classroom Assessment Standards 173–174
Clifford, G. 139–140
climate change 117–118
"climate strikes" 114
"clinical supervision" 147–148
The Cognitive Domain (1956) 167–170
colonies see settler colonizers
Colored Teachers Association 142–143
Commissioner of Indian Affairs 93
Committee on Historical Foundations of the National Society of College Teachers of Education 20
Common School Era 90–91, 92–93, 138–139
communism 42
competency-based education 32, 78–79
complexity 25–26
comprehension and cognitive function 167–168, 169
Congress, US 92–93, 95–96, 102–103
Constitution of the Fifth Republic 119–120
construct validity 166
content standard, rise of 78–80
context 25–26
contingency 25–26
continuity and change 26
COPPA see Children's Online Privacy Protection Act
Corbett, M. 2
Council for the Accreditation of Teacher Education (NCATE) 146
Council on Measurement in Education (NCME) 160
Council of Teachers of English 79–80

Council of Teachers Mathematics 79–80
Council of Teachers of Social Studies 79–80
Count, G. 19–20, 45–46
COVID-19 pandemic 39–40, 59–60, 103
Cox, L. 116
Cremin, L. 4–5, 88
Crenshaw, K. 52–53
"The Crick Report" 117
critical race theory (CRT) 42
Cronbach, L.J. 163, 165–166, 171–172
Cuban, L. 6–7
culture, historical mindedness 30
Cunningham, S. 116
curricula 39–40, 65–85
    bans on 42
    Eurocentric and unsettling of 50–57
    formation of educational experience 74–82
    psycho-social screen and experiential continua 69–74
"Curriculum of Historians" (Cuban) 6–7
cyber-bullying 128–129
cyber-libertarianism 126–127

Davis, H. 59
Declaration of Sentiments 98
deculturalization 96, 97
Dei, G.J.S. 55
deliberative tradition and rethinking curricula 80–83
democracy and democratic process
    public schooling 41–42, 45–46
    teacher evaluation during progressive era 144–145
    values and aims of society 72
Department of Classroom Teachers 142, 145
Department of Education 89, 98–99, 102, 103
developmental stage theory 72
Le Développement du langage observé chez un enfant bilingue 121
Dewey, J. 3–5, 10–11, 15, 66
    deliberative tradition and rethinking curricula 82
    educational experience 66–67
    experiential continua 67–74, 78
    nature of the learner 71

psychometrics and standardization 164
schools and education systems 87–88, 91
settler colonizers and public schooling 45–46
social efficiency/particularizing of school experience 75–76
subject matter 74
Tyler rationale and role of the objective 77, 78
v. Thorndike 164
values and aims of society 72
didaktik 82
digital environments 124–129
    see also social media
digital literacies 39–40
"Digital Natives, Digital Immigrants" (Prensky) 124–125
diversity 39
Donald, D. 40–41, 49–50, 54, 57–58
double consciousness (DuBois) 52
DuBois, W.E.B. 52
Dunne, Á. 128
Durant, W. 1–2

Earth Day 117–118
economic progress and education 45
Education for All Handicapped Children Act (EHA) 89, 99
Education in the Forming of American Society (Bailyn) 4–5
education systems *see* schools and education systems
Education Testing Service (ETS) 171
educational experience *see* curricula
Eliot, T.S. 3
embryonic democracy 72
Emilsson, K. 117–118
Emirbayer, M. 112
Engendering Curriculum History (Hendry) 41
Enlightenment 40–41, 56
enslavement *see* slavery
equity and access to education 89–104
Este, D. 55
ethical dimensions of "historical thinking" 26
ethics and education 21
ETS *see* Education Testing Service
eugenics movement 164–165

Eurocentric curricula
    unsettling frameworks/(re) purposing 50–57
    see also Canada; United States
Europe of the 18th and 19th centuries 162
European countries 159
    accountability practices 175–176
    see also settler colonizers
evaluation and cognitive function 167–168, 169
evaluation of teachers
    accountability era 150–151
    progressive era 144–145
    sixties and postwar posterity 147–148
    system-building era 141–142
Every Student Succeeds Act 151
evidence 26
"exclusivity" and Facebook 127
"executive ability" assessment 147–148
experience *see* curricula
experiential continua 67–74, 78
Eynon, R. 124–125

Facebook 127, 128–129
Fair Housing Act 1968 102–103
Fanon, F. 52
Faulkner, W. 11
"Favorite" buttons 128
feminism 98–100
feminization of teaching 28
Fenton, E. 16
field-mapping 15–37
    beyond teacher education 23
    foundations in varied forms 21–23
    as habits of thought 23–25
    knowledge and its foundations 27–31
    metaphor of foundations 18–21
    new foundations for historical foundations 31–32
    teacher education 17–18
Finland and assessment criteria 159
Finn Jr., C. 88
First Nations individuals 44, 57
    see also settler colonizers
five C's of "historical thinking" 25–26
Florida and CRT bans 42
formative evaluative judgment 173–174
forms of reasoning about teaching (Westbury) 82

Forrest Gump (1994) 2–3
Foundations Division at Teachers College
    Columbia 19–20
French nation-state and Revolution
    119–120
French settler colonies 43–48
Froebel, F. 71
Fultz, M. 144

Galante, A. 122
Gaztambide-Fernández, R.A. 53–54
gender
    eugenics movement 164–165
    historical mindedness 30
    purposes of education 39
    see also women
Generalizability theory (G theory)
    165–166
GI Bill 145
Gidney, R.D. 46
Glanz, J. 141
Gleser, G.C. 165–166
Google 39–40
Granatstein, J. 24–25
Grant, M. 118
"great equalizer" of public schooling
    90–91
Greene, M. 17–18
Grégoire, A. 119–120
Grigg, R. 114–116
Gronlund, N.E. 176
Guilford, J.P. 165
Gutek, G.L. 43

habitus (agency informed by the past) 112,
    122, 130–131
Hall, G.S. 71
The Handbook on Formative and
    Summative Evaluation of Student
    Learning 168
Handicapped Children Act, Education for
    All 89
Hannah-Jones, N. 94
Harper, W.R. 141–142
Harvard College 90
"hashtagged" 55, 126
    see also Twitter
Hastings, J.T. 168
Haugen, E. 121
Heiser, W. 165–166

Helsper, E.J. 124–125
Hendry, P. 41, 56
Herbart, J.F. 71
Hirsch, E.D. 46–47, 88
Hispanic Americans' access to
    education 95–96
historical mindedness 29–31
"historical thinking" 23–24, 25–27
"house histories" 24–25
housing 102–103
human intelligence 164–165
    see also IQ tests; standardization
humanism 24
Humphries, S. 115

Ibrahim, A. 54, 57–58
ICCS *see* International Civic and
    Citizenship Education Study
IDEA *see* Individuals with Disabilities
    Education Act
'ideal child' concepts 111, 130–131
identity 119
    historical mindedness 30
    settler colonizers and public
      schooling 43
IEA *see* International Association for
    the Evaluation of Educational
    Achievement
"imagined community" concepts
    (Anderson) 24–25
incarceration 41
Indian Act of 1876 44
"Indian Education: A National Tragedy, a
    National Challenge" 93
Indian Education Act of 1972 93
Indian Residential and Day Schools
    legacy 17
Indian Self Determination and Education
    Act of 1975 93
Indigenous communities 40, 52–53
    Indigenous Americans' access to
      education 92–93
Indigenous Métissage 49–50, 56–57
"In(di)genuity" (Brant-Birioukov) 59–60
Individuals with Disabilities Education Act
    (IDEA) 99
Industrial Revolution 90–91
industrialization 28
industrialized towns 114–116
Instagram 126

institutional factors shaping access and
     equity 100–104
  school attendance areas 102–103
  school funding 101–102
  school oversight 100–101
  school structures and processes
     103–104
"institutions of promise" (Blount) 56
instructional models and rise of content
     standard 78–80
"instructional skills" assessment 147–148
International Association for the Evaluation
     of Educational Achievement
     (IEA) 158–159, 170–171, 172, 173
International Civic and Citizenship
     Education Study (ICCS) 170–171
international climate summits 117–118
Internet (World Wide Web) 124–129
intersectionality 52–53
Invitation to History (Durant) 1
iPads/iPods 39–40
IQ tests 104
Iraq War 114, 116–117
*Iraq War Day X: The largest school strikes
     in UK history* (2015) 116–117
Irish women 139
iterative dimensions of agency 112

James, C. 54
Jefferson, T. 90
Jewish women 139
Jim Crow 101
     see also segregation
Johansson, H. 117–118
Journal of Curriculum Studies 82
journalism 115–116
Judd, C. 76
Judeo-Christian religious organizations 44

Kagan, D. 10
Kane, R. 51–52
Karn, S. 59
keju system 160–161
Kendi, I.X. 41
Kentucky Instructional Results and
     Information System (KIRIS)
     173–175
Kifer, E. 170, 174
Kliebard, H. 2, 78

knowledge
  challenges of unsettling 58–59
  cognitive function 167–169
  field-mapping 27–31
Kovach, M. 55
Krug, E. 4–5

Labaree, D. 140
large-scale standardized assessment
     169–175
Lau v. Nichols 97–98
Laurie, S.S. 120–121
Lavalette, M. 116
Lawlor, M.-A. 128
learning and human development 111–135
  digital child 124–129
  plurilingualism 119–124
  school strikes 113–118
  structure and agency 112–113
Leurs, K. 129
Lewin-Jones, J. 127
Lexington, Massachusetts school 140
LGBTQ+, access to education 99
libertarianism 126–127
"Like" buttons 128
"linear progressive narrative" of
     freedom 41–42
linguistic purism 119–120
Livingstone, S. 125–127
Llanelli, Wales 114–116
Lorenz, C. 24
Lorenzetti, L. 55
The Lost Education of Horace Tate
     (Walker) 94

McCarran-Walter Act of 1952 94–95
Macdonald, J.A. 11
McGregor, H.E. 59
Madaus, G.F. 168
Mann, H. 90–91
Maoism 42
Marxism 42
mass incarceration 41
Massachusetts
  the first "normal school" 140
  school attendance areas 102–103
Masters of Arts in Teaching program 147
mastery learning 78–79
Maxwell, B. 22–23

measurement driven instruction 173–176
mediation 125–126
Meehl, P. 166
metaphor of foundations
    field-mapping 18–21
    new foundations for historical
        foundations 31–32
Métissage 49–50, 56–57
Mexican Americans 97
Mexican-American War of 1848 95–96
Microsoft 40
Milewski, P. 39
Millar, W.P.J. 46
Milloy, J.S. 44
Mische, A. 112
missionaries 92–93
modernist views of freedom 41–42
monolingualism 119–120, 122
Montessori, - 71
Morton, T. 25–26
Mosteller, F. 171
motherhood 138–139
Mount Saint Vincent University 22
multidisiplinarity 39
multilingual learners' access to
    education 96–98
multilingualism 122–123
Murray, C. 116
Musk, E. 1

narratives 28, 40–42
nation, historical mindedness 30
National Assessment of Educational
    Progress (NAEP) 168, 171, 172,
    173
National Association Teachers in Colored
    Schools (NATCS) 142–143
National Center for Education Statistics
    (NCES) 168
National Colored Teachers
    Association 142–143
National Council for the Accreditation of
    Teacher Education (NCATE) 146
National Council on Measurement in
    Education (NCME) 160
National Council of Teachers of
    English 79–80
National Council of Teachers
    Mathematics 79–80

National Council of Teachers of Social
    Studies 79–80
A National Crime (Milloy) 44
National Education Association (NEA)
    progressive era 142, 145
    sixties and postwar posterity 145–146,
    147
National Science Teachers Association
    79–80
National Teacher Corps 147
"national unity" (unitarisme) 119
"native mechanism" of education
    (Dewey) 45–46
Naturalization Act of 1790 92, 94–95
nature of the learner 70–72
NCLB see No Child Left Behind
NEA see National Education Association
Nelson 8 History textbook 55
Nemausus (today Nîmes), France 27–28
neophobia/neophilia 2
"networked publics" concepts 126
The New Social Studies (Fenton) 16
"New World" 90, 162
    see also settler colonizers
New York City Department of
    Education 103
New York City and protest against
    standardized test scores 151
New York City Teacher's Association
    141–142
New York Times Magazine's 1619
    Project 94
New Zealand
    accountability practices 175–176
    and assessment criteria 159
Ng-A-Fook, N. 51–52
nihilism 128–129
Nilsen, A.G. 116
No Child Left Behind (NCLB) 101, 151
Nobel Committee 118
non-policy historians 6–7
North America
    deliberative tradition and rethinking
        curricula 80–82
    instructional models and rise of content
        standard 78
    public schooling 41
    and settler colonizers 40, 43–60
    see also Canada; United States

occupational professionalism 137–156
Ogren, C. 140
Old Deluder Laws of 1642 and 1647 90
Ontario Black History Society (OBHS)
    55–56
Orientalism and otherness 30, 52
Osborne, K. 9, 10, 29
otherness 30, 52–53
    anti-racism 40, 42, 48–60, 93–94

"Parenting Order" 113–114
Parrott, A.L. 145
particularizing of school experience 75–76
Peace Corps 147
people of color
    NATCS 142–143
    racial agendas and reform 139
    student demographics 148–149
    see also Black communities
"personal qualities" assessment 147–148
perspective 26
Pestalozzi, J.H. 71
Piaget, J. 72
Picardo, E. 122
Pind, J. 59
PIRLS *see* Progress in International
    Reading Literacy Study
PISA *see* Programme for International
    Student Assessment
plurilingualism 119–124
police brutality 93–94
policymakers 102, 103–104
    teaching and teacher education
    137–156
policy-sensitive historians 6–7
Pont du Gard aqueduct bridge, France
    27–28
Popham, J. 79
pornography 128–129
postcolonial theorists 48–60
    see also anti-racism
posterity, postwar 137, 145–148
power/privilege 122
practical-evaluative dimensions of
    agency 112
"practice schools" 143–144
pragmatism and public schooling 45–46
praxis 49–50
Prensky, M. 124–125

presentists 6–7
prisons 41
privacy 127–128, 130–131
problem-solving skills 72–73
Programme for International Student
    Assessment (PISA) 160
programmed instruction 78–79
Progress in International Reading Literacy
    Study (PIRLS) 170–171
progressive education 46–47
progressive era of teaching 137, 142–145
projective dimensions of agency 112, 118
protest against standardized test scores 151
Protestantism 44–45, 90, 92–93
"pryto-epistemiology" (Steeves) 59
Psychometric Society and
    Pyschometrika 165
psychometrics 162–166, 171–175
psycho-social screen for curricula 69–74
public schooling 41–42
    racial agendas and reform 139
    racial demographics 148–149
    school attendance areas 102–103
    settler colonizers 43–48
    tracing the history of access 90–91
Puerto Rican Americans 95–96, 97
purpose 173–174
purposes of historical education 39–64
    challenges of unsettling 57–60
    settler colonizers and public
        schooling 43–48
    unsettling frameworks/(re)
        purposing 50–57
    unsettling of settler colonial
        education 48–50

Queen's University 20–21

race
    anti-racism/racism 40–42, 48–57
    eugenics movement 164–165
    historical mindedness 30
    racial agendas and reform 139
    racialization of Blackness 54
    unsettling frameworks/(re)
        purposing 52–53
Race to the Top (RTT) initiatives 150,
    151
radicals/extremists 5–6

Radovic, A. 120, 128
Rajaratnam, N. 165–166
Ravitch, D. 4–5, 47
Relay Graduate School of Education
    149–150
religion 44–45
rematriation/refusal 53–54
"republican motherhood" 138–139
Requiem for a Nun (Faulkner) 11
rhetoric and xenophobia 124–125
rise of content standard 78–80
role of the objective 76–78
Ronjat, J. 121
Rousseau, J.-J. 70–71
Rowley, J. 128
RTT *see* Race to the Top initiatives
Rugg, H. 19–20, 71
Ryerson, E. 11, 45

"safeguarding powers" 113–114
SAGE Guide to Curriculum in Education
    (Gaztambide-Fernández) 53–54
Said, E. 52
Said, E.W. 30
San Antonio Independent School District v.
    Rodriguez 101
Sato, C. 55
School Attendance Order 113–114
Schooling in Transition (Burke &
    Milewski) 39
schools and education systems 87–109
    access 89–104
    attendance areas 102–103
    funding 101–102
    historical interpretations 88–89
    institutional factors shaping access and
        equity 100–104
    oversight 100–101
    strikes 113–118
    structures and processes 103–104
    tracing the history of access 90–91
    see also public schooling
Schwab, J. 80–82
Scriven, M. 157–158, 167, 172–174
search engines 39–40
Seattle and the WTO 116
segregation 41, 93–94, 102–103, 139,
    142–143
Seixas, P. 25–26

Self Determination and Education Act
    1975, Indian 93
Senate, US 93
Seneca Falls Convention 98
Seneca (Roman stoic) 9–10
Sentiments, Declartion of 98
settler colonizers
    challenges of unsettling 57–60
    deconstructing/unsettling 48–50
    public schooling 43–48
    unsettling frameworks/(re)
        purposing 50–57
sexism 98–100
Shelley, P. 32
Shumaker, A. 71
significance, historical 26
sixties and postwar posterity 137,
    145–148
slavery 42, 94, 97
    see also settler colonizers
2SLGBTQI+ curricula 42
smartphones 39–40
Smith, L.T. 48
social efficiency of school experience
    75–76
social foundations 22–23
The Social Foundations of Education
    (Count) 19–20
social justice teacher education (SJTE) 56
social media 1, 39–40, 55, 126, 127–129
social progress and education 45
sociology of technology and
    education 124–125
Socratic method 160–161
South Carolina and school funding 101
Southern states and Black inequality 94,
    142–143, 146
Spanish-American War of 1898 95–96
Spearman, C. 163, 164–165, 171–172
Spivak, G. 52–53
Spring, J. 88
standardization 144–145, 151, 158–160,
    162–166, 169–171
standards and accountability era of
    teaching 137, 148–151
Stanley, T.J. 54–55
Stearns, P.N. 24–25, 30–31
Steeves, P.F. 59
stereotyping 95

stoicism 9–10
Stop the War movement 116
The Story of B (Donald) 40–41
strikes 113–118
Stull Act of California 148
subject matter and experiential
        continua 73–74
summative evaluative judgment 173–174
Supreme Court, Senate 93
Supreme Court, US 89, 94–95, 97–98,
        101, 146
Sweden and climate initiatives 117–118
synthesis and cognitive function 167–168,
        169
system-building era 137, 138–142
systemic anti-racism and racism 42, 93–94
systemic oppression of women 98–100

"tagging" 126
Tanner, D. & L.N. 69–70
*Taxonomy of Educational Objectives
        Handbook I: The Cognitive Domain*
        (1956) 167–170
teacher evaluation
    accountability era 150–151
    progressive era 144–145
    sixties and postwar posterity 147–148
    system-building era 141–142
teacher training
    accountability era methods 149–150
    progressive era training methods
        143–144
    sixties and postwar posterity 146–147
    system-building training methods
        139–140
teaching and teacher education 137–156
    accountability era of teaching 137,
        148–151
    field-mapping 17–18
    progressive era 137, 142–145
    sixties and postwar posterity 137,
        145–148
    system-building era 137, 138–142
theories 80–81
thinking skills 72–73
Third International Mathematics and
        Science Study (TIMMS) 170–171
Thorndike, E. 163–164, 165, 171–172

Thunberg, G. 117–118
Thurstone, L.L. 163, 165, 171–172
TikTok 39–40
Todd, Z. 59
Tomkins, G.S. 45
Toronto University 20–21, 29–30
traditionalism 46–47
Trail of Tears 92–93
Tremblay-Laprise, A.-A. 22–23
Truth and Reconciliation Commission
        (TRC) 44, 57
Tuck, E. 53
Tukey, J. 171
tuning out and nihilism (digital
        world) 128–129
Twitter 1, 55, 126, 127, 128–129
Tyack, D. 6–7, 140, 143
Tyler, R. 76–78, 82
Tyler rationale 76–78, 82
Tyler, R.W. 166–167, 171–172

under-resourcing of Black
        communities 93–94
United Kingdom
    five C's of "historical thinking" 25–26
    school strikes 113–118
United Nations Educational, Scientific
        and Cultural Organization
        (UNESCO) 170
United States
    access to education 89–99
    American Historical Association and
        historical mindedness 29
    American Revolution 90
    banning of curricula 42
    Brown v. Board of Education 89, 94,
        101, 146
    challenges of unsettling 57–60
    Congress 92–93, 95–96, 102–103
    digital environments 126
    five C's of "historical thinking" 25–26
    funding 101–102
    instructional models and rise of content
        standard 78–80
    NAEP 171
    school attendance areas 102–103
    school oversight 101
    schools and education systems 87–109

and settler colonizers 40, 43–60
settler colonizers and public
    schooling 43–48
subject matter 73
Supreme Court 89, 94–95, 97–98, 101,
    146
teaching and teacher education 137
unsettling frameworks 51
unsettling of settler colonial
    education 48–50
universities 20–21, 22, 29–30
upper classes, school strikes 114–115
Urban, W. 141–142

value-added measures (VAMs) 150, 151
values and aims of society 72–73
virtual realities 39–40
    see also social media

Walcott, R. 41–42, 55
Wales, school strikes 114–116
Walker, S. 94, 143
Walker, V.S. 88
Warren, D. 140
Waugh, C.K. 176
Weinrich, U. 121

Wennerhag, M. 117–118
Westbury, I. 81–82
Western eurocentrism
    unsettling frameworks/(rc)
        purposing 50–57
    see also Canada; United Kingdom;
        United States
White supremacy 53–54
    anti-racism/racism 40–42, 48–57
Willinsky, J. 47
Wilson, S. 55
Wineburg, S. 25
"winner" and "loser" schools 175–176
women
    access to education 98–100
    racial agendas and reform 139
    "republican motherhood" 138–139
working classes, school strikes 114–115
World Trade Organization (WTO) 116
Wragg, W. 118
Wrong, G.M. 29–30

xenophobia 124–125
    anti-racism/racism 40–42, 48–57

YouTube 39–40, 126